THE

TROY

DECEPTION

THE
TROY
DECEPTION

VOLUME 1. FINDING THE PLAIN OF TROY

JOHN CROWE

Matador
5 Weir Road
Kibworth Beauchamp
Leicester LE8 0LQ, UK
Tel: (+44) 116 279 2299
Fax: (+44) 116 279 2277
Email: books@troubador.co.uk
Web: www.troubador.co.uk/matador

ISBN 978 1848765 498

British Library Cataloguing in Publication Data.
A catalogue record for this book is available from the British Library.

Typeset in 11pt Aldine 401 BT by Troubador Publishing Ltd, Leicester, UK
Printed and bound in the UK by TJ International, Padstow, Cornwall

Matador is an imprint of Troubador Publishing Ltd

This book is dedicated to John Lascelles,
whose inspiration and hard work made it possible.

'And this grey spirit yearning in desire
To follow knowledge like a sinking star,
beyond the utmost bounds of human thought.'

From 'Ulysses'. Alfred, Lord Tennyson (1809-1892)

CONTENTS

CONTENTS

ACKNOWLEDGEMENTS

My romance with Homer started at Sydney airport on 29th January 2002, where I was met by my fellow chronologists Eric Aitchison and Dale Murphie. They had each agreed to share their homes near Newcastle with me while we discussed the issue which had brought me to Australia – a possible revision of ancient history and chronology. As I shook Eric's hand he proffered me an A4 sized package. It contained a draft book about a new location for the Trojan War, by a good friend of his called John Lascelles. This I read over the next few days, and was soon hooked. Later when Eric drove me to Canberra to meet John, a friendship started which has grown with time. Soon after my return to England, John generously agreed that we should pool our resources in an endeavour to ensure that his discoveries would eventually reach a wider audience. This later included sharing our collection of photographs. Several of his are included in my two volume book, the Troy Deception, which is the product of this initial collaboration.

Over the next nine years many people have helped me in different ways as I struggled to understand something of Homeric studies and ancient Greek history. I must first thank Noel Worswick, a retired Oxford University tutor and lecturer in Greek and Roman studies, for his generous support while acting informally as my mentor, and for carrying out an academic appraisal in 2004/5 of my first study – a draft thesis building upon on Lascelles' discovery. His kindness in trying to impart some of his vast knowledge of ancient history to me was always appreciated, even when the message was not always understood. Professor Walter Radt, head of excavations at Pergamon, was both kind and helpful, albeit unconvinced, when I met him in Istanbul to discuss the possibility of Troy at Bergama. I am grateful to both him and his publishers, Wissenschaftliche Buchgesellschaft, for giving me permission to reproduce one or two images from his magnificent book 'Pergamon'. I am much indebted to Prof. Dieter Hertel for generously providing much information about the discovery of Bronze Age pottery on Pergamon. This has given valuable archaeological support to our equation of Pergamon with Homer's Ilios. I also found the excellent 'Dictionary of Classical Mythology' by Dr. Jenny March a most valuable resource, and must thank her for allowing me to reproduce the two maps of the ancient Mediterranean and Greece. A big thank you is also due to the staff supporting the Google Earth website, who allow the use of their images for educational purposes. In an area where few good maps are readily available, their gradual improvement since 2003 of image quality over the areas between Pergamon and Candarli has led to a much better understanding of the true nature of what was once Homer's Trojan plain. I hope the reader will take full advantage of this great resource.

I would also like to thank Robert Bittlestone for showing the world, in his splendid book Odysseys Unbound (2005), that the Ithaca of the Odyssey has probably been found on Cephalonia. Against all the odds he has convincingly shown that the poet's descriptions of the Ithaca landscape may now be found on the western part of Cephalonia known as Paliki, which was once a separate island. Taken together with my own findings, these show that the poet's detailed descriptions of the Ithaca and Trojan landscapes are real, and are not poetic imaginings as has previously been believed.

An amateur outsider seeking interest and support for an unwelcome and at first sight outlandish theory can expect short shrift from today's busy academics. In my case, among some notable exceptions who were willing both to read short sections of my work and comment on them, I must particularly thank Professors Anthony Snodgrass, Richard Seaford, George Huxley, Walter Burkert, Peter Frei, Oliver Dickinson, and most recently, Gregory Nagy. Thanks are also due to Eric van Dongen, Rosemary Baines and Sophia Fisher for much needed help with German translation. Thanks also to Paul Martin and Andrew Tatham for their generous help in producing some of the sketch maps. I would also like to thank the staff at the great libraries of the Bodleian (Oxford), Cambridge University and especially London University's Senate House, who have always been most helpful, friendly and tolerant. Thank you also to Jeremy Thompson and the staff of Troubador Publishing Ltd for their help and support in getting this book ready for publication. And many thanks also to Joanna and Sarah Griggs for help with proof reading, and to my son Chris for getting my web sites, www.troyatbergama.com and www.thetroydeception.com, up and running.

Thanks must also go to all those scholars, past and present, whose work has contributed to my greater understanding of questions concerning Troy and Homer. Responsibility for all errors of fact and misunderstandings, however, is entirely mine.

My lengthy studies have meant that family relationships have been much neglected for far too long, and for this my apologies and thanks for their understanding go to all concerned, especially to Jane. I look forward to resuming a normal retirement as soon as possible.

INTRODUCTORY NOTES FOR READERS

General comments. Dates. Proper names and pronunciation. General maps.

General comments

Some who read this book will be familiar with the subject of Troy and its history. Some will have visited the site called Troia or Ilium near the mouth of the Hellespont. Of these, many during their tour of the region will have visited the magnificent acropolis of Pergamon. However, those reading about the subject for the first time may be unfamiliar with the geography of western Turkey, its place names and its language. They may know little or nothing of the history of Troy, or about Homer, or about the later Greek and Roman historians and commentators who wrote about the Trojan War. Also, archaeological terms may be unfamiliar. For these readers, it is hoped that the Glossary at the end of this book will prove helpful.

Dates

This book is mainly concerned with ancient history, archaeology, and the events of the Trojan War. Please note therefore that **all dates should be assumed to be 'Before the Christian Era' (BCE)** unless otherwise stated, or the context makes it obvious that the event is fairly recent.

Proper names and pronunciation

Readers may be confused, at least initially, by the fact that some Turkish cities and rivers had different names in the past to those we use today. The western coast of Turkey has, at various times throughout its history, been occupied by Greeks, Romans and Persians. In the last century, after the first world war, parts of this coast were occupied for a short period by Greece, until full sovereignty was finally restored. Since then, the older Greek names which are more familiar to western scholars have been replaced by less well known Turkish names. For example Smyrna is now called Izmir, and the Kaikos and Hermus rivers are now the Bakir Çayi and the Gediz Nehri respectively. The Bakir Çayi takes its name from the village of Bakir in the upper catchment, some 15km southeast of Soma. Where appropriate in this study I have used the modern names, but the older ones are also used when referring to the writing and times of ancient Greek and Roman authors.

Greek and Roman names may also differ, often because the Greek ending 'os' is changed to the Roman 'us' or 'um'. Also the Greek 'ai' can change to the Roman 'ae'. The Romans came to adopt most of the Greek Pantheon, but had their own names for some of the gods. For example, the Greek chief god was Zeus, and the Roman chief god was called Jupiter or Jove. Athene was identified with Minerva, and Herakles was called Hercules.

For all these reasons, a place, river or person may be referred to by two or more different names, according to which author is being quoted. In this book I use the names that seem best suited to their context, and hope that this does not present the reader with any serious problems. The modern Turkish names will be used when referring to recent times.

As a general rule, the letter 'c' in early Greek names is pronounced as 'k'. I have spelt such names as Herakles, Skamander, Kaikos, Kilikians, etc. with a 'k' rather than with a 'c', to help ensure their correct pronunciation. There are one or two exceptions, such as Mycenae and Mycenaean, where the 'c' is more commonly pronounced like an 's'. In Turkish, the letter 'c' with a cedilla (a small comma below it) is pronounced 'ch'. For example, the word 'Çayi', meaning a river, is pronounced 'Chai'.

Below are some of the names most frequently mentioned in this study, along with their most common variants. Where an author is quoted, the names will normally be given as written by that author.

This study	Other variants
Aigai	Aegae.
Alcaeus	Alkaios, the Greek spelling of the name.
Asklepion	Asclepieum, Asklepeion.
Bergama Çayi	Greek – Selinos. Previous Turkish name – Uç Kemer Çayi. The word 'Çayi' (river), is sometimes locally spelt 'cay'.
Bogazkoy	Boghaz Keui, Boghazkoi.

Elaia	Elaea.
Erigol tepe	Molla Mustafa tepe. Homer's tomb of Ilus?
Hisarlik	Ilion, Ilium or Ilium Novum, whose people were Ilians.
Homer's Ilios	Ilium.
Kaikos	Caicos, Caicus, Turkish - Bakir Çay or Çayi.
Kalarga hill	Prophet Elias, Sultan tepe, Homer's Kallikolone?
Kara Dagh	Kara Dag, ancient Kanai, Sappho's Aega, The Aigai of the Iliad?
Myrine's tomb	Bataeia, Thorn Hill, Tomb of the Dancing Myrine.
Pisistratus	Peisistratos or Peisistratus. Pronounced Pi (as in pie)-sis-trar-tus, accent on the second syllable.
Sigeum	Sigeion.
Skamander	Scamander, 'Xanthus' or 'the waters of Xanthus'.

Note – when pronouncing Turkish names, the accent should generally be spread evenly across the syllables. Stressing the penultimate syllable should be avoided.

General Maps

Fig.I.1 shows the countries round the Mediterranean.

Fig.I.2 shows the ancient Greek countries in and around the Aegean Sea in the Hellenistic era.

Note — Mysia on Fig. I.2 is shown too far inland. It should refer to the Kaikos / Bakir Çayi valley.

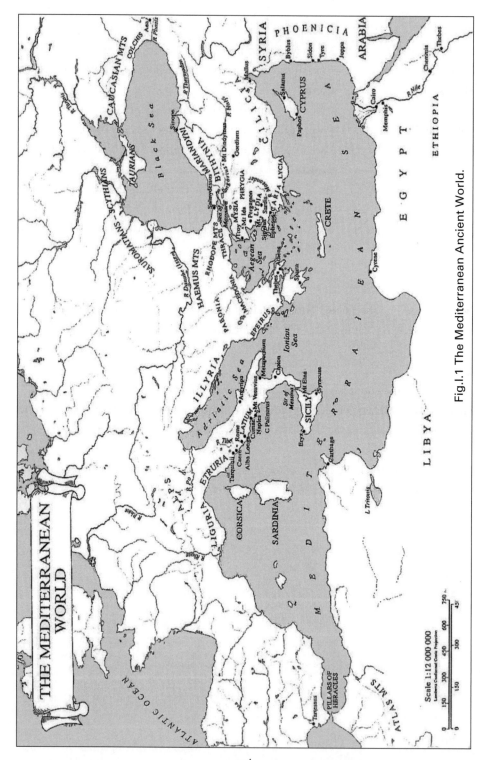

Fig.I.1 The Mediterranean Ancient World.

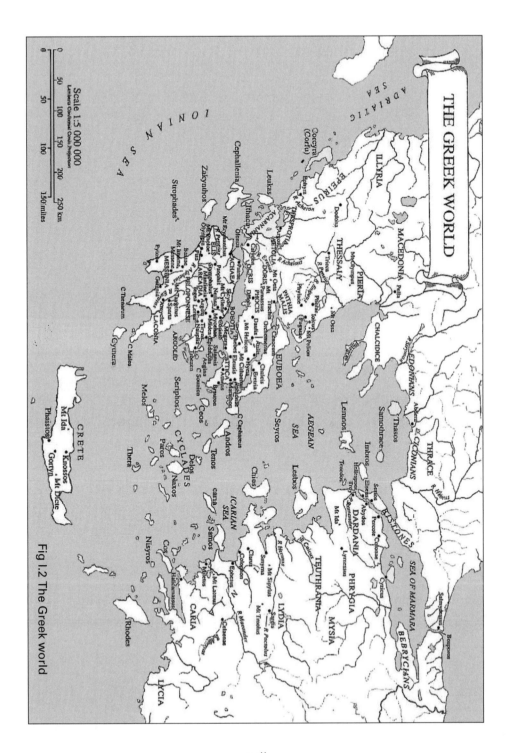

Fig I.2 The Greek world

PROLOGUE

Breakfasts in the courtyard at the Athene Pension in Bergama are the social highlight of the day. Here, behind high stone walls and cooled by the brown façade of the Ottoman townhouse, guests can meet the new arrivals and share their travel experiences. They start any time between nine and ten, not because this suits the guests, but because Aydin gets up late. Our young bachelor host has fully embraced the Internet as the only readily accessible form of nightlife in Bergama. While this results in late breakfasts, it did not appear to diminish his ability to make all-inclusive omelettes. Coming from a sizzling pan, these are augmented with copious quantities of local seasonal vegetables, olives and various cheeses. One generous portion, accompanied with all the usual (and unusual) Turkish breakfast trimmings and any amount of bread, tends to render lunch obsolete. His modest pension, full of Ottoman character, lies in the heart of the old city. The famous acropolis of Pergamon towers above it on the eastern side. It is also not far from a low-lying hill on the city's north-western edge known locally as Musalla, or by its full name Musalla Mezarlik. This, roughly translated, means 'Cemetery Hill'. It was used as a cemetery for some 400 years up until some time in the 1920s. It then remained almost devoid of houses until the 1960s, but today it is covered with a variety of modest homes. And, although two prominent Roman arches still stand on opposite sides of the hill, it is almost never visited by tourists. Their attention is focused on the magnificence of Pergamon, generally acknowledged as perhaps the finest acropolis in Western Anatolia. Yet it was to the far side of Musalla that I walked before breakfast one sunny morning in June 2003.

I started out on the road which led from Bergama to Kozak, which lies some 22km away in the hills to the north. These hills are at the eastern edge of a large area of mountainous country covering most of the north western corner of Turkey. In ancient times, these uplands were known to the Greeks as Mount Ida. Beside the road runs a small river, the Bergama Çayi, which flows through Bergama, across the plain, and into the much larger Bakir Çayi on the southern side of the valley. Being summer, the flow was barely a trickle. This is because water is taken from the river further upstream, and pumped into the river on the other side of Pergamon. Here, a new reservoir helps to maintain the water supply to this rapidly expanding town. But the wide banks, and the two large ancient culverts that carried the river under the Roman 'Kizil Avlu' (Red Hall), bear silent witness to the great volume of water it once had to carry when heavy winter rains fell on the uplands to the north.

Bergama once nestled into the foothills of Ida on the north side of the valley, but today it spills far out across the plain. On the outskirts of the town I came to a small jutting outcrop of natural rock some 7 metres high, on the left hand side of the road. Into this rock some ancient stone-worker had carved out some recesses, which may have served as places to stand small statues, or a carved relief. Perhaps here was once an ancient shrine. Just beyond this rock I turned left along a rough gravel pathway that leads round to the northern side of Musalla. A few hundred metres along this rain-eroded path brought me to a large Roman arch. On this side of the hill, away from the town, the Romans had built an amphitheatre. This one was rather unusual. It had straddled a small stream that ran in a valley along the north side of the hill. According to my old 'Fodor' guidebook, the stream was called the Teledere. The amphitheatre was built in such a way that the flow in the stream could be shut off, allowing water to build up within the amphitheatre to form a small lake. In this lake, the spectators could be entertained by what Fodor called 'combats involving crocodiles and hippopotami.' It was built to hold an audience of some 50,000 people, which gives an indication of the size and prosperity of the city at the height of the Roman Empire.

I stood there for a while under the clear blue morning sky, taking in the scene, and trying to imagine what this hill must have looked like some three thousand years ago, long before the coming of the Romans and their blood sports. My attention was then caught by two thin young bullocks, which appeared from between the houses on the hilltop. They were followed by a man waving a stick. He proceeded to run behind them, driving the animals down the steep side of the hill, across the almost dry stream in the bottom of the valley, and up the other side. There, in the brown grassy field at the top of the bank, they drank their fill from a white cattle trough, fed by a natural spring flowing from the hillside. For me this scene had a special significance. If a new theory about Troy was right, this scene may have been enacted countless times since the hill was first occupied in Trojan times, some three thousand years ago. I imagined

I was perhaps only the second person in modern times to stand here, in this rather impoverished corner of Bergama, knowing the secret of this brown and dusty hill.

Musalla is not yet promoted as being of any interest to tourists who come to Bergama. It had long been the site of a cemetery, and photographs taken in 1958 showed that it was not yet built on. It is not even shown on most of the Bergama street maps that are reproduced in the popular international guidebooks. However, archaeologists have long recognised it as being of some interest. In the late 1950s the hilltop was subjected to some brief shallow excavations, but little was found to suggest that it was occupied much before Attalid times. After the second world war Bergama started to grow rapidly. It offered a home and some land to many refugees from Eastern Europe, who preferred to leave their homelands rather than live under a communist regime. After these preliminary excavations were completed in 1958, houses started to be built on this hill. I thought that its name, 'Cemetery Hill', was rather appropriate, given what may still lie buried deep within it.

From where I stood I watched the first tourist bus of the day wind its way up the road leading to the top of the acropolis. Acropolis is a Greek word meaning high (acro) city (polis), and this certainly applies to Pergamon. It rises to a height of over 300m, and is crowned with some fine Hellenistic and Roman ruins. It is particularly well known for its open air theatre auditorium, carved into the hillside. This is the steepest and one of the largest found in the western Mediterranean. The steep hill, a natural outcrop of volcanic rock, stands less than a kilometre from Musalla, on the other side of the Bergama Çayi. With its northern and eastern sides almost sheer in places, it seemed to tower over its smaller neighbour. At its summit, I could see the re-erected white marble columns of Trajan's temple glinting in the morning sun. On this hill once stood the capital city of the Attalid kings, successors of Alexander the Great, who ruled the region from around 281 to 133. Here the acropolis dominates the broad flat plains of the middle and lower valleys of the Bakir Çayi.

From about 8-6C, the Greeks colonised most of the west coast of Turkey. The early Greeks knew this region as Mysia, and the Bakir Çayi as the river Kaikos. It was the northernmost of four major rivers that flow westwards from the central plateau of Anatolia, passing through wide and fertile plains until it reached the Aegean Sea. This plateau was once home to ancient Phrygia, whose capital, Gordion, lies some 400km to the east of Bergama. In its heyday Phrygia was ruled by the rich and powerful King

Midas. Who does not know the legend of Midas, whose touch turned everything to gold? Once he was thought of as a mythical character, but now many believe he was a real historical king. This is because the name 'Mitas of Mushki', Mushki being an early Asiatic name for Phrygia, has been found in the royal annals of the ancient Assyrian kings.

The next major river to the south is known in the history books as the Hermus river. It flowed past ancient Sardis, the once famous capital of Lydia, and into the sea a little north of Smyrna. Today the Hermus is called the Gediz Nehri [1], and Smyrna is now called Izmir, a vast sprawling industrial city. The ancient acropolis there is still called Old Smyrna. The early Greeks believed that Homer once lived near Smyrna in the late 8th and early 7th C. He was believed to be the author of two great epic poems, the Iliad and the Odyssey. These are the earliest known poems which tell us something of the immortal story of the Trojan War, fought between the Greeks and the Trojans. The Greeks had come to Troy in a thousand ships to rescue the beautiful queen Helen of Sparta. The special quality of these epics ensures that today Homer is still regarded as perhaps the finest of all the early epic poets.

The story of how Pergamon became the chosen residence of the Attalid kings deserves a brief mention. It began when Alexander the Great died unexpectedly in 323. His vast newly won empire, stretching from Greece to India, was then divided up between his most senior and trusted generals. One of these was the young Lysimachus, who had amassed a huge personal fortune from gold mines of Thrace, and also as plunder from conquered cities. After Alexander died, and some years later when the historical dust had begun to settle, Lysimachus was given charge of this region of NW Anatolia. At Pergamon he left a large fortune for safe keeping in the care of Philetaerus, one of his most trusted commanders. This fortune was his share of the riches captured during the conquest of Asia. But Lysimachus was himself killed in battle in 281, and Philetaerus then claimed ownership of both the treasure and the city. With the help of this fortune, and with considerable skill and diplomacy, he became accepted by the superpowers of the day as the ruler of a kingdom there. Thus he founded a new ruling dynasty. When he died he passed his kingdom on to his nephew Eumenes I (263-241), who in turn passed it to his adopted son Attalus I (241-197). Attalus won a famous victory over the Celts, bringing a measure of peace and prosperity to the young kingdom. As the power of Rome grew steadily in the west, so Pergamon became a staunch ally of Rome in the east. Successive kings displayed their wealth by building great monuments on the acropolis. Larger and more formidable walls were built to defend the city on the hill. During its heyday, it became a centre of learning to rival Athens and Alexandria. It had a library that grew in size and stature until it was recognised as second in importance only to the library of Alexandria. Pergamon also had a fine harbour some 25km to the west at Elaia, in a wide bay just east of the mouth of the Bakir Çayi. The fertile lands produced an abundance of food, especially wheat, which ancient records confirm was sometimes exported to Greece. The lush pasture of the plains enabled the Attalids to establish a reputation for breeding fine horses. By the time the last Attalid king, Attalus III (138-133) came to the throne, Rome was extending her power ever further eastwards, and he bowed to the inevitable. When he died, he left a will handing over his kingdom to the Romans. Soon afterwards, Pergamon became the Roman capital of a large region of western Turkey that the Romans called 'Asia'.

During the next three centuries of peace under the Roman Empire, Pergamon prospered. Its population grew at one point to some 200,000, and extensive aqueducts were built to bring more water to the city. With no external threat, fortification walls were not needed, and some were pulled down so their stone could be used for new buildings. But with the eventual decline of the Roman Empire, Pergamon also fell into decline. A major earthquake in 262AD destroyed the Roman aqueduct bringing water to the city from the northern hills. And, as with many of the once great cities on the western coast of Turkey, such as Miletus and Ephesus, its decline was hastened by the loss of its harbour. The large western Anatolian rivers flowing into the Aegean brought down with them huge quantities of silt every year. This built up around the river mouths, extending the river plain, and causing the old harbours to silt up and become unusable. Pergamon also suffered from being away from the main trading routes between east and west. Lying out of sight from the rest of the world, up until the 19th century much still remained of its ancient buildings. By then, the Ottoman Empire, itself well into terminal decline, had little interest in the preservation of antiquities.

Western interest in Pergamon was rekindled when a German archaeologist, Carl Humann, visited it in around 1870AD. There he found that sections of beautifully carved stones, which once adorned the face of a great altar of Zeus, were being broken up and fed into lime kilns for the production of fertiliser. He managed to obtain permission to rescue as many of these as possible, and these he sent back to Berlin. There the great altar was reconstructed to form the centrepiece of Berlin's now famous Pergamon Museum. Today, much of our understanding of the layout and succession of these civic buildings derives from the meticulous work of a succession of German archaeologists. Professor Radt, who supervised teams of archaeologists here for over 30 years until he retired in 2005, deserves special praise for his book, entitled simply 'Pergamon'. [2] This gives a brilliant exposition of the site, its history, and its environment. Tourists come here to see the splendour of the towering acropolis with its fine views, and the ruins of the many Hellenistic and Roman buildings upon it. Professor Radt and his predecessors have naturally focussed their archaeological studies on the Hellenistic and Roman buildings on the acropolis. The obvious need to preserve these ruins means that they cannot be swept away, as Schliemann did with the upper layers at 'Troy', to discover what, if anything, lies beneath them. At the time of my visit, only a few finds as yet could be dated to the pre-Attalid period. The most important of these was a recently found 'archaic wall', which encircled much of the area occupied during the Attalid era. This was dated by Radt to roughly to 8C or 7C. But this 'archaic wall' makes it clear that the acropolis was occupied long before Attalid times.

My attention was brought back to Cemetery Hill by a group of small children, pushing past me on the narrow path to play near the animals by the spring. Again I pondered over this mysterious mound and its possible secret. I believed then that this low hill, lying here in this forgotten corner of the city, may have once lain within the ancient city of Troy. Thanks to 'The Iliad' and 'The Odyssey', Troy was one of the most famous of all the world's ancient cities. By studying these epics we can learn a great deal about Troy and the Trojan War. The war, which led to the destruction of Troy, is commonly believed to have taken place between 1300 and 1200. Both epics are generally thought to have been composed around 700. If so, they must contain much traditional poetic material about the war. This must have been handed down over the intervening centuries to the time of Homer by many generations of ancient bards. It was the task of these bards to remember traditional poems, both mythical and legendary, and they earned a living by reciting them to their audiences.

And yet, before we go any further, we run into our first difficulty. From the Iliad we learn that Troy had another name, Ilios. These two names, the scholars tell us, both refer to exactly the same place. In the epics, these are apparently used interchangeably, perhaps according to whichever name best fitted the poetic line in the composition. But is this really true? A careful reading of the Iliad shows that the name Ilios was only used when referring to the holy and towering acropolis. Ilios was high and windy, and had steep streets. Troy, on the other hand, seemed to be the well-walled lower town, with lofty gates, fine towers, and broad streets. Ilios, we learn, was where the king and other members of the royal family lived in marbled splendour. There too lived the servants of the royal household, and the priests of the temples and altars dedicated to the gods who protected the town. Today's Troy and Ilios are at a small site, some 150km away at the southern end of the Straits of the Dardanelles, known locally as Hisarlik. The problem is that Hisarlik could never have fitted the descriptions in the Iliad. Before the famous Heinrich Schliemann first dug at Hisarlik, anyone using the Iliad to find Troy and Ilios looked for a spacious walled and towering acropolis, with an adjacent lower town, also walled, and with a hot spring nearby. The history books tell us that Musalla Mezarlik was walled in the days of the Attalid kings, but today this wall has disappeared and its extent is unknown. So here, at Pergamon and Bergama, there was once a spacious walled acropolis and a walled lower town. Could these places match the Iliad's descriptions of Ilios and Troy? After his first visit here in 1980 my Australian friend, John Lascelles, believed they did. This was what I had come to see for myself.

John Lascelles was the man responsible for my being in Bergama. He had trained as an architect in Oxford in the 1950s, around the time when another British architect, Michael Ventris, announced he had deciphered the ancient Linear B tablets. These tablets, with their strange script, were first found at the Minoan palace of Knossos on Crete by Sir Arthur Evans. Despite more tablets being found later at Pylos by Blegen, for fifty years they defied all efforts to decipher them. Then, against all expectations, Ventris discovered that they were written in an early form of Greek. The Minoans were regarded as a separate civilisation with their own language, who were eventually wiped out by some natural catastrophe and replaced by the Mycenaeans from mainland Greece. So to discover that the Minoans also spoke an early from of Greek caused a sensation. Suddenly, these Linear B tablets threw open a new window onto the heroic world of the Mycenaean Greeks, a world previously known to us only through the epics of Homer and the findings of archaeology. John was fascinated by this discovery by a fellow architect, and it inspired him to take a life-long interest in the history of ancient Greece and the Homeric world. It was his detective work that led him to claim he had discovered Troy at Bergama after he first visited here in 1980. He had long been dissatisfied with the popular belief that Hisarlik was the site of Troy. He believed that neither the archaeology of the site, nor its topography, seemed to match what we should expect from the story of the Iliad. John was convinced that here, upon Cemetery Hill where the man and his cattle now live, once stood the city that Homer called Troy. Here and on the acropolis, the Trojans stood firm and safe behind their fortified walls for more than nine years against a mighty Greek army.

He was to return to Bergama for a second visit in 1991. By this time he believed he had found almost all of the features of the Trojan landscape that were described in the Iliad, many of which were absent at Hisarlik. He then wrote a draft book about his discovery. However, he failed to excite any academic interest in his discoveries, and in its original form this book remained unpublished. Not surprisingly, contributions from amateurs which dispute the conclusions of generations of expert scholars are not welcomed by the professionals. If we stop to consider just how much has been invested in the belief that Troy was at Hisarlik, it is easy to understand that many people would find such a revolutionary proposal extremely unwelcome. Over the last century, thousands of scholars have devoted millions of scholarly hours to the study of Homer, and to formulating theories about his work, based on the belief that Troy was at Hisarlik. German and American scholars, as well as the Turkish authorities, have invested millions of dollars in promoting Hisarlik as Homer's Troy. Although no hot spring has been found there, this is explained by saying that the hot spring, and other features of the Trojan landscape not found there, must have been invented by a poetic imagination. Thousands of tourists visit it every year. Why should scholars waste their time bothering to look at an amateur study claiming to show that Troy was not at Hisarlik, but at a site some 120 miles away where no-one had ever thought of looking before? Surely the world could not, and would not, believe that the experts had been wrong about its location for over 2,500 years? How could the true site of Troy have remained undiscovered, when it had been sought by so many for so long?

From the Roman archway, I walked over the earth bank that bridged the small stream in the valley bottom, and took a closer look at this spring. There was little sign of any flow in the stream, and only a trickle of water appeared to come from the spring. The small group of children had started playing with a kite, and took no notice of me as I came closer. There I found that there were, in fact, three springs, all quite close together, and the cattle drank from the middle one. The water feeding them was obviously flowing out from the side of the hill. I wondered if this cattle trough might mark the place where, in the climax of the Iliad, Hector was killed by Achilles. Hector was the greatest of the Trojan warriors. The Iliad tells us that he was killed close to two springs, one warm and the other cold, found not far from the Dardanian Gates of Troy. Today, the water in the trough felt disappointingly cold to the touch, and I wondered if I would find any warm springs nearby that would lend credence to the Iliad. Later, on the same day, yet another piece of supporting evidence revealed itself. There, on a map of Bergama bought at the local museum, I saw 'Cleopatra's Spring' shown less than 2km away from Cemetery Hill. It was described on the map as a thermal spring with a temperature of 35 degrees C. So today, over 2,500 years later and only some two kilometres away from where I was standing, was evidence for all to see of local geothermal activity. The 'hot spring' of the Iliad may possibly therefore have been more than just a poetic invention.

I walked slowly over to the upper spring, then stopped and stared in amazement. There, beside the collecting chamber, with cement around it to keep it in place, lay an old white stone washing trough. Half of a second trough had been placed alongside it for good measure. This was completely unexpected. They were not there when Lascelles came here in 1980 and 1991, although he did find half of a trough buried under a nearby bush. At once, the Iliad's description of the place where Hector died sprang to mind. Achilles had chased Hector three times around the walls of Troy, passing close to the Dardanian Gate and the springs on each circuit. By the time Hector reached the springs for the fourth time, he was exhausted. There, resigned to the fate ordained for him by the gods, the greatest of the Trojan heroes stood, fought, and died. The Iliad has this to say: 'And there, near the springs, are broad washing troughs, fair and wrought of stone, where the wives and lovely daughters of the Trojans were used to wash bright clothes formerly in the time of peace.' (Il. 22.144ff.) Now who would have thought that here, by the place John Lascelles claimed was once Troy, and some 2,700 years after Homer lived, we would find not only a spring, but an old stone washing trough beside it. Here it seemed, in this small and rather isolated corner of western Turkey, some aspects of daily life had not changed very much over the last three thousand years.

Looking back at the archway, I could see that the Dardanian Gate of Troy may once have stood on the northern edge of this town. From its name we might expect that it once opened on to a road leading towards Dardania, close to Hisarlik and some hundred or so miles away to the north-west. At the time of the Trojan War, Dardania was ruled by Trojan princes related to King Priam. Some of these nobles came to Troy to fight for their king in his hour of need. If they came here from Dardania, they would have travelled across Mt. Ida, past Adramyttion (ancient Thebe), headed SE towards Kozak, and then turned south to reach Troy at Bergama. Here, the Dardanian Gate would have been hidden from the plain of battle. This explains why Trojan reinforcements could have arrived at Troy unseen by the Achaeans.

Not wishing to be late for breakfast, I started to make my way back to the Pension. On the way I bought a large ripe water melon from a huge pile blocking the pavement in front of a corner shop. This I would share with Aydin and his guests later in the day. When I arrived, breakfast was already laid out, and three other guests were sitting at the table in the small courtyard. Soon our genial host brought his famous vegetable omelette from the kitchen, and we all feasted. Later, over a mug of apple tea, we discussed my Troy project, in which Aydin took a keen interest. I had already told him that this discovery was first made by John Lascelles, whom I'd met when I visited Canberra, Australia, in 2002. At that time John had almost given up trying to persuade scholars that he had made a discovery worthy of their serious attention. He had heard, through a mutual friend, of my pending visit to Australia, and of my interest in ancient history and chronology. It was this friend who had given me a copy of his manuscript to look at. I read it during my visit, and found his arguments, both against Troy being at Hisarlik, and in favour of Troy at Bergama, quite compelling. But, at that time, I knew little about Homer and his epics. Since then I have carried out wide-ranging research on many aspects related to Homer and his world. And everywhere I looked, I found more and more evidence that appears to support his theory. I told Aydin that, as a result of the discoveries made during my present visit, supported by much photographic evidence, I now believed I had a strong enough case to convince any open-minded scholar that Lascelles' theory was correct. My plan was to assemble all this evidence into a thesis for academic appraisal, and to ask my friend Noel Worswick, then a senior lecturer and tutor in ancient Greek and Roman history at Oxford University, if he would be willing to review it. If the results were encouraging, I hoped then to publish a book about it. When I left the pension, Aydin wished me luck, and asked me to send him a copy of my book when it came out. I thanked him very much for his warm hospitality, assured him I'd mention his pension, and of course I'd send him a copy of my book. If he wished, I said, I would send him a stock of them that he could sell to his guests. He just smiled.

All that happened over eight years ago. After much further study and research, and many interruptions, the book I discussed with Aydin is now before you. Whatever your verdict, I hope you get as much interest and pleasure from reading it as I have done during the long process of its creation.

PART I

REJECTING TROY AT HISARLIK

CHAPTER 1

SETTING THE SCENE

Introduction. Sketch map Figure1. Introducing Homer, the Iliad, the Odyssey.
Introducing Hisarlik. Troy's general location from the Iliad. Finding Troy at Hisarlik.
Hisarlik as a coastal fortress. Did Troy exist at Hisarlik? – an old debate. Hisarlik on trial.
Achilles tells us where to find Troy. Hisarlik as Troy – more faith than fact.
Addressing the problems.

Introduction

Today, finding the site of Troy is easy. Open any map of Europe and there it is, a black dot on the western edge of Turkey. It sits beside the outlet of the Straits of the Dardanelles, earlier known as the Hellespont. Here, the waters of the Danube and several other great rivers from western and central Russia finally reach the Mediterranean, after flowing through the Black Sea, the Bosphorus and the Sea of Marmara. Beside the black dot is the name 'Troy', or perhaps 'Troia'. Sometimes it is even marked on maps of the world, such is deemed to be the measure of its fame.

A simplified sketch map of the region around Troy is shown as Figure 1. This map stretches from the island of Samothrace in the north-west, to Izmir, ancient Smyrna, in the south. The great mountain range known to the Greeks as Mount Ida covers the whole of the Troad, and extends down as far as the northern side of the lower Kaikos valley. Its highest peak, about 1300m above sea level, was known as Gargarus. This peak lies some 50km to the south-east of Troy, and some 85km north-north-west of Bergama. The island of Samothrace, dominated by Mount Fengari, is in the top left hand corner of the

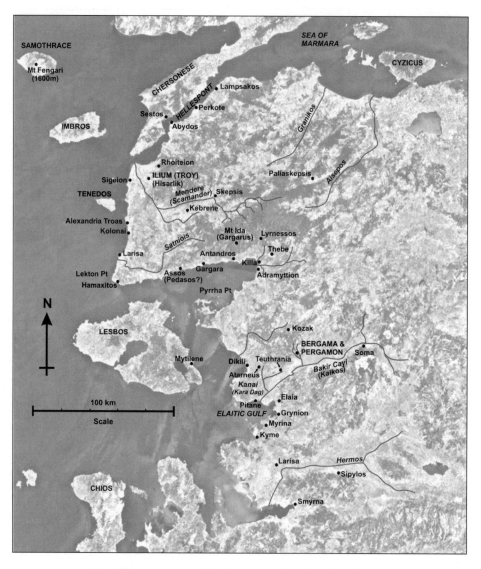

Fig.1. Sketch map of the Troad as described by Strabo.

map. The top of this mountain is clearly visible from Troy over the low lying island of Imbros. The island of Tenedos lies just off the coast to the south of Sigeum.

Today's Troy was discovered by Heinrich Schliemann, who first started excavations in 1870 on a site known locally as Hisarlik. The name means 'the place of the fort'. It lies due north of the island of Lesbos, once home to one of Greece's most famous women, the poet Sappho. Due east of Lesbos, on the southern edge of Mt. Ida, lies Bergama and the magnificent acropolis of Pergamon. They are on the northern edge of the plain of a river known to the Greeks as the Kaikos, but today called the Bakir Çayi. This region was called Mysia by the ancient Greeks, home to ancient Teuthrania.

The earliest mention of Teuthrania is found in one of the Trojan legends, in the unlikely tale of the Mysian war. [1] This tells us that the Achaeans lost their way when they first set sail for Troy. They reached Mysia thinking they were at Troy, and then attacked and destroyed the walled city of Teuthrania. They were then driven away by an army led by a local hero called Telephos, whereupon they returned to Greece. Some two or ten years later, according to which legend you choose to believe, they sailed for Troy again, and this time arrived successfully. Teuthrania is thought to have been the home of the Teucrians, also called Trojans by Herodotus.

The next large river valley to the south of the Kaikos valley is that of the Gediz river, once known as the Hermus. Here we find the great industrial city of Izmir on the site of the ancient city of Smyrna, once regarded by the ancients as the birthplace of Homer. Also marked are the locations of other places, some mentioned in the Iliad and some described by Strabo, the ancient Greek Geographer, in his study of the Troad. He thought that Mount Ida and the Troad, the lands over which King Priam of Troy held sway, extended as far south as the lower Kaikos valley. All these places are mentioned at some point in later chapters.

But did the legendary Troy really once stand at Hisarlik? Here there was certainly once a fortress, first built perhaps a thousand years before the Trojans would have lived there. Here, perched on the edge of a ridge and overlooking the plain at the mouth of the Mendere, its guardians could keep watch for marauding bands of pirates, and observe the ships that sailed up or down the Straits. Why does the world in general take it for granted that this was once the site of Troy? What is the evidence, both for and against, this assumption? Where is the great acropolis of holy Ilios as described in the Iliad? Can a larger and more impressive site be found which gives us a better match with the Iliad's descriptions of Troy, Ilios and the Trojan plain? If Teuthrania was the home of the Teucrians, and Teucrians were also known as Trojans, surely Teuthrania and Troy should lie in the same valley? I will be addressing these and many other questions during the course of this study. One of my aims is to try to convince you that the 'Troy' marked on today's maps was not the home of the Trojans. The principal aim of this volume will be to show, with a very high degree of probability, that the plain of Troy as described in the Iliad may be found much more convincingly in the lower valley of the Bakir Çayi, between Pergamon and the river mouth near Candarli.

My task will not be easy. Most people find it very hard to change their beliefs, especially if taught to them as fact at an early age. The evidence presented here will have to be very good if it is to convince the sceptics. I believe that it is, and hope that, when considered as a whole, this new theory will be accepted. It offers a plausible explanation of much of the diverse evidence about Troy and the Trojan War. I am greatly encouraged by the fact it has already gained a measure of support from a few senior professional scholars. I hope that, when you have finished reading this book, you also will agree with me that the case for the Trojan plain at Bergama is entirely credible, and deserves to be heard and considered seriously by as wide an audience as possible.

Introducing Homer, the Iliad and the Odyssey

In this book I aim to recreate the landscape of the Trojan plain as described in the Iliad, and compare this with the landscapes at Hisarlik and Bergama. Yet the Iliad did not tell the whole story of the Trojan War. It told mainly of events during some two months in the tenth year of the war, ending with the death of the Trojan captain Hector at the hands of Achilles. Much of what happened before and afterwards is told in the Odyssey, and in other Troy-related epics not credited to Homer. [2] It will therefore be important to make sure that the descriptions of the landscape in both the Iliad and Odyssey are consistent with each other, and also with my findings. Since these epics are the principal sources for my study, I should first give some general background information about what we know of their origin and authorship.

The ancients believed that both epics were composed, wholly or largely, by a poet they called Homer. They kept no convincing record of when he lived, but today many think the Iliad and Odyssey originate from around 720 to 680 BC. It is also generally accepted that the version of the Iliad we have today has come down to us not much changed from a version produced in Athens in 6C BC. This version was developed and produced for their great festival to Athena, the Panathenaica, in the eras of Solon and Pisistratus, the first tyrant of Athens. How much of these epics is the work of Homer, or of bards who came before and after him, is a matter of endless debate, but the influence of the Athenians is clearly seen in some passages.

Today some scholars, in the absence of what they regard as positive proof, refuse to believe that such a person as Homer ever actually existed. This illustrates how little we really know with any certainty about the origins of the epics. Other uncertainties abound. If he did exist, when and where did he live? How did he know so much about the Trojan War? How much of the two long epics did he compose, and how much came from traditional poems which existed in his time? How much has been added in later? Did he write them down as he composed them, or were they originally composed, learnt by heart, and recited to audiences as oral poetry? At one extreme, are the two epics simply mythical stories, made up and embellished over the centuries to produce the poems we have today? Or, at the other, is the action a vivid and accurate description, by a poetic genius, of real historical people taking part in a real historical war? Scholars have been debating these questions for some 2,500 years, but we actually have very little firm evidence, and even less proof, to help us supply the answers.

So what do we know? We know that the Iliad was believed by the ancients to be the work of a bard they called Homer. It had a sub-title, 'The wrath of Achilles'. Some believe that this was, in effect, the core poem of the Iliad, the earliest part, to which later sections have been added. This suggests that the great epic we know as the Iliad has developed by accretion.

We know that Strabo, perhaps the best known geographer of the Roman era, had a very high regard for the geographical information contained in the Iliad. This knowledge should at least help give the story of the Trojan War some geographical credibility. The Iliad tells us that the Greek army at Troy was led by Agamemnon, king of Mycenae. We know that a real historical walled royal city in southern Greece called Mycenae existed from earliest times, and its ruins were never lost in antiquity. Nearly 2,000 years ago a Greek travel guide and historian, called Pausanias, wrote that he had seen the royal graves of Agamemnon and his family lying just inside the gates of Mycenae. In the Iliad, Mycenae is described as 'rich in gold'. When Schliemann dug there in 1876 he discovered some deep shafts containing multiple burials, together with large quantities of objects made of gold and bronze. So here is evidence that suggests that both Pausanias and the Iliad were telling us the truth. Mycenae was a real place which at one time was indeed 'rich in gold'. There is no reason to doubt the legends that a king named Agamemnon once ruled there, and Schliemann believed that he had found his tomb. As in Egyptian burials, some of the bodies were buried wearing gold face masks. However, current dating methods lead archaeologists to claim that these burials are some 200 years earlier than the time of Agamemnon. So we must reluctantly accept that Pausanias had been misinformed as to the occupants of the graves.

The names of many other places in different parts of the Greek world are found in the Iliad. These appear in Book 2, in a section known as the 'Catalogue of Ships', which is a long list of places which sent troops to Troy. [3] A knowledge of the history of these places from the time of Strabo, supported by recent site investigations, strongly suggests that the composer of the Catalogue of Ships had a good knowledge of many places that really did exist at the time of the Trojan War.

The geography of the Odyssey is much more uncertain. Odysseus describes many places where he stayed, or was shipwrecked, during his return from Troy to his home on Ithaca. Unfortunately, the names of some of the places given in the Odyssey are not recognisable today, so they cannot be identified with any certainty. This means that, although many have tried to reconstruct this journey, none of these reconstructions are convincing.

Our initial impression is therefore that the evidence of geography supports the belief that the Trojan War, with participants from places known to have existed at that time, may possibly have been an historical event. On the other hand, some of the fabulous adventures of Odysseus on unknown islands appear to owe more to myth than to history.

Introducing Hisarlik

For centuries the site at Hisarlik lay largely unnoticed, an unimposing low grassy uneven mound not more than 10m high on a spur of a plateau on the eastern side of the broad flat plain of the river Mendere. This plateau is fairly flat, and stands not more than some 25m above the level of the plain. The road which approaches the site from the east slopes gently downhill towards it. From a strategic viewpoint, the site was not as strong as it appears from the plain. Any attacker planning to capture a fortress here would first gain the higher ground, probably by marching up one of the several valleys cutting into the plateau. Once on this level ground, all the defensive advantage of being at the top of a steep cliff overlooking the plain is lost, and only the height of the fortress walls would stand between the defenders and their attackers. Yet in the Iliad, such an obvious strategy seems never to have crossed the minds of the combined military intelligence of the Achaeans, or of Odysseus, their master tactician.

Today, visitors to the site are greeted by the sight of a large wooden horse, the internationally famous logo for Troy. This can be seen in one of five photographs of the site shown in Chapter 5. It stands in front of the reception buildings, in which some excellent maps and models are on display. The walled site itself is called the citadel, and is supposed to be the holy acropolis of Ilios. To the uninformed tourist, it appears as a rather bewildering and uninspiring succession of ancient walls. Its size is difficult to appreciate, but it is actually roughly circular and no more than about 180m across. This is much too small to be Ilios, the holy city with wide and steep streets as described in the Iliad. Here there was no natural acropolis to justify the epithets 'towering' or 'beetling'. Here there was no room also for all the grand buildings of Priam's palace, temples and temple precincts. No room either for housing for the priests and servants, accommodation for horses, chariots and soldiers, and storage rooms for food and water. No columns of the Athene temple have been reconstructed to help visitors appreciate the grandeur of the ancient city.

Since there is no dominating acropolis to climb, visitors cannot gain an appreciation of the much disputed size of what is today called 'the lower town' on the plateau away from the ridge. Many visitors regard the site as rather uninteresting. To those who do not appreciate the architectural subtleties of ancient wall-building, perhaps the most memorable sight at Hisarlik is of the ships, in the distance across the flat plain, sailing up and down the Straits of the Dardanelles.

Troy's general location from the Iliad

In 1985 Michael Wood[4] published his informative and well illustrated popular book 'In search of the Trojan War.' In it he wrote :

'Of its (Troy's) general location there has never been any dispute'.

There are good reasons for this confident statement. The Iliad, the Odyssey and the myths and legends relating to the Trojan War all take it for granted that there was once a city called Troy on the west coast of Anatolia. Since a few well known places are named in the Iliad which are not far from Troy, it should not be hard to find. I call the mentions of these places 'offsite signposts', since they indicate the direction in which Troy should lie. For example, the Iliad names the sea near Troy as the 'Hellespont'. This name today is taken to refer to the Straits of the Dardanelles, and most people assume that in Trojan times it referred exclusively to the Straits. So the mention of the Hellespont is like a signpost that points us in the direction of Troy beside the Straits. But are we right to assume that the name 'Hellespont' really did refer only to the Straits in the time when the Iliad was written? This is one of the assumptions I will be challenging in a later chapter.

The Iliad mentions some islands not far from Troy, such as Tenedos and Imbros, which retain their Homeric name to the present day. Also nearby was a mountain range with many springs called Mount Ida and this, as we have already seen, was well known in the time of Strabo. And most importantly for all those trying to find Troy, it was visible from Samothrace over the top of Imbros. At the start of the Iliad Book 13, we find Poseidon watching the battle at the Achaean ships from the topmost peak of Samothrace. When he sees their ships being attacked he takes pity on them and hurries to help them resist the Trojan onslaught.

The Iliad also tells us that the Trojan War takes place on the plain of a river called the Skamander. This river is fed, at least in part, from Mount Ida and its springs. Today Hisarlik supporters tell us that the name 'Skamander' is ancestral to the name of the Mendere, but with the prefix 'Kara', which means 'black' in Turkish. So in the most recent archaeological reports we read the name Kara Mendere, where earlier excavators had known only the Mendere. [5] To some, this may seem a rather unconvincing explanation of the first two consonant sounds, 'Sk', in Skamander. However, it is beyond dispute that collectively, these offsite signposts do point inexorably to Troy lying somewhere in the lower Mendere valley.

Finding Troy at Hisarlik

For some 90 years before Heinrich Schliemann, a wealthy, successful businessman, first dug there in 1870, Troy was thought to lie some 10km further up the valley, at a place called Burnabashi. Here there was a natural acropolis with a reported warm and cold spring nearby. But in due course, excavations there confirmed that this could not have been Troy, mainly because the site was not occupied in Trojan times. Before Burnabashi, several other places were at one time or another believed to have been Troy. Much confusion was caused by the fact that people searching for Troy were naturally trying to find, above all else, a towering acropolis within sight of distant Samothrace, standing beside a plain, and with hot and cold springs nearby. It gradually became accepted that no such site existed in the lower Mendere valley. The composer of the Iliad must have used poetic licence when describing the size of Troy and its citadel, and some of the features of the Trojan landscape.

It is a sad fact that almost all sites of ancient cities and burials have suffered at regular intervals from the depredations of local people scavenging for antiquities and building stone. Apart from this activity, Schliemann was actually the third person to excavate on the mound of Hisarlik. The first was John Brunton, a railway engineer from London, employed to build a new hospital for casualties of the Crimean War. [6] By late 1855, the hospital was finished and the war was drawing to a close. Brunton, who was interested in exploring the ancient sites which might be connected to the Trojan legends, found himself for a short while with some 150 idle soldiers under his command. He decided to set them to work digging for antiquities at several sites, one of which was Hisarlik. There, at no great depth, he found some remains of Classical Ilium, including the foundations of a temple, a beautifully carved white marble capital of a Corinthian column, and a fine marble mosaic floor depicting a boar hunt. He later gave his collection of finds from various sites to the British Museum.

The second was Frank Calvert, a sometime American consul, merchant, farmer, gentleman archaeologist and antiquarian. He had been exploring the archaeology of the Troad for many years before Schliemann arrived on the scene. At first he thought Troy was at Bunarbashi, but after digging there he decided that the site was not occupied early enough to date back to the Trojan War. He later tried to buy the site at Hisarlik, quite close to his farm, in the expectation that Priam's city might be found in its lower layer. But he managed to acquire only the eastern half, which did not include the highest part of the mound. In 1864-5 Calvert dug intermittently on his side of the tell. 'Everywhere he dug he hit Classical remains. Nowhere did he reach virgin soil.' [7] He dug three trenches down to between 3 and 4m., reaching in places as far back as the 6th and 7th centuries BC. He found the remains of a temple to Athena [Roman Minerva], including Doric columns and lion head water spouts, and a massive wall built by Lysimachus, one of Alexander the Great's generals. Lack of funds then forced him to stop. Afterwards he said he had missed a Late Bronze Age wall by only a meter. It was Frank Calvert who persuaded Schliemann that Hisarlik was probably the site of Troy.

Schliemann first arrived in the Troad in 1868. After meeting Calvert, he decided they should join forces to excavate the site. He also tried without success to buy the other half from the local owners. Then a law was passed making excavation of antiquities and their export illegal without government permission. Nearly two frustrating years passed without obtaining the necessary government permission or securing the purchase of the site. With his patience exhausted, Schliemann finally decided to act. In April 1870 he put together a small workforce of 10-15 workmen and started excavation on the highest part of the site without buying the site, without permission from the Turkish landowners, and without a government licence. Within about two weeks he had uncovered many interconnecting walls. Cement was used in the more recent walls, but some earlier ones were built with open joints using cut stones of various sizes. The outlines of some buildings were exposed, along with an assortment of coins and fragments of pottery of different kinds. Schliemann was looking for cyclopean walls, built from huge blocks of stone like those still visible at Tiryns and Mycenae, and was bitterly disappointed when none appeared. What he had found were mostly some remains of Classical Novum Ilium. Yet from this confused and unpromising beginning, Schliemann eventually prevailed. His energy, cunning and wealth enabled him eventually to triumph in his many battles with the Turkish authorities. In 1873 he announced the discovery of 'Priam's treasure'. The photographs of his beautiful young wife wearing the Trojan necklaces and other jewellery were seen around the world, capturing the imagination of the world at large and bringing him the international fame and acclamation he had long craved. Henceforth, scholars and the general public alike began, in increasing numbers, to believe that Troy really had been found. By 1882 he had secured the services of a brilliant architect, Wilhelm Dorpfeld, who worked with him on the excavations, helping to establish a greater level of scholarship and archaeological integrity to the often confused and mistaken archaeological conclusions previously reached by Schliemann. After he died in 1890, Dorpfeld worked at Troy for two further seasons in 1893 and 1894. The site was revisited between 1932 and 1938 by a team of archaeologists from the University of Cincinnati, led by Carl Blegen. Work resumed again in the late 1980s and has continued there ever since. From 1991 reports of site activities have been published annually in 'Studia Troica', with articles in both English and German.

The focus of this volume is on the geography and topography of the Trojan plain, so I will dwell only briefly on archaeology. It was naturally hoped that archaeologists would soon reveal a long and prosperous settlement period for the Trojans in the Mycenaean era, followed by a destruction layer with evidence of war and fire, then a long period of abandonment. This would then help confirm both the reality of the war and its date. Alas, such hopes soon vanished. Instead, many different layers of settlement and occupation were revealed, which proved difficult both to identify and date.

Of the nine main occupation levels found there, the level 6th from the bottom, with some fine sloping walls and around 500 years of occupation, was regarded by Dorpfeld as the city of the Trojans. This long period was later divided by Carl Blegen [8] into several subdivisions. The final layer of Troy 6, called Troy 6h, was apparently destroyed by an earthquake, judging by cracks and lateral displacement found in some of the walls. After this destruction came Troy 7a. This was a layer with smaller, less well built houses, which, from its thickness, lasted probably not much more than a generation. The pottery evidence suggested that the survivors of the earthquake had resettled the habitable parts of the mound with no obvious cultural break. Troy 7a was destroyed by fire. 'The blackened debris left by the fire was heaped up everywhere to a height ranging from 0.5m to above 1m above the former ground level, and the new houses were superimposed over the ruins of their predecessors.' [9] Blegen chose this settlement, despite its small size and impoverished appearance, as the Troy captured by the Greeks. After Troy 7a came Troy 7b1, a short period of occupation by the survivors of the fire. Then came Troy 7b2, when the site was taken over by people of a different culture, including a new style of pottery.

Dating these different settlements was not easy. Small pieces of Mycenaean pottery, some imported, were found in the four layers from 6h to 7b2, but identifying different styles from which they could be dated proved controversial. Grey pottery was much more abundant. This included a glazed type, called Grey Minyan Ware, first discovered by Schliemann at Orchomenos, home of King Minyas, some 90km north-west of Athens. 'In Troy VIIa, Grey Minyan Ware occurs in profusion in the identical fabric, finish, and shapes that prevailed in Phase VIh.' [10]. Opinion seemed to veer back towards Troy 6h for a time, but the date of its fall, c1300, seemed too early for the Trojan War. So at present Priam's city is identified as Troy 7a.

The most popular traditional date of the fall of Troy, still broadly accepted by some, is 1194. This was derived by Eratosthenes in 3C BC, mainly from two separate but parallel genealogies of the Kings of Sparta. It was dismissed by Professor Page in 1959 as pure speculation. [11] Today scholars prefer a date c1250-1200, assuming that the war must date to shortly before the destruction of the Mycenaean palaces and the collapse of Mycenaean power. We may conclude therefore that there is broad agreement between history and archaeology at Hisarlik, where Troy, either Phase 6h or 7a, fell around 1300-1200.

However, looked at more closely, the choice for Priam's city at Hisarlik appears unconvincing. It seems to lie between Phase 6h, which fell as a result of an earthquake, or Phase 7a, which seems much too small and impoverished to be regarded as Troy of the Iliad. No significant evidence of war was found at either destruction layer. No evidence of a Greek attacking force has been found. It is now agreed that Classical Ilium was indeed discovered at Hisarlik. Our overall conclusion, however, is that nothing has been found in the excavations which convincingly links the site at Hisarlik to the Troy of the Iliad, or to the story of the Trojan War.

Hisarlik as a coastal fortress

In the late 1970s another bombshell seriously damaged the illusion of Hisarlik as Troy. Working quietly away near the mouth of the Mendere, a soil survey team made a crucial discovery. They found that, at the time of the Trojan War, there was a great bay at the mouth of the river. This meant that the plain that now lies between Hisarlik and the river mouth simply did not exist some 3,200 years ago. Hisarlik at that time was not the site of a great fortified and palatial city far from the sea. It was merely a small fortress on a ridge overlooking a large bay at the mouth of the Straits. In the Iliad the great river plain, which stretches between Troy and the ships, is the stage for most of the action of the Trojan War. Here two large armies fought hand to hand as the battle swayed back and forth between Troy and the Greek ships. At one point the Trojans had, at the end of a hard day's fighting, pushed the Greeks back to their camp by the ships. Here the Trojans were so far from Troy that they decided to risk camping out on the plain rather than return to the safety of their walled city. So to find that this plain could never have existed at Hisarlik was a stunning blow. Finding Troy a few hundred metres from the coast made a mockery of the story of the Iliad. Why would 'Homer', or anyone else for that matter, compose a poem about a great war fought on a plain before Troy when no such plain existed? Surely no-one would believe that Troy could have stood upon such a site?

But a century's worth of investment in Troy at Hisarlik was not to be abandoned overnight. An alternative site for the Greek camp was quickly adopted. This lay on the coast some 9km southwest of Troy, at a place called Besik Bay. When Manfred Korfmann [12] found a few Late Mycenaean remains there, he argued that it was actually a more credible site for the Greek camp than the one, generally accepted since antiquity, at the mouth of the river Mendere. But, from the Iliad, we should be able to follow the Scamander from near the Greek camp, then along the length of the plain until it approaches Troy. Yet from Besik Bay, the Mendere crosses the plain at right angles fairly close to Hisarlik. So, as a possible location of the Greek camp, Besik Bay lamentably fails to match Homer's Trojan plain.

Did Troy exist at Hisarlik? An old debate

We now know where Novum Ilium was, but then so did the Greeks and Romans. This is nothing new. We know it did not compare at all well with Homer's Troy, but Strabo also knew this 2000 years ago. So are we really any further forward in our quest for the true Trojan plain? It seems we are left with the same questions that confronted Strabo. If Ilium was not Troy, was there ever a real site for the Trojan War as described in the Iliad?

Schliemann's discovery of 'Priam's treasure' at Hisarlik ignited some fierce debates among Greek and Homeric scholars. One example was between two eminent professors, Mahaffy and Jebb, as revealed in papers published in the Journal of Hellenic Studies in 1882. [13] These papers are still interesting to read, and some of the points made are still relevant.

Mahaffy was certain that Ilion lay on the site of Troy. Strabo, from Demetrios of Skepsis, his principal source relating to the history of the Troad, had disputed the claim of the Ilians that they lived on the site of Troy. He cited a tradition (Strabo 13.1.25-26.) that the Aeolic colony now there had changed its seat in the Troad more than once, before taking up its final abode on Hisarlik 'in about the time of Croesus', c560-546BC. [14] These claims of Demetrius and Strabo were adopted by other scholars. But the great Greek scholar George Grote found them to be 'novel, paradoxical, and based on no real evidence.'

Now, in answer to the question 'was historical Ilion on the site of the mythical Troy?', Mahaffy [15] said that both he and Dr. Schliemann had concluded 'yes' independently; he from a study of texts, and Schliemann with the spade. Schliemann had shown irrefutably that Ilium was now found to have been occupied in Classical, heroic and prehistoric times, so the alleged new foundation for Troy at Hisarlik was not true. Mahaffy concluded:

'As there is no other site in the Troad for which the least evidence of this kind has been, or can be, produced, the argument that Troy and Ilium occupied the same site is as surely established as any thing in ancient history.'

Jebb disagreed. In an earlier paper [16] he had concluded that a) the general belief in antiquity was that Troy had been utterly destroyed and that the site had remained desolate; and b) the claim of the Greek Ilion at Hisarlik to occupy the site of Homer's Troy was merely a local legend, destitute of evidence. In reply to Mahaffy, Jebb accepted that Hisarlik dates back far enough possibly to have been 'the site of that town, the capture of which gave rise to the story of Troy.' But he then asked 'where did Homer conceive his Troy as standing? Here we can judge only from the topographical data given in the Iliad.' Jebb divides this information into 1) the general and 2) the particular. Regarding the latter, a poet might make slips or permit himself some licence. 'And the probability of such oversights or such licence is indefinitely increased if we suppose the poem or parts of it to have been composed without a detailed knowledge, or an exact recollection of the ground.' No one place, he assures us, satisfies all the general data for the site of Troy. At Hisarlik there was no lofty acropolis, and the site was too small. He concluded:

'The city of Troy, as described in the Iliad, is a creation of the poet's fancy, suggested by handsome cities of his own time. The spacious palaces and wide streets of the Homeric Troy point to a city totally different, both in scale and in character, from anything of which traces exist at Hisarlik. In this sense,' concluded Jebb, 'Homeric Troy has *not* been found, and never can be found, because it never existed.'

To sum up, Mahaffy believed that the case for Troy at Hisarlik was as surely established as anything in ancient history. Jebb, on the other hand, concluded that, even assuming the war was a real event, the mismatch between Hisarlik and Homer's Troy showed that either the real site of Homer's Troy has not yet been found, or Homer (or his sources) invented the whole geographical background for his epic. Jebb concluded that Homeric Troy can never be found because it never existed.

Hisarlik on trial

I have quoted these opinions from over 130 years ago because they are well expressed, and because they summarise effectively the opposing views of scholars today. The mismatch between the Trojan landscape of the Iliad and that at Hisarlik is generally accepted. Part of the problem is that, until now, no-one has ever proposed a convincing alternative site. The Hisarlik supporters therefore have to follow Jebb, and argue that what is not found at Hisarlik must have been imagined by the poet of the Iliad. This book will show that Jebb's supposedly non-existent alternative site does actually exist in the plain at Bergama and Pergamon. I hope that this discovery will also lead to a whole new understanding of the epics about the Trojan War.

Does this sound so incredible that it will be a waste of time reading any further? I can imagine Counsel for the Defence of Hisarlik as Troy jumping to his feet and saying just that. He tells the jury that the very idea of Troy being anywhere else is preposterous. 'Troy must be visible from Samothrace. Tenedos and Imbros must be close by. Hisarlik, like Troy, lay beside the Hellespont, which has always been another name for what is now called the Straits of the Dardanelles. Hisarlik is the only ancient walled site in this narrowly defined area which has been proved by archaeology to have been settled long before, and throughout, Trojan times. The Classical city of Ilion was on this site. Ilion was generally accepted by antiquity, from at least the time of Herodotus and Alexander the Great, to have been the site of ancient Troy. Anything described in the Iliad, but not found at and around Hisarlik, must therefore have been imagined by the Poet. No site anywhere else can possibly fit the geographical requirements demanded by the Iliad. On these grounds alone, the case for Troy anywhere other than at Hisarlik falls at the first fence, and must be dismissed.'

'How do you reply'? asks the Judge.

My advocate rises slowly to his feet. He quietly points out that Counsel for the Defence has overlooked one rather important fact. 'The only basis for assuming Troy was at Hisarlik/Ilion is the acceptance as true of a very few place names, including Samothrace, in the Iliad. This acceptance is the sole reason why no alternative site for Troy was thought possible. Yet it has been known for over 2,500 years that all we read in the Iliad was not written by Homer. The epics today include many lines that have been added in by others. The subject matter, the language used, and the variable quality of the poetry, have all convinced many scholars that parts of the Iliad were composed at different times by different authors. This is not difficult to explain. Stories about the heroes will have been told and retold by many different bards, and the original versions may not be the ones finally enshrined in the Iliad. The heroes themselves were so famous that some later rulers and great families wanted to claim descent from them. For example Alexander the Great had a genealogy invented for him that showed that he was descended on his mother's side from Achilles, and Julius Caesar claimed descent from Aeneas. Homer was also accepted as a great authority on geography in Trojan times. Places named by him gained the honour of immortality, and this was much envied by places that were not. His geography may have been tinkered with by some later rulers, so as to claim entitlement to, or hegemony over, lands they wished to possess. The Defence Counsel will therefore, for example, have to prove that Homer, and no one else, was the most likely author of the references to Samothrace, Imbros and Tenedos. And that is just the beginning of their difficulties.'

Achilles tells us where to find Troy

It is a fact, known to few outside the world of Homeric scholars, that in the Iliad, Achilles tells us exactly where the Trojan plain lies. [17] And it is not at Hisarlik. From a natural translation of Book 24, lines 543-546, we learn from Achilles that Priam's kingdom lay between the island of Lesbos and 'Phrygia in the uplands'. As it happens, we know that the ancient capital of Phrygia was at Gordion, a site on the central Anatolian plateau some 400 kilometres inland due east of Pergamon. If we look at a map of Turkey to see what lies between Lesbos and the ancient lands of Phrygia, our eyes alight on Pergamon and Bergama. Here is the great fertile plain of the Bakir Çayi valley, once ancient Mysia. Hisarlik lies due north of Lesbos, not due east. Now whether or not the lower Bakir Çayi valley was the plain of Troy, it is certainly not visible from Samothrace. So something is seriously wrong. Troy cannot be both east of Lesbos and visible from Samothrace. On the face of it, Homer is giving us two pieces of geographical evidence that are contradictory. So one of them, if not both, must be false. Those believing in Troy at Hisarlik are forced to find different translations for the lines 24.543-6, some adding in the word 'north', although this is not used in the text. [18] But to an untrained eye, these seem contrived and unconvincing.

In later chapters I will present further examples of apparent conflicts of evidence which throw serious doubts upon the assumption that Troy was at Hisarlik. The Hisarlik Defence Counsel may repeat their argument that Homer probably did not know the site of Troy very well. And if Homer was blind, neither his descriptions nor his geography would be reliable. Yet each claim that Homer's descriptions are unreliable helps to undermine their own case for Troy at Hisarlik.

Hisarlik as Troy – more faith than fact

I hope that by now you will begin to appreciate that the case for Troy at Hisarlik is not nearly so cut and dried as modern writers would have us believe. Perhaps you are wondering why little or nothing is heard of these problems in today's books about Troy and Homer. The reason is that the matter was considered settled when a majority of scholars decided over a century ago to follow Schliemann and accept Hisarlik as Troy. The matter had been debated by the leading scholars of the day, and a consensus had been reached. Hisarlik was either the site of Troy, or of the city whose fall inspired the tales of Troy. No better site could, or would, ever be found. Although Wood was not quite correct when he said that the general location of Troy has never been doubted, it is true that the case against Troy at Hisarlik is no longer heard.

After Schliemann, the next generation of scholars proclaimed the opinion that Troy was at Hisarlik as a fact. This is what Professor Leaf told a cruise ship audience of prominent scholars and archaeologists during an onboard lecture in 1912, just before they visited Hisarlik:

'Now let me say, once and for all, that there is not the least doubt that this is Homer's Troy, because it corresponds in every respect with the scene of the Iliad.' [19]

Now to anyone familiar with both Hisarlik and the Iliad's descriptions of the Trojan plain, this statement was palpably untrue. Leaf was even contradicting himself, since he had accepted in 1892 that Homer's topography was partly imaginary. Yet no one seemed to mind. As so often happens, faith had become fact. Yet, in truth, the statement that Hisarlik was once the Troy of the Iliad is not one of fact. It is merely an expression of a personal belief.

Addressing the problems

By now you are aware of some of the many questions that confront us when we study the Iliad and the Odyssey, and try to relate the information they contain to the real world and the site at Hisarlik. This volume is confined to providing evidence that the Trojan plain as described in the Iliad is best found at Bergama, not Hisarlik. The case as presented does not depend upon Troy and Ilios being real places, nor upon the Trojan War being a real event. Our overall conclusion is based upon what we read in the Iliad as we have it today. It is therefore independent of whoever wrote this epic. It is also independent of the existence or otherwise of a real poet called Homer. However many people had a hand in creating it, today's version of the Iliad exists as a matter of fact. That it is possible to reconstruct a layout of the landscape of the plain of Troy from this Iliad is also a fact. When looking for this Trojan landscape at Hisarlik and Bergama I will be appraising geographical and topographical evidence. Normally when assessing evidence from ancient historical sources, unequivocal proof is seldom available. Here, however, the evidence of topography is easily proved, for it is there for all to see. Seeing, at least in this case, is believing. When we look in the right place, all the main features of the

Trojan landscape are still there. They are plainly visible for the tourist to see and admire, in the place where the poet tells us we should expect to see them.

If I can convince you that the Trojan plain was in the lower Bakir Çayi valley, then you will at once want to know how well Pergamon and Bergama can match the Ilios and Troy of the Iliad. You will also want to know what archaeological evidence, if any, is available to support these identifications. The case for Ilios at Pergamon and Troy at Bergama will be made in Volume 2 of this study. There I hope to be able to tell you that the discovery of Grey Minyan Ware on Pergamon, the same type of pottery as found in the layers equated with Priam's Troy at Hisarlik, has now been published.

Many questions remain to be asked. Having shown that, in a few key places, the Iliad we have today contains some misinformation as to the whereabouts of Troy, you will want to know who was responsible for this deception. Who wanted to show that the Trojan plain was at Hisarlik rather than at Bergama? Who would benefit from such a deception? Could this beneficiary have had sufficient control over the early texts of the epics to make such minor alterations? These and other related questions will also be discussed in Volume 2. There I will argue that the most likely perpetrators of such a deception were the Pisistratids, who ruled as the first tyrants of Athens, c560 – 510. And if ever there was a case which demonstrates the truth of the old saying 'Oh what a tangled web we weave when first we practice to deceive', this is it.

CHAPTER 2

THE STORY OF THE TROJAN WAR

Introduction. The Judgement of Paris. The Trojan War from the Iliad.
The Trojan War from the Odyssey. The Epic Cycle and the Trojan Cycle. The Mysian misadventure.
Laomedon and Herakles. The mythical origins of Troy. The Cretan Troy foundation legend.
The verdict of Robert Graves. Are any of the Troy-related legends historical?
The Iliad and Odyssey – recent translations.

Introduction

Before we start looking in detail at the Iliad, perhaps I should give the general reader a brief outline of the story of the Trojan War. In the Troy-related ancient myths and legends, the cause of the war can be traced back to the lust of Zeus and Poseidon towards a young sea nymph named Thetis. Thetis lived in the depths of the sea with her father Nereus, and her sisters. She was brought up by Hera, the wife of Zeus. Being very beautiful, she was desired by both Zeus, whom she declined out of loyalty to Hera, and by Poseidon, the great god of the sea. Then it was foretold by an oracle that she would have a son, and he would one day become even greater than his father. This immediately made Thetis rather less desirable, since neither Zeus nor Poseidon wished to be upstaged by one of their sons. So they agreed she should be married to a mortal, and a suitably distinguished hero, Peleus, was chosen to be her husband. He was king of Phthia in Thessaly, and had earlier sailed with Jason and the other Argonauts to Colchis to recover the Golden Fleece. After he had proved his worth in contest, Thetis agreed to marry him. Many gods attended the wedding on Mount Pelion, but Eris, the goddess of strife, was not invited because the theme of the event was harmony. Angered at this rebuff, she dreamed up a scheme to get her own back. She went to the wedding place and threw a golden apple into the assembled crowd, inscribed with the words 'to the fairest'. The three goddesses, Hera, Athene and Aphrodite, all claimed it as theirs, causing strife between them exactly as Eris had intended.

The Judgement of Paris

Zeus decided on a way to settle the issue. His son, the messenger god Hermes, took all three ladies to see a fair youth called Paris, a son of King Priam, who was tending his flocks on Mount Ida, and Paris would decide who was the fairest. [1] When Hermes arrived on Ida with the apple and the three goddesses, Paris was fearful of the task asked of him. 'How' he cried, 'can a simple cattle man like myself become an arbiter of divine beauty?' Then he begged the losers not to be vexed, for, he said, 'I am only a human, and liable to make the stupidest of mistakes.' Hermes reassured him, saying he need only rely on his native intelligence. The goddesses all agreed to abide by his decision, but each tried to bribe him to choose them. Hera offered to make him king of all Asia, and the richest man alive. Athene offered him victory in all his battles, and to make him the most handsome and wisest man in the world. Aphrodite, the goddess of love, called him the most handsome young man in Phrygia, and promised him the hand of Helen, the most beautiful woman in the world. Paris had never heard of Helen, and was worried when Aphrodite told him she was already married to the king of Sparta. But Aphrodite assured him that Paris should make a tour around Greece, and when he met Helen, she would fall in love with him. Paris then, without further hesitation, gave Aphrodite the apple. And thus it was that the young Trojan prince incurred the abiding wrath of Hera and Athene, who then went away, arm in arm, to plot the downfall of Troy, his native city.

The Trojan War from the Iliad

This story is a familiar one, known in many countries around the world. It has captured the imagination of people, children and scholars alike, for over 2,500 years. According to the Iliad, the war started after Paris, also called Alexander, a son of the Trojan King Priam, came on a trading mission to Sparta. There he stayed as a guest in the palace of King Menelaus of Sparta and his beautiful queen, Helen. On the day before Paris was due to leave, Menelaus was called away to the funeral of his grandfather, leaving Helen in charge of his household and his guest. During his visit, Paris had contrived to win the love of Helen, and the absence of Menelaus on the last day of his visit made their immediate elopement possible. They both sailed away from Sparta to Troy, bearing with them many of Helen's household treasures.

Before she married Menelaus, Helen had been courted by many noble suitors. Her father, Tyndareus, became concerned that, since so many of these influential and powerful young men would find themselves rejected by Helen, they might turn against him or his daughter's chosen husband. So, taking the advice of Odysseus, he made them all swear an oath, binding them to protect the suitor she chose against any wrong that might afterwards be done to him. Partly with the support of many princes bound by this oath, Menelaus persuaded his brother Agamemnon, King of Mycenae, to help him get Helen back. So the brothers gathered together a large confederation of Greek nations to sail to Troy with the aim of securing her safe return. They arrived at Troy at the second attempt, having landed in Mysia and fought the Mysian war at Teuthrania on the first trip. The Trojan King Priam refused to return Helen and the stolen property to the Achaeans. He also managed to muster military support from many of his neighbouring states to oppose the Achaean invaders. Thus the scene was set for what today we would call a major confrontation.

The Iliad describes the action during an approximate 50-day period in the tenth year of the war. It is divided into 24 books, although this division is thought to have been made not by Homer, but nearly 500 years later by the Iliad's Alexandrian editors in the 3rd century BC. In Book 2, as already mentioned, the 'Catalogue of Ships' lists the troops and captains of the Achaeans who sailed to Troy. The allies of the Trojans are also listed. We learn that in the epics, following the epic tradition, Homer's Trojans spoke Greek and worshipped some of the Greek gods. [2] Some of their allies, who came from other parts of Western Anatolia, spoke different languages. Past events that took place before the action of the Iliad are sometimes mentioned. Also, some future events are predicted, the most notable of which are the imminent death of the hero Achilles, and the eventual fall of Troy.

Very briefly, the Iliad begins by explaining the quarrel between Agamemnon and Achilles over a captured prize woman, Briseis. Agamemnon took her from Achilles when his own prize woman had to be returned to a local priest of Apollo to pacify the God's anger. Achilles refused to fight until Briseis was returned to him, which Agamemnon refused to do. The Trojans saw a chance to defeat the Achaeans, who had lost their leading warrior, and the war began. After many battles, with the armies charging back and forth across the plain, the Trojans pushed the Achaeans back to their ships, and managed to set one alight. The situation for the Achaeans became even more desperate when Patroclos, Achilles' best friend, was killed. Then Achilles made his peace with Agamemnon and entered the fray. The Trojans, with their most dreaded foe back in action, immediately started to flee back across the plain to the safety of Troy.

The Iliad ends with the death of Hector at the hands of Achilles, and Priam's visit to Achilles to plead for the return of Hector's body in return for a large ransom. There is then a truce to allow Hector's burial rites to be observed and for the building of a tomb mound. After this, the war resumes. The Iliad contains no account of the death of Achilles, or of how the Achaeans eventually achieved their victory.

The Trojan War from the Odyssey

Fortunately, more about the end of the Trojan War is told in the Odyssey. This epic is about the return of the Greek hero Odysseus to his home on the island of Ithaca after the war. The journey took ten years to complete, during which time Odysseus and his men were shipwrecked and washed ashore in a number of different places. In some of these he was given a friendly reception, and in return for hospitality Odysseus would tell his hosts some of his own stories about the war. In one such interlude, we learn of his role in the ruse of the wooden horse and the fall of Troy. He explained that, after the death of Achilles, the Greeks grew weary of the war. They pretended to give up trying to take Troy, and built a great hollow wooden model of a horse, designed by their chief craftsman Epeios. Then, leaving the horse on the beach, they sailed away, and anchored out of sight behind the offshore islands, including Tenedos. Unknown to the Trojans, the horse contained a number of Greek soldiers, including Odysseus. When the Trojans came down to the beach and saw the horse, they were tricked by the lies of Sinon, a solitary Greek left behind, into thinking it was an offering to Athene who had saved Troy from destruction. So they brought the horse into the city, and to do so they tore down a section of the city wall because the horse was too large to pass through the gates. Then they dragged it up the acropolis to the Temple of Athene, to whom it was to be dedicated. There it was allowed to stand outside the king's palace while the Trojans relaxed, celebrated their victory, and then finally fell asleep. During the night, Sinon crept out of the city to light a beacon on the top of Achilles' tomb. Luckily it was not raining, and the flames were seen from the islands by the Greeks. More fortunately, the direction of the wind must have changed, allowing them all to sail swiftly back to their old abandoned camp. Meanwhile the Greek soldiers climbed out of the wooden horse, killed their sleeping guards, and set fire to the buildings on the hilltop. Having alighted from their ships, the Greeks marched quickly across the plain and joined forces with their comrades. The city was soon captured and Helen was rescued. The Trojans who did not flee were all killed, and the city was then sacked, burnt and destroyed. Agamemnon finally pronounced a curse upon the site, so that it would forever remain abandoned. Then the victorious Achaeans loaded their ships with looted valuables and prize women, and sailed for home.

The Epic Cycle and the Trojan Cycle

Much more information about the wider events relating to the war was contained in a series of minor epic poems that collectively are referred to as the Epic Cycle. [3] These were a series of compositions by different authors, telling myths and legends which covered the whole Heroic period. Incorporated within the Epic Cycle was a series of works known as the Trojan Cycle, which included the Iliad and Odyssey, both credited to Homer. [4] The others are lesser literary works. After Homer the quality of the epic style of poetry generally declined. The later epics told of the causes of the war, of its initial stages, of how it ended, and of the returns of the Greek heroes. Such accounts may or may not have agreed in points of detail with what Homer wrote. All these epics are assumed to contain inaccuracies and embellishments, not least because they were based on stories handed down by oral poets over several centuries before they were written down. Further changes were made after they were written down, some deliberate and some from careless copying. Of the poems which make up the Epic Cycle only scant fragments have survived. These are mainly in the form of short summaries of each poem by a later writer popularly known as Proclus.

In summary, fragments of The Epic Cycle have been collated into the following separate stories:

a) 'The War of the Titans'. This tells of the union of heaven and earth, and of their offspring the Cyclopes and one hundred-handed giants. It is ascribed to Arctinus of Miletus.
b) 'Theban Cycle'. This tells the story of the wars against Thebes in Boeotia in three poems, including the story of Oedipus.
c) 'The Epigoni'. This story is ascribed to Antimachus of Teos, and tells of the sack of Thebes.
d) 'The Trojan Cycle'. This is a cycle of 8 epics including the Iliad and Odyssey. The eight epics are The Kypria, The Iliad, The Aethiopis, The Little Iliad, The Sack of Troy, The Returns, The Odyssey and The Telegony. Apart from the Iliad and Odyssey, these are all generally believed to be later than Homer, and their general structure is considered purely imitative.

For those who are interested, more information about these Cyclic poems, and of other early literary sources about the Trojan War, is given in Appendix 1.

The Mysian misadventure

Early in the first chapter I mentioned the improbable story in the Kypria that the Achaean fleet got lost when it first sailed for Troy, and ended up fighting a war in Mysia, where they captured and destroyed Teuthrania. They soon discovered they were not at Troy, and found themselves opposed by a local army led by Telephos. They then decided to sail from there to Troy, but a storm blew up and dispersed the fleet. Those that could eventually limped home to Greece. They finally reached Troy at the second attempt some years later. More about this important story is given in Appendix 1, and its significance is discussed further in Chapter 6.

Laomedon and Herakles

There is another Troy-related legend to relate here. This mentions a feature of the Trojan landscape that we will be looking for at Hisarlik and Bergama. It explains how Laomedon came to lose all but one of his sons to the sword of Herakles. It was Laomedon, son of Ilus, who decided to build the famous walls of Troy. For this task Zeus gave him the services of Poseidon and Apollo, as a punishment for both gods because, on an earlier occasion, they had plotted against him. In the Iliad (21.441-457) we are told that Poseidon built the walls while Apollo 'tended the king's cattle on the wooded glens of Mount Ida.' [5] Another story adds that Poseidon was helped in one place by a mortal, Aeacus. This was a necessary addition to the story, since Troy was doomed to fall, and if the walls had been built by the gods alone, it would have been impregnable. This in turn led to the notion of there being a 'weak spot' in the wall, where it was eventually breached. Some archaeologists and commentators on Hisarlik, keen to link their site to the Trojan legends, have claimed in all seriousness to have identified the location of this 'weak spot'.

When the walls were finished, Laomedon angered the gods by refusing to pay them their promised wages, and expelled them from his dominions. The gods were greatly affronted by this breach of promise. So as a punishment, Apollo sent a plague upon the land, and Poseidon sent a sea monster into the territory of Troy which ravaged the whole country. Oracles foretold that Troy could only be released from these horrors by the regular sacrifice of a maiden to the sea monster. On the occasion of one such sacrifice, it chanced to be decided by lot that Hesione, a daughter of Laomedon, should be the victim. But after she was tied to a rock, and as the monster approached, Herakles appeared on the scene. He was returning from his expedition against the Amazons after successfully performing his ninth labour, which was the recovery of the girdle of the queen of the Amazons. He promised Laomedon that he would try to save Hesione on condition that, in return, Laomedon would give him the immortal horses that his grandfather, Tros, had received as compensation from Zeus for taking his beautiful son Ganymede to serve him as a cup bearer at Olympus. Laomedon agreed, but after Herakles had killed the monster and saved Hesione, he again broke his word. So Herakles departed empty handed. Later, however, he sailed back to Troy with a squadron of six ships, ransacked the city, killed Laomedon and all his sons except Podarces, and gave Hesione to Telemon, one of his captains. Hesione pleaded for the life of her brother Podarces, and Herakles agreed to ransom him in return for her veil. Podarces' name, which meant 'swift-footed', was then changed to Priamus, meaning 'the ransomed one'. What happened to the immortal horses is not revealed. Laomedon's tomb, according to this story, existed in the region of the Scaean Gate, and it was believed that Troy would be safe as long as his tomb remained uninjured.

The mythical origins of Troy

How Troy came to be built, and why its people apparently spoke Greek, are explained by the Troy foundation myths and legends. The origins of most of these are obscure. 'Troy' and 'Ilios' were apparently named after Tros and his son Ilus, two early kings of Troy. According to Robert Graves [6], the two best known Troy foundation legends are quite different. The most popular one, given briefly in the Iliad, provides the foundation of the Athenian version. A lesser known version explains that Troy was first settled by a colony from Crete.

The Iliad (Il. 20.199-240) tells us that when Aeneas and Achilles faced each other on the battlefield, they both recounted their lineage before they fought. Aeneas was descended from Dardanus, founder of Dardania 'at a time before the sacred city of Ilium had been built to shelter people on the plain.' Dardanus had a son, Erechthonius, who in turn had a son, Tros, the king who gave his name to the Trojans. Tros had three sons, Ilus, Assaracus and Ganymede. Ilus succeeded Tros as king, and built the acropolis of Ilios. He was followed by his son Laomedon and finally Priam. Assaracus had a son, Capys, who was the father of Anchises and the grandfather of Aeneas.

The full Athenian version of the foundation of Troy is given by Graves. In essence, the Athenians claimed that a man called Teucer, who came from a district in Attica called Troes, emigrated from Athens to Phrygia. He welcomed Dardanus to Phrygia, not the other way round. Then, in an attempt to make their story more credible, they claimed that Erechthonius, the son of Dardanus, was a descendant of both the Athenian and Trojan royal houses. They also claimed that Erechthonius had a brother called Ilus, and a son of the same name. Thus in the Athenian version, Erechthonius seems to have replaced Tros in the lineage of the Trojans, and the name 'Trojans' apparently came from Troes, a district in Attica.

The Cretan Troy foundation legend

The Cretan version is less well known. This tells of a time of famine in Crete, when a third of the population left to establish a new colony. They were led by Prince Scamander. When they came to Phrygia, they pitched their tents not far from Hamaxitos, below a high mountain that they called Ida, after the mountain home of Zeus of that name on Crete. Apollo had told them to settle wherever they were attacked by earthborn enemies under cover of darkness. That same night a horde of hungry field-mice invaded the camp. They nibbled at the bow strings, the leather shield straps, and all other edible parts of the Cretans' war gear. So Scamander called a halt, dedicated a temple there to Sminthian Apollo, and married Idaea, perhaps a local girl, who bore him a son named Teucer. Apollo helped them defeat their new neighbours, the Bebrycians, but during the fighting Scamander leapt into the Xanthus, which then took his name. Teucer succeeded him, and the settlers took the name Teucrians. Some say that it was Teucer who led the colonists, but either way Teucer was welcomed to Phrygia by Dardanus, who gave him his daughter in marriage. Teucer eventually inherited the kingdom and called his own subjects Teucrians. This Teucer would then have been succeeded by Tros, Ilus, Laomedon and Priam.

The verdict of Robert Graves

Which story do you think is the more credible? The simple story of colonisation by Cretans fleeing their famine-stricken homeland, applying Cretan names to their new landscape, or the more elaborate Athenian version? Graves did not hesitate to pronounce his verdict. He said that the Athenian claim to have founded Troy 'may be dismissed as propaganda.' [7] That Mount Ida in the Troad was named after Mount Ida on Crete seems quite plausible. Finding the god Sminthian Apollo there also points to Crete, since 'sminthos' is a Cretan word for 'mouse', a sacred animal at Knossos. Graves also pointed out that

Erechthonius was a name for the fertilising north wind, which was worshipped in Pelasgian Athens and in Thrace.

If Graves is correct, and there seems no reason to doubt his authority on this point, then we have here our first example of a myth invented by the Athenians. It is worth asking why the Athenians should go to so much trouble to invent a long and complex series of interwoven myths concerning the founding of Troy by an Athenian. Why did Athens regard it as so important to have such strong links with Troy? The reader should remember the Greek propensity for inventive story telling, for it plays a key part in our discovery of the real site of Troy. More importantly, we find the early Athenian king Erechthonius mentioned in the Iliad as an early Trojan king. This piece of Athenian propaganda, as Graves called it, has somehow found its way into the Iliad. And once in the Iliad, the story can claim the authority of Homer. As we shall see in Volume 2, he who had control over the text of Homer had a powerful political weapon at his disposal.

Are any of the Troy-related legends historical?

Many scholars believe, as I do, that behind some of these ancient stories lies a grain or more of historical truth. This is why they are so important to the ancient historian, since often he has nothing else to work from. And, when exploring this possibility, he needs to know when and why these stories were created. For example, was the 'Judgement of Paris' story invented long after the Trojan War? Was its purpose to absolve the Trojans from blame for their defeat, by claiming instead that defeat was preordained by the gods? The Troy legends raise many interesting questions. For the present, it is worth remembering that, whenever we come across Troy-related legends, we should ask what, if any, aspects of them might have a historical, chronological, or even a geographical value.

The plain of Troy from the Iliad and Odyssey

In the next chapter we will take an introductory look at the two epics, the Iliad and Odyssey, to see in outline what we can glean from them about the plain of

Troy. For much of this study the popular translation of the Iliad by Rieu [8] is our main source, published as 'Homer The Iliad' by Penguin Classics. This is probably the version most widely available. I have compared it in places with the translation of Murray [9], which is more true to the original Greek. Rieu, like most scholars, has assumed that the names Troy and Ilium are interchangeable at will. So in one or two important places he writes 'Troy' where the original Greek has 'Ilios'. Other authors also make this mistake. For example, the great Homeric scholar Sir Maurice Bowra [10] writes of 'beetling Troy' when the text names Ilios. Homer's Iliad is divided into 24 books. Rieu retains this, but he prefers to maintain an uninterrupted flow of the story line rather than stick to Homer's line numbers. For reference purposes therefore, where a specific translation is discussed, I give the book number and line from Murray.

The version of the Odyssey used here is the translation by W.H. Shewring. [11] Like Rieu, he does not specify the line numbers, so the book and page number are quoted from Murray's translation. The geographical detail concerning Troy and its plain contained within the Odyssey is, with one or two notable exceptions, generally consistent with that in the Iliad. However, the Iliad remains our primary source of geographical information.

CHAPTER 3

THE FEATURES OF THE TROJAN PLAIN

Introduction. Identifying the landscape of the Iliad.
The beach and the Greek Camp. The Harbour. The wall defending the Greek Camp.
The plain of Troy. The distance from Troy to the ships. The 'rising in the plain'.
The rivers of the plain – general comments. The Skamander. Locating the Skamander in the plain.
The Simois and the layout of the two rivers. The ford, the coast road, and the bend in the river.
Hills and tomb mounds on the plain - general observations. Kallikolone. The Wall of Herakles.
The great barrow of Ilus. The tomb of Old Aesyetes. Thorn Hill or the tomb of Myrine.
The barrow of Patroclus. The barrow of Hector. Concluding comments.

Introduction

In the first two chapters we have looked at some introductory information about the Trojan War myths and legends, and the how the site at Hisarlik came to be generally accepted as Troy. A few of the reasons for doubting Hisarlik as the site of Troy were also explained. In this chapter I aim to show that the Iliad yields a good general picture of the Trojan plain. This picture will then be compared with the landscape at Hisarlik, to see how well it fits.

My search for the Trojan plain of the Iliad is based on three underlying assumptions:

1. That Troy and Ilios were real places and the Trojan War was a real historical event.
2. That the detailed descriptions of Troy, Ilios and the Trojan landscape as given in the Iliad are generally accurate, and are not simply the product of

a poetic imagination. One test of this will be their consistency; if they are accurate, they will be consistent rather than conflicting.

3. That by using these descriptions, and the site location clues, we should be able to find a real setting for the Trojan War of the Iliad.

The first assumption, that the war was an historical event, was accepted by intelligent antiquity. Across the Greek world there are countless shrines and temples built to honour the heroes of this war, and it is hard to believe that such effort and expense would be lavished for so long on imagined heroes of an imagined war. There are also many genealogies, some credible and some not, which lead back to the families of these heroes, and again it is hard to believe that all of these are inventions. Opinion today is divided, but I think the majority of scholars accept that there is at least some historical truth underlying the Trojan War stories. My search for the Trojan plain will, in due course, uncover more evidence supporting the view that the war was historical.

The last two assumptions are really hypotheses, statements of beliefs for which I will be providing supporting evidence as the book proceeds. These hypotheses can bring a smile of incredulity to the faces of Homeric scholars today. They know that the geography of today's island called Ithaki, generally accepted as the home of Odysseus, does not match the descriptions of Ithaca in the Odyssey. They are also well aware that the ancient walled city at Hisarlik fails to match the descriptions of Troy in the Iliad. Yet this is only to be expected. How could anyone think that minor and even trivial details of the Ithacan and Trojan landscapes could have been handed down to Homer unchanged through some 500 years of oral poetic tradition? And how could anyone expect that the words composed by Homer, if it was he who composed these epics, could have remained unchanged during the 150 or more years before they came to be written down in Athens around the mid-6th century BC? These considerations lead them to agree with Professor Jebb that, given the circumstance of the epic's survival, such places as Ithaca and Troy, as described in the Odyssey and Iliad, will never be found, because they never existed.

My job in this book is to convince you that this consensus view is wrong, at least as far as the Iliad is concerned. I will start by showing that the onsite descriptions of the Trojan plain are consistent, and therefore credible. Then we will compare these descriptions with those found at Hisarlik. This will show the extent to which Hisarlik fails to match the Iliad's Trojan plain. Then we must find a plausible alternative site that offers a demonstrably better match than we found at Hisarlik. If we can do this, and offer a convincing explanation for any inconsistencies in the offsite signposts, we can claim that our assumptions were correct, and that here, at last, is the real Trojan plain.

At the beginning of our study we will heed some advice from Professor Taplin, a Homeric scholar at Oxford University. [1] First he tells us that 'The poems themselves are our firm evidence, and they contain everything worth knowing about Homer. An internal approach (to the study of Homer) is needed.' He then quotes an ancient Latin motto: 'Homeron ex Homerou saphenizein', which means 'You should elucidate Homer by the light of Homer'. I believe that by following this ancient adage, the Iliad will lead us eventually to the real Trojan plain at Bergama.

One further point. In this book, when I use the name 'Homer', I refer to the poet believed by the early Greeks to have composed the core poems of the Iliad. While interpreting the landscape information in the Iliad we will be aided in places by a special facet of Homer's genius, namely his economy. I believe Homer's original poems contained little if any surplus information. If Homer mentions something it is because it is worth mentioning, of some merit or distinction, or served a particular purpose in relation to the action of the epic. On the other hand, if something is not mentioned, this does not mean that it did not happen or was not there. It means only that it played no part in the action, and was therefore irrelevant to his story. This principal of the economy of Homer will guide us in our attempts to recognise and interpret some of his descriptions.

Identifying the landscape of the Iliad

We will start our study of the Iliad where the epic starts, at the camp by the ships. We will then proceed from the ships towards Troy, crossing the plain and collecting topographical information as we go. Once we have the descriptions of the Trojan plain before us, we will combine them with those for Troy and Ilios, check them for consistency, and set them out in a list. Then we will produce a similar list from Homer's off-site location information. Both lists will help confirm the identity of the real site of Troy.

The beach and the Greek camp

The first two books set the stage for the war. On the beach by the Greek camp, we are told that over a thousand ships stood propped up, 'high on the sands' (Il. 1.485-6) in long lines, three ships deep, on a wide and gently sloping beach. This sandy beach lay within a bay, between two headlands, and near the mouth of the river Scamander. 'For though the beach was wide, yet it could in no way hold all the ships, and the men were confined; so they had drawn up the ships row behind row, and had filled up the wide mouth of the shore that the headlands shut in between them.' (Il.14.30ff) With the bay full up with ships, and no mention of deposits of river mud, there is no hint here that the mouth of the Scamander was also within this bay.

If we add up the total number of ships that went to Troy as given by the Catalogue of Ships in Book 2, we get a total of 1,186 ships. So, if these numbers are not exaggerated, [2] we must look for a bay long enough for nearly 400 ships to have been drawn up out of the water, where they stood side by side in three long curved rows. When the Achaeans were called to their battle stations, Homer writes (Il. 2. 464ff) '…their many tribes poured out of the ships and huts into the plain of Scamander…and they stood in the flowery meadow…, countless, as are the leaves and flowers of their season.' Here we find no mention of any cliffs beyond the beach, only of grassy meadows full of wild flowers.

The harbour

A question now arises. The Iliad does not tell us that Troy had a harbour. If it did, did the Greeks land there? The early legends about Paris say that, for his trip to Sparta, he persuaded Priam to build him a small fleet of ships. The Iliad [Il. 5.59ff] tells us that these ships were made by the Trojan Phereclus. Troy, as an important capital city, would no doubt have traded goods with other countries, and some of this trade with distant places such as Greece and

Phoenicia would have been by ship. Thus it seems reasonable to expect that Troy had a harbour with wharfs and shipbuilding facilities. A harbour is usually found within a bay between two headlands, since these afford it some protection from the weather in the open seas. It seems likely that the Greek ships would have planned to land at or near this harbour, provided the bay was big enough to hold all the ships.

The wall defending the Greek camp

Homer tells us in the second part of Book 7 that, after the Trojans had fought their way close to the Greek camp, the Achaeans then decided to build a wall and a ditch to defend it. But the story of its building and later destruction has caused much controversy among scholars. We must look briefly at this controversy, since we need to know whether or not we should expect to find evidence for such a wall when we find Homer's Troy. The question is important, since no evidence of harbour defensive walls has been found near Hisarlik.

So what does the Iliad tell us about it? First, the Achaeans burnt their dead brethren with full honours on the customary funeral pyre. Then, using carts drawn by oxen and mules, they raised a single barrow over them, 'using such material as the plain provides.' No doubt this would include rounded stones rolled down across the plain by the river when in flood. Using this mound for a base, they then built high walls to protect the ships and themselves, with strong gates let into them, probably as a carriage-way for the chariots. Then outside the walls they dug a deep parallel trench, with a line of stakes along it as an obstruction to chariots and infantry, should the Trojans press them hard against their ships. In Book 11 we learn that there were places where the Achaeans had left a causeway between the trenches for the safe passage of their own troops, which were protected by gates. Then in Book 12 we read that '…all along the stone walls fierce fires had broken out…' The mention of stone walls suggests that the earthen wall was either protected by stone facing or topped by stone walls. The 'fierce fires', however, suggest perhaps a timber palisade at the top. Here there is a hint of inconsistency about the nature of this wall, so I must put a question mark against these lines having been written solely by Homer.

Also in Book 12 we read about the later demolition of the wall by Poseidon and Apollo. These two gods directed a torrent of all the combined rivers of Ida at this wall, so that it was washed out to sea, including 'all the wooden and stone foundations that the Achaeans had laid down with such labour...' This suggests that the defences involved major construction works, with the wall having some stone foundations.

Lastly, in Book 16 (395-400) we find another mention of this wall. Patroclos has managed to divert a group of Trojans before they fled towards Troy. Having trapped them 'in the space between the ships and the river and the high wall he rushed among them and slew them, and exacted vengeance for many a slain comrade.' This confirms what we had suspected – that the Skamander flowed close to the Greek camp but did not discharge into the bay which accommodated the ships.

Now why should we be suspicious about the lines in Book 12 telling us that all traces of this wall were later destroyed by the gods? Firstly, there are the circumstances of its building. Even a first-time reader of the Iliad may find himself puzzled by the apparent speed with which these important and complex defences were built. The timetable for this seems unclear, but it took less than two days to complete. Could such extensive works realistically have been built in one or two days? More importantly, why did the Greeks wait for over nine years before building some form of protection for their camp and their beached ships? Can we also believe that this wall was completely destroyed by the gods, and by such unlikely means? This affront to our common sense also failed to convince two scholars over 2,000 years ago. Two famous Alexandrian grammarians, Aristarchus and Zenodotus, studying the texts in 3-2C, rejected the passages about the wall's destruction. They thought these were only introduced to account for the fact that no sign of it was ever found at Ilion. So here we come across another example of a possible addition into the Iliad, inserted after Homer's time by a later author, who may have had Hisarlik in mind as the site of Troy. [3]

So where does this leave us in our search for the real site of the Greek camp? Should we expect to find evidence of old defensive walls there or not? I think it likely that the Achaeans, as soon as they arrived and knew that a war was inevitable, would have built a wall to defend their beached ships as a matter of standard practice. I suggest that Homer knew the wall was there, but that the lines about its sudden building and its impending demolition by Poseidon and Apollo were added in by those who wished to move the site to a place where no wall could be found. All things considered, and if the story is historical, evidence for its existence at the site of the real Greek camp may still be found.

The plain of Troy

The Trojan War took place on the plain of the river Skamander between the coast and Troy. Chariots and foot soldiers were used by both sides. The chariot riders seem unafraid of such dangers as crashing into trees or being overturned after hitting rocks on the ground. So we can deduce that the plain, apart from a few old tomb mounds, was relatively flat, grass covered, with not too many large boulders. But smaller rocks and stones were found in some places, since these were used in building the Greek defensive walls, and stones were regularly used as weapons in the general fighting.

The Iliad mentions the grassy meadow near the Greek camp, and that Troy's wealth came largely from rearing horses, an activity that needs large wide open grassy plains and water meadows. Nearer the town there were wheat fields, but as we would expect with the farmers safe behind the city walls, there is no mention of any standing crops during the war. Parts of the plain near Troy would therefore have been cleared of rocks and trees prior to cultivation. Some of the fields at least appeared to have been defined by boundary stones, since in Book 21 during the battle of the gods, Athene picked up what may have been one of these and hurled it at Ares.

The distance from Troy to the ships

The size of the plain is of considerable interest. This has an added significance since it was discovered in 1982 that there was no plain of the River Mendere between Hisarlik and the sea at the mouth of the river. Its width is impossible to estimate, since it is not spoken of as offering any constraints to the battlefield. So the plain was obviously wide enough to accommodate a full scale battle with thousands of troops and charioteers on both sides. There are also references to the Greeks fighting far from their ships, and to the Trojans camped far from their walls, but how far is 'far'? I think the only way to make an intelligent guess about the distance between Troy and the Greek camp is to estimate how long it took to travel between them.

In the Iliad, there were ten crossings of the plain as the battle swayed to and fro. Some of these crossings apparently took very little time, so they are not all consistent with each other. Taken together, they have given rise to the popular view that Troy was not more than 10 kilometres or so from the sea. There were two more crossings of the plain which did not involve advancing or retreating troops. These were by Priam when he ransomed Hector's body from Achilles. To estimate the distance travelled, I needed to estimate roughly how long the journey took, and the speed of travel. Looking at the ten battle crossings, I could not help wondering if so many chases back and forth were really a necessary part of the central story of the wrath of Achilles. It is entirely possible that some of the forays across the plain were written later, perhaps to please a particular audience by honouring a particular hero featured in the battle. There is also some confusing information about the length of some of the days when fighting is taking place. With these thoughts in mind, it seems preferable not to use these crossings of varying durations to estimate the distance travelled. It is only Priam's journeys that are free of any battle heroics from either side, so we will look at these first.

In Book 24, Priam travelled in a horse-drawn cart to collect the body of Hector from Achilles. Accompanying him was a mule-drawn cart laden with treasure as ransom. He left Troy late one afternoon, and reached the ford by the time it got dark. There he stopped to let his horses and mules drink from the river. He reached the hut of Achilles before the Achaeans had gone to bed. He stayed only for a few speeches and a short sleep, before he was woken up and told to get back to Troy as soon as possible. He left in the middle of the night, and arrived home in daylight the next day. He was first spotted in the distance by his daughter Cassandra from the top of Pergamos, the precinct of Apollo on the highest part of the acropolis of Ilios. Now in order to estimate the distance he travelled, I must make some guesses that appear reasonable about his start and finishing times, the length of time he spent with Achilles, and the speed at which his cart travelled. So, let us say he started out at 6.00pm, reached the ford by nightfall, spent say 4 hours with Achilles, and got back to Troy at 8.00am the next morning. This gives a total travel time of around 10 hours. If the loaded wagon travelled at about walking pace, say 5-6km per hour, the distance travelled would be 50 to 60km. If I deduct say half an hour each way to give the horses time to drink at the ford, then the distance travelled would be around 45 to 55km. This would suggest that the distance between Ilios and the Camp was, in round figures, somewhere between 20 and 30km. This is broadly consistent with the statements in the Iliad that Troy was 'far', or 'a long way', from the ships. I accept that this estimated distance is purely speculative, but it does not seem unreasonable.

The rising in the plain

Book 8 describes the Trojan's most successful attack. As night fell, Hector withdrew his troops. Only the failing light had prevented them from destroying all the Achaeans and their ships. So the Trojans collected food by chariot from the town, and camped across the corridors of battle, between the ships and the streams of Xanthus. They pitched their tents on an area of higher ground, called the 'throsmos' in the Iliad. Murray translates this ancient Greek word as 'the rising ground of the plain'. Yet no such hill or area of significantly higher ground, large enough to accommodate the Trojan army, could be found in the plain at the mouth of the river Mendere near Hisarlik. Hence, during the search for Troy in the 19th century, this word caused much controversy. Some thought it was really a hill. They wondered how big and how high it might have been, and could it have been washed away in a great flood? So what should we be looking for? As always, our first step towards understanding this problem is to see exactly what the Iliad has to say about it. The word 'throsmos' is used in three places.

On the first occasion (Il. 10.160) Nestor woke up Diomedes, so he could go on a night spying mission with Odysseus. He reminded Diomedes that the Trojans were close at hand. 'Do you not realize that the Trojans on the rising ground of the plain are camped hard by the ships, and but scant space still holds them off?' In the next mention, (Il. 11.56) we are told that, just before the two great armies clashed in front of the Greek camp, 'the Trojans facing them on the rising ground of the plain were arrayed about great Hector...'

42

The last mention, (Il. 20.3) is similar to that in Book 11, simply telling us that while the Achaeans lined up for battle by the ships, the Trojans took up their positions 'on the rising ground of the plain.'

Our final piece of evidence concerning the 'throsmos' comes from Book 10. Dolon, a Trojan spy, was captured at night by Odysseus and Diomedes while the Trojans were camped on the 'throsmos', and he told them (Il. 10.426ff) where the Trojan allies were lying. Five groups of allies, including the 'noble Pelasgi', were lying towards the sea, and another four, including the Mysians and Phrygians, were situated towards 'Thymbre'. The Thracians, 'newcomers', were lying apart, 'the outermost of all'.

Collectively, this evidence implies that the 'throsmos' was on the same side of the Skamander as the Greek camp, and near the ships (Il 10:160). It was also spoken of simply as being a part of the Trojan plain. Hence it is not a hill as such. From Il. 20.3, the 'throsmos' must have covered an extensive area, for it applied to the whole area of ground occupied by the Trojan army. One wing was at or near the sea, and another part lay 'towards Thymbra', which probably lay in the opposite direction, towards the sides of the valley. I will mention Thymbra again in a later chapter. Here it seems safe to conclude that the 'throsmos' was an extensive tract of ground generally higher than the plain around it, on the Greek side of the Skamander and near the ships. We will look for such a feature in our new Trojan plain.

The rivers of the plain – general comments

Next we must look at what Homer has to say about the rivers. If I can determine some sort of layout for these, I can then see how this compares with the river layouts at Hisarlik and Bergama. Troy, we are told, had 'a pair of noble rivers' called the Skamander and the Simois. These rivers joined somewhere not far from the Greek camp. They are mentioned together (Il. 5.773-776), when Hera and Athene agreed to join the battle to help the Achaeans. Riding from Olympus on Hera's 'fiery chariot', they soon came to 'the land of Troy and the two flowing rivers, where the Simois and Scamander join their streams, there the goddess, white armed Hera, stayed her horses, and loosed them from the chariot...' The two goddesses then set out on foot to help the Achaeans, and soon came upon Diomedes and his group of supporters. Hera told them (Il. 5.788-791) 'So long as noble Achilles fared in battle, never did the Trojans come out even in front of the Dardanian gates; for they feared his mighty spear; but now far from the city they are fighting at the hollow ships.' From these lines we can see that the two rivers joined 'far from the city' and close to the camp. This joining place is sometimes called 'the watersmeet', and I will also use this term.

The Skamander is found near Troy, and also near the defensive wall and the ships. It is crossed only once on the journey from the Greek camp to Troy, so they lie on opposite sides of the river. No crossing of the Simois is mentioned, and there is no reference to the Simois anywhere near Troy. Remembering Homer's economy, this means that either it did not extend as far as Troy, or that, if it did, it did not play any part in the action of the epic. I will assume therefore that the Skamander is the main river of the plain, and the Simois is a tributary.

The Skamander

The Skamander carries water from Ida, and flows past Troy on its way to the sea. It is sometimes called 'Xanthus', or 'the waters of Xanthus', which is a name of a river god, a son of Zeus, but also has the meaning 'yellow'. There seems to be some difference of opinion as to its source, which deserves our attention. In one popular translation [4] these two springs outside the walls of Troy become the source of the Skamander. As a retired water engineer I find this difficult to believe, since we are told that the waters came originally from Mt. Ida, and at Troy the Skamander was already regarded as a 'noble river'. The flow from two springs beside the walls of Troy that were used for washing clothes could hardly, while still near Troy, have become a 'noble river'. However, both Rieu and Murray read the Iliad as saying that the two springs 'feed the Skamander', as distinct from being its source. This seems much more likely.

It is interesting to note here that in 1892 Leaf [5], certain that Hisarlik was Troy, wrote 'The two springs of Skamandros have naturally been the foundation of all attempts to fix the site of Homer's Troy. It is now settled that no such springs are to be found in the plain of the Skamander. Either they have disappeared, or the topography is to some extent imaginary. There can be no doubt that the latter solution is the true one...' Leaf went on to say that two such springs, one hot, the other cold, were actually found high up in the catchment near the summit of Ida. From this coincidence, he concluded that Homer must somehow have known about them, and introduced them as part of the imagined scene outside the walls of Troy. Here we see that, as a result of believing that Hisarlik was Troy, Leaf condemns Homer for giving us misleading information by inventing landscape features at Hisarlik that did not really exist. Yet if one starts with a false premise, the application of sound logic to it is of no avail, and the wrong answer beckons.

The Iliad also gives us a clue about the size of the Skamander. Apart from an isolated incident of a flash flood brought down on Achilles by Xanthus, the description of the river, with its pools described as 'silver' or 'deep', suggests the battles took place when the river was low. This is consistent with the events of the Iliad taking place during the summer. It is true that in Book 7 the Trojans were said to have held an assembly beside the eddying river, which could imply there was a summer storm in the uplands, but this book is regarded by Leaf as a later addition. Then in Book 21 we read that a flood caused a full-grown elm tree to fall and span the river from side to side. Now a fully grown elm tree close to a river bank, where its roots need not be very deep, would perhaps reach a height of say 25-35 meters. So if we are to take Homer literally on this point we might expect the river channel where the tree fell to be not much more that say 20 – 30 meters wide. It is interesting to note from early travellers to the Troad that the channel of the lower Mendere in flood was in one case reported to be over 200 feet wide, say some 65 metres. This is too wide to be spanned by an elm tree. River banks generally provide a good spot for trees and shrubs to grow that need plenty of water. In Book 21 the Iliad mentions that trees such as elms, willows and tamarisks were growing there. To conclude, at Troy we would hope to find a river not much more than say 30 metres wide, and with plenty of trees and shrubs along its banks.

Locating the Skamander in the plain

There are one or two clues in the Iliad which help to locate the river on one side of the valley or the other. One example is found in Book 11, where the Trojans have rallied after being pushed back to Troy. With Agamemnon and some other heroes wounded, the Greeks have retreated past the tomb of Ilus and are now approaching their camp. There Aias was even singlehandedly mounting a counterattack. 'But Hector as yet knew nothing of this, since he was fighting on the far left of the battle by the banks of the river Skamander…' (Il. 11.497-499). This tells us that the river in front of the Greek camp was on the left hand side of the battlefield. But 'left' from which viewpoint, and can we say what compass point direction was meant by this 'left'?

There is a very early tradition in Homeric studies, dating back to Aristarchos of Alexandria, that when the poet referred to left or right, we should picture this as meaning to the left or right as seen from the beach looking towards Troy. In other words, looking south towards Ilion from the mouth of the Mendere, 'right' from this viewpoint meant to the west. So, according to this canon, right became synonymous with 'west' and left with east, whatever the viewpoint in the story or whoever is the viewer. Because Troy was always assumed to have been at Ilion, this canon was derived from an attempt to explain the actions and words of the epic in terms of the plain at Hisarlik. Many scholars accept that this canon still applies today.

In this book however, we are keeping an open mind, and must not be bound by anything derived from the assumption that Troy was at Hisarlik. I also find it hard to believe that this canon of Aristarchos ever had any place in the performance of a very long oral epic poem, a performance which might be spread over more than one day. By definition, a 'right hand' is attached to a body which can move to face in any direction, not to a fixed compass point. When he uses the expressions 'left' and 'right', the poet, a master dramatist, generally makes it perfectly clear from the principal actor and/or the action being described, to whom the left or right hand belongs. In this example from Book 11, where we are concerned with the Achaean defensive battle not far from the Greek camp, the 'far left' would logically refer to the view of the battlefield as seen by Achilles from his beached ship. So here we learn that, when viewed from the beach, the Skamander near the ships lies on the left side of the plain. The river mouth will thus be to the left of the harbour bay containing the ships and the Greek camp. Here we conclude from Homer that, if the river flows from south to north as at

Hisarlik, the ships are on the west side of the river mouth. Alternatively, if the river flows westwards from Troy to the sea as in our sketch plan, the Greek camp would be on the south side of the river mouth.

Since the river is crossed once between Troy and the ships, Troy and the Greek camp will be on opposite sides of the river. So, when viewed from the ships near the mouth of the Mendere, Troy will be on the left (east) of the river as it flows from south to north. Alternatively, if the river flows from east to west as in our sketch plan, Troy would lie to the north of the river.

Finally, and just to confuse the reader even further, if we reverse the viewpoint and look downriver from Troy, we find the river on the left side near Troy, and on the right side of the ships near its mouth. With the Greek camp where Strabo suggests, this is true for Troy at both Hisarlik and in Mysia. However, the poet has not yet revealed whether left here is to the east or the west.

The Simois and the layout of the two rivers

Now we come to the Simois. The watersmeet is near the ships, where the Skamander is on the right of the camp as viewed from Troy. We expect the Simois to be a smaller river, either fed from a smaller separate river valley, or collecting runoff from one side of the valley. But there is no mention of any crossing of the Simois between Troy and the ships. Therefore the Simois must drain an area on the right hand side of the valley below Troy. This could be from a smaller separate valley as at Hisarlik.

However there are problems with this idea. Firstly, in Book 6 we learn that, after Athene and Hera had revived the fortunes of the Achaeans, and the Trojans had been pushed back a little from the ships, the battle continued to sway to and fro across the plain, 'midway between Simois and the streams of Xanthus' before the Achaeans got the upper hand. This implies that, at some point not too far from the watersmeet, the Simois flowed roughly parallel to the Skamander, and the battlefield lay between the two. So the Simois and the Skamander share the lower part of the same valley.

Secondly, in Book 20.50-53, Homer tells us that Ares, the god of war, came to give strength and resolve to the Trojans when they needed it after they had fallen well back from the ships. He incited them to greater efforts, one moment from the top of the citadel, the next 'from the banks of the Simois, as he ran along the slopes of Kallikolone'. Now 'Kallikolone' means 'beautiful hill' in Greek. So, from these lines, we discover that there was a hill in the plain some way inland from the ships, and the Simois ran beside it on the side facing the battlefield. And from our earlier considerations, this would have to be on the right side of the plain as we look down-river from Troy.

Although the Simois is called one of the noble rivers of Troy, there is no mention of the Simois between Kallikolone and Troy. As already explained, this may well be because, over this part of its length, it played no part in the action of the epic.

The ford, the coast road and the bend in the river

While estimating the distance between Troy and the Greek camp, I mentioned the ford where Priam stopped to let his horses drink. This was mentioned again during Priam's return journey, after he had collected Hector's body from Achilles. It is also mentioned in Il.14.433. Here we learn that after fighting against the Greeks, who were advancing from their ships, Hector was wounded by a stone from Aias and taken by chariot away from the field of battle. 'But when they had come to the ford of the fair-flowing river, eddying Xanthus, that immortal Zeus begot, there they lifted him from the chariot to the ground and poured water over him.'

Homer mentions the ford again in Il.21.1, after Achilles had caused the Trojans to flee back towards Troy, killing any stragglers that he caught. Then '...when they had now come to the ford of the fair-flowing river, the Xanthus...', Achilles split the Trojan forces into two groups. '...one he drove to the plain towards the city', and the other half '...were forced into the deep flowing river with its silver eddies...' There, in the river, '...cowered the Trojans in the streams of the dread river beneath the steep banks.' There Achilles killed many Trojans, and took 12 youths alive '...as the blood price for dead Patroclus...'

So where should we place this ford? The Trojans reached it some time after retreating across the battlefield, after being watched over by the gods sitting on Kallikolone and the Wall of Herakles. Rieu translates the lines where Trojans are trapped in the river slightly differently. He tells us that some of the Trojans fleeing from Achilles '…were chased into a bend in the river where Xanthus…ran deep… the Trojans cowered under the overhanging banks of that terrible river.' Here I must agree with Rieu that, even if the Iliad does not specifically mention a bend at this point, it is hard to imagine Trojans being trapped in the river and cowering under overhanging banks unless they were caught in a bend. River banks tend to overhang where they are undercut by the faster currents on the outside of a bend. So the mention of overhanging banks supports Rieu's belief that there was a bend in the river here. It must have been large to entrap many of the fleeing soldiers. I will therefore conclude, with Rieu, that the ford was just downstream of a large bend in the river. Perhaps, with his famed economy, Homer thought the great bend here was so well known, possibly from other stories then in circulation, that to mention the word 'bend' here specifically would be unnecessary.

Now we must look more closely at what the Iliad tells us about Priam's journey. On the way to see Achilles at the ships Priam drove his own chariot, and Idaeus drove the ransom wagon. 'Now when they had driven past the great mound of Ilus, they halted the mules and the horses in the river to drink; for darkness had now come down over the earth.' (Il. 24.349ff). While the animals drank in the river, which Homer's audience would assume was at the ford, the god Hermes came to Priam in disguise. He had been sent by Zeus to act as a guide and protector to Priam, so the old king could enter the Greek camp and reach Achilles' tent without being seen. On the return journey Priam was also initially accompanied by Hermes. 'But when they had now come to the ford of the fair-flowing river, eddying Xanthus…' (Il. 24.693), Hermes left Priam and returned to Olympus, home of the gods. Priam then continued on his homeward journey. Cassandra, who had been keeping watch from the Pergamos, was the first to see them in the distance in the early morning light.

On his outward journey, Priam passed the 'tomb of Ilus', a 'great mound', just before reaching the ford. The ford was therefore just downstream of this 'great mound'. We can get some idea of where this 'great mound' is from a passage in Book 11. Here, Agamemnon is leading a charge against the Trojans, who are being chased back towards Troy. 'And past the tomb of ancient Ilus, son of Dardanus, over the middle of the plain, past the wild fig tree they sped, straining towards the city, and always did the son of Atreus follow…' (Il. 11.136). From this and the other passages, we may reasonably assume that the tomb of Ilus, the ford, and the large bend, are all close together somewhere around the middle of the plain between Troy and the ships.

Our picture of the rivers in the plain is now as complete as the Iliad's descriptions allow. If it is a reliable witness, then in the Trojan plain we should find the site of an old ford close to 'a great mound', and just downstream of a place where there was once, and still may be, a large bend in the river. To find a cluster of these three features near the middle of what we suspect is the Trojan plain would be strong evidence that we were looking in the right place. However, we should not expect too much. A bend is an inherently unstable section of river, where erosion due to the faster currents occurs on the outside of the bend, which can cause a river bend to change position over the centuries. Unless, that is, there were good geological reasons for it to remain stable.

Hills and tomb mounds on the plain - general observations

In the Iliad there are references to several hills and tomb mounds, some of which were used as observation points or meeting places. Three tomb mounds are named that existed before the Trojan War, those of Ilus, Myrine and Old Aesyetes. These all lay between Troy and the sea. At least a further three were built for heroes during the action of the epic. It is also apparent that the earlier three, Old Aesyetes, Myrine and Ilus, lay between Ilios and the coast. But, while the hills will remain, should we also expect to find the tomb mounds mentioned by Homer at the real site of Troy? Or might it be impossible to identify these among many later mounds?

If, as the Greek legends claim, Troy was really destroyed and deserted for centuries, then we may not find any more tomb mounds of the Trojan era in the plain. But assuming that Troy was well sited, commanding a well-watered fertile and pasture-rich region, we would expect people to settle there again sooner rather than later. New towns would spring up, if not on the abandoned site of Troy itself, then not far away. We know from the region around Hisarlik that several large tomb mounds were built there during the Classical and Hellenistic periods, some of which were named after Homer's heroes. We should also expect that tomb robbers in later periods may have robbed some of these mounds, especially if they were thought to have contained rich burials. Yet in Anatolia many such mounds have survived un-plundered. Perhaps this is because superstitious local people were reluctant to disturb the spirits of the dead. It is only in recent times that the invention of the bulldozer, allied to the demands of the developer or of mechanised agriculture, has become a serious threat to the existence of many of these mounds. The archaeologist at Pergamon, Professor Radt, [6] told me that many tomb mounds in the region have been robbed and razed to the ground over the last century, so evidence for their existence may now be lost.

All we can safely say at this stage is that, if the practice of raising mounds for the rich or royal dead continued around Bergama after the end of the Trojan era, then we may expect more, and later, tomb mounds to be in the plain, not just those mentioned in the Iliad. This could make an initial identification of those named in the Iliad much more difficult.

Kallikolone

From earlier references, we have already discovered that the beautiful hill, Kallikolone, may be found somewhere past the ford, on the right hand side of the plain as we look from Troy towards the ships. It should also have a smaller river, the Simois, running at its foot on its side facing the battlefield. This river should be flowing in the direction away from Troy, since it does not join the Skamander until it is nearer the ships.

One mention of Kallikolone deserves our particular attention. Zeus was fearful that, once Achilles took the field, the Trojans would give up the fight, and Achilles 'may lay waste the wall' of Troy (Il. 20.30), before the appointed time. He therefore allowed the gods to join the battle on whichever side they chose, so this would make the two sides more even. The gods fought on their chosen sides for a short while, then withdrew to watch the battle from a safe distance. The Achaean supporters, Poseidon, Hera and Athene, sat on a hill called the

'Wall of Herakles', while '…they on the other side sat opposite on the brows of Kallikolone, around you, archer Phoebus (Apollo) and Ares, sacker of cities.' (Il.20.146-151). We may guess that these vantage points were both quite high, as they were chosen by the gods to give a good view of the battle in progress. From the Iliad it seems that Kallikolone had 'brows', which suggests a distinctive hilltop feature, something rather more than just a hill with a smooth flat or rounded top. This feature may help us identify Kallikolone from other hills, once we find the right site.

The 'Wall of Herakles'.

The 'Wall of Herakles' is another feature we would expect to be able to identify on the Trojan plain. The Iliad tells us about the 'heaped up wall of god-like Herakles, the high wall that the Trojans and Pallas Athene had built for him so that he might flee there and escape from the monster of the deep when it drove him from the sea shore to the plain' (Il 20:145ff.). This legendary event happened in the time of Laomedon, as told briefly in Chapter 2. There is no need to search for a man-made hill. The poet tells us it was built by Athene with help from mortals, so we may assume the 'wall' was too large to have been built by men alone. At Hisarlik, the generally accepted Wall of Herakles was a natural hill. Here we should look for a natural hill shaped as if by man.

The wall was 'opposite' the brows of Kallikolone, but where should we look for it? Again, the Iliad does not disappoint. Earlier, Poseidon had told Hera (Il. 20:135) 'But for our part let us then go apart from the track to some lookout spot and sit there, and the war will be the concern of men.' Now the main track mentioned in the Iliad is the one that goes from Troy across the ford to the Greek camp, so we will assume this is the one to which Poseidon refers. Poseidon is suggesting sitting down on a wall-like hill, which is 'a look-out spot', which lies beyond the track on the other side of the battlefield from Kallikolone. With these clues to guide us, we may therefore hope to find this 'Wall of Herakles' in the foothills opposite Kallikolone. If it was used by Herakles as an escape from a sea monster, we may expect to find it not too far from the coast.

The great barrow of Ilus

This barrow has already been discussed in relation to its position by the ford and the bend in the river, so we know roughly where to find it. Two references to this barrow were given. One was from Book 11, where the tomb of Ilus was found roughly half way across the plain (Il. 11.166). The second was from Book 24 (Il. 24.349), where it was described as a 'great mound' just upstream of the ford.

Another reference is found in Book 10. Here we are told that, with the Trojans camped close by the ships, Dolon, the captured Trojan spy, told Odysseus and Diomedes that Hector was '…holding council by the tomb of godlike Ilus, away from all the turmoil.' (Il. 10.415). This passage confirms that the tomb of Ilus was some way inland, away from the noise coming from the Trojan camp on the rising ground in the plain before the ships. This information is consistent with this tomb being near the ford, and some halfway across the plain between Troy and the ships.

The one reference to the tomb of Ilus not yet discussed is also from Book 11. Here, Zeus had granted Hector a day of glory. Agamemnon's assault was halted, and the Achaeans then started to be pushed back. Then another of their heroes was put out of action when Paris shot Diomedes in the foot with an arrow.

'But Alexander (i.e. Paris)…aimed an arrow at Tydeus' son, shepherd of men, supporting himself against a pillar on the mound that men's hands reared for Ilus, son of Dardanus, an elder of the people of old'. (Il. 11.370-372).
This tells us nothing new about the position of the mound, but is of interest in being the first mention of a pillar being placed on the top of a tomb mound in the Trojan plain. Homer later mentions such a practice for the great Trojan hero, Sarpendon, son of Zeus, who was killed by Patroclus. The twin brothers 'Sleep' and 'Death' transported his body to Lycia, and there 'his brothers and kins-people [will] give him a burial with mound and pillar; for this is the privilege of the dead.' (Il. 16.675).

This practice reminds us of the stele placed above the shaft graves at Mycenae, and raises a number of questions. The first thing a raised mound of earth will do is settle. What steps were taken to stop the pillar from leaning or falling as the ground settled beneath it? Were these pillars placed on stone foundations on top of the tomb and, if so, has any evidence been found of this practice? Is it possible that such pillars bore written inscriptions, or the name of the dead, and have any like this been found in western Anatolia? At Mycenae, the Shaft Graves within the later city walls had headstones with carved reliefs, one even showing a single-axel chariot with a 4-spoked wheel, but with no writing on them. Certainly, such stones would be vulnerable to theft and re-use in later times, so we should not expect to find any still in place today in the Trojan plain.

The tomb of old Aesyetes

Outside Troy, in the direction of the ships, there were two tomb mounds. The first is called the Tomb of Aesyetes. Polites, a son of Priam, 'sat as a lookout of the Trojans, trusting in his fleetness of foot, on the topmost part of the grave mound of aged Aesyetes, watching for the time when the Achaeans should start out from their ships.' (Il. 2.791-794). From this description, we imagine a tomb mound well out in the plain, so that when Polites saw the enemy advancing, he could, provided he was a good runner, get back to Troy in time to warn the city of a pending attack. The Iliad says nothing of its size or shape.

Thorn Hill or the tomb of Myrine

The second of the two tombs outside Troy is the Tomb of Myrine.
'There is in front of the city a steep mound far out in the plain, with a clear space round it on all sides; this men call Batieia, but the immortals call it the grave mound of Myrine, light of step.' (Il. 2.811-815). It was here that the Trojans and their allies first lined up to do battle.

Remembering Homer's famed economy, we should especially note his use of the epithet 'steep', and hope that such a mound may still be found. From the mention of both mounds, I will speculate that Old Aesyetes' tomb, as a lookout post for a fast runner, was probably further away from Troy than Myrine's tomb. He would have chosen the mound which gave him the earliest opportunity of seeing the movement of the Achaeans from the ships, and of getting an early warning of whether or not Achilles was among them. Myrine's tomb would then be the nearer of the two to Troy. I must hope that the real Trojan plain will yield present or past evidence of both these mounds.

The barrow of Patroclus

The building of this barrow is mentioned in Il. 23:253. I will therefore hope to find it, if it still exists, somewhere not far from the Greek camp. Walter Leaf, however, believed the episode of the recovery of the body of Patroclus may not have been part of Homer's original story. If he is correct, then clearly no such tumulus will be found there. Also, if a tomb mound is found here, its owner may not have been Patroclus.

The barrow of Hector

This barrow was built by the Trojans during an eleven day truce after he was killed. Homer tells us that Hector's body was first cremated on a large pyre. Then were '…the bones placed in a golden urn…the urn laid in a hollow grave, and covered it over with great close-set stones. Then they quickly heaped the mound…' (Il 24.795-800). We are not told where this barrow was, but it must have been quite close to Troy, as a keen watch was kept in case the Achaeans broke the truce and attacked without warning. Since the Trojan practice was apparently to erect mounds on the plain between Troy and the ships, we may hope to find evidence of Hector's tomb in this direction also, albeit not very far from Troy. If one day it could be found, what a treasure this golden urn would be.

Concluding comments

We have now identified all the main and durable features in the Trojan plain between Troy and the mouth of the river. In the next chapter we will try to use our information to reconstruct a sketch map of the Trojan plain. We can then compare this map with what we find at Hisarlik.

CHAPTER 4

RECONSTRUCTING THE TROJAN PLAIN

Introduction. A theoretical reconstruction of the plain of Troy.
Reconstructing the river layout. Reconstructing the Trojan landscape.
Twelve features for comparison purposes. Concluding comments.

Introduction

In the last chapter I commented that one of my basic assumptions is that the detailed descriptions of Troy, Ilios and the Trojan landscape as given in the Iliad are generally accurate, and are not simply the product of a poetic imagination. Despite the reasonable scepticism of professional scholars, I was encouraged in this belief by a few lines from Hilda Lorimer, a leading Oxford scholar who devoted much of her life to the study of Homer. In 1959 she published her classical study in a book entitled 'Homer and the Monuments'. Referring to Homer's landscapes, this is what she had to say:

'The story-teller who develops a complicated plot involving frequent changes of scene must, if he aims at producing an impression of reality, carry a map of operations in his head. Modern writers of this type…generally select a countryside with which they are well acquainted, sometimes equipping it with fictitious names, and thus attain a consistency in their setting which, although few readers are consciously aware of it, contributes to the illusion of actuality achieved.' [1]

This is equally true today. Most of today's radio and TV soap operas have a geographical location setting that is consistent and recognisable to the audience.

One test of the accuracy of the landscape descriptions will be to test their consistency. If they are accurate, they will be consistent rather than conflicting. And if they are consistent, it may be possible to reconstruct a credible Trojan landscape from the Iliad. In this chapter I will attempt such a reconstruction.

A theoretical reconstruction of the plain of Troy

The first point to make is that in this theoretical reconstruction I am only concerned with the on-site topography as abstracted from the Iliad. Clues about Troy's general location, i.e. the geographical signposts pointing in the direction of Troy, will be considered separately once a plain matching these onsite features has been found.

Secondly, in this reconstruction, as throughout Volume 1, I am principally concerned with the Trojan plain. The topographical features of Troy and Ilios will not be included at this stage. My assumption is that the Iliad describes the geography and sufficient features of the Trojan landscape for us to identify it among the main river valleys of western Anatolia. Once the Trojan plain is found, it will lead us to Troy, as we will see in Volume 2.

We will start by representing the plain as the valley of a river which flows in a straight line from east to west. This is a gross simplification because we know that, in nature, most large rivers do change their directions in some places before they reach the sea. In general, however, the major rivers from the Anatolian uplands to the Adriatic Sea do flow from east to west. This applies to the Bakir Çayi, the Hermus and the Maeander rivers.

The plain is shown with a flood plain which gradually widens as it gets nearer the sea. In other words, the distance between the foothills on either side of the valley increases towards the sea. So we can start our reconstruction by drawing a straight line representing the river, running down the centre of a gradually widening valley.

In Chapter 3 we concluded from the Iliad that the ships did not land in the mouth of the Skamander. The dangers from flood waters and silt, and the breach of communications between the two halves of the army would not make this a preferred choice for landing. We should look instead for the Greek camp beside their ships in a large bay between two headlands. And since the river is crossed only once between the ships and Troy, this bay will lie on the opposite side of the river from Troy. We also concluded that, when viewed from the beach, if the river flows from east to west as in our sketch plan, Troy would lie to the left (north) of the river, and the ships would lie to the right of the river mouth. This also makes it credible for Troy to have a Dardanian Gate, unseen from the Greek camp, from which a track led northwards into the foothills and across Mt. Ida to Dardania.

Reconstructing the river layout

Having drawn the line of the main river in relation to Troy and the Greek camp, we can now complete the layout of the two rivers. When we look seaward from Troy, we find the Skamander on our left near Troy. It crosses the road to the harbour at a ford perhaps around halfway to the coast, then continues towards the right hand side of the valley. Also, as deduced in Chapter 3, the Simois must drain the right, or north, side of the valley. In the plain, it also runs along the side of a hill, Kallikolone, and in one place it runs on the opposite side of the battlefield to the Skamander. So we will show the Simois running roughly parallel to the Skamander, before it turns south and joins it at the watersmeet, not far from the coast. The Greek camp must be on the left, i.e. the south, side of the river mouth.

Also near the camp we should find the 'throsmos', an area of higher ground overlooking the ships, upon which the Trojan army camped overnight before launching their final attack. This 'rising in the plain' may have been a low ridge of higher ground running from the southern foothills towards the river mouth.

The cart track running between Troy and the Greek camp can now be added to the sketch map. This crossed the river at a ford, roughly halfway across the plain, and just below the site of a large bend in the river. Here, the information gleaned so far has been consistent. A simple study of the Iliad has enabled us to reconstruct a primitive, but consistent, sketch map of the river layout in the Trojan plain. This is shown as Fig. 4.1. below.

Having developed this theoretical plan, we can now use it to add more features.

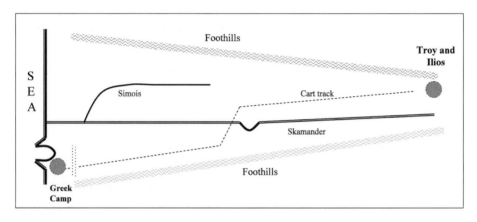

Fig. 4.1 Homer's Trojan plain – reconstruction of river layout.

Reconstructing the Trojan landscape

All the important information about the geography and topography of the Trojan plain, the field of battle, was extracted in Chapter 3. To Fig. 4.1. we can now add in the main hills and tomb mounds in their correct positions according to the Iliad.

The beautiful hill, Kallikolone, lies on the north bank of the Simois probably somewhere towards the middle of the plain. Opposite it, on the other side of the battlefield, and 'apart from the track', we should find a wall-shaped hill, the Wall of Herakles, in the foothills on the southern side of the plain.

Just upstream of the ford, and close to the bend in the river, we should find a great mound, which in the Iliad is called the 'Tomb of Ilus'.

Then as we approach Troy we should find two tomb mounds outside the town. Perhaps the one furthest away from Troy would be the tomb of Old

Aesyetes, the lookout point for Polites, Priam's young son. A little nearer and further out in the plain we may hope to find the tomb of Myrine. Here, 'far out on the plain', and with Achilles sulking by the ships, the two great armies first lined up opposite each other and prepared to do battle. If Homer's epithet is true, this mound may have steeper sides than the other tomb mounds.

The descriptions of the Iliad have now enabled me to piece together a reasonably coherent picture of the Trojan plain including the main rivers, hills and tomb mounds featured during the action of the epic. This picture is seen below in Fig. 4.2.

Twelve features for comparative purposes

Perhaps the easiest way to compare this notional map with other sites will be to list the main features we should expect to find as we travel from the Greek camp towards Troy. I will now draw up this list with the help of Fig. 4.2.

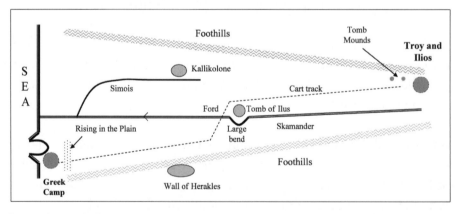

Fig. 4.2 Homer's Trojan plain – theoretical reconstruction showing the main features.

1. The bay and beach

As we stand at the river mouth facing Troy we should find, not far away to our right, a separate large sandy bay between two headlands. This bay should be large enough to accommodate all the ships in three rows, with some 3-400 ships in each row. Within the bay, the sandy beach should back onto fields and meadows, rather than onto hills or cliffs.

2. The rising in the plain
The beach should be overlooked by an area of higher ground, large enough for the whole Trojan army to camp upon it. This would be the 'throsmos' mentioned in the Iliad.

3. The watersmeet
Not far from the camp the Simois should flow into the Skamander from the left hand side looking upstream towards Troy. This would be the 'watersmeet' mentioned in the Iliad.

4. The Simois
The Simois is a tributary draining the left hand side of the plain looking upstream. For part of its course it will run roughly parallel to the Skamander, with the battlefield between them.

5. Kallikolone
Some distance across the plain will be Kallikolone, a notable hill in the plain. This may have a distinctive brow. The Simois will flow beside this hill on the side facing the battlefield.

6. The Wall of Herakles
Opposite Kallikolone, on the far side of the cart track on other side of the plain, will be a distinctive high wall-shaped hill or large mound. This will be the Wall of Herakles.

7. The distance between the camp and Troy
As a measure of the scale of the Trojan plain, the distance between Troy and the ships was estimated as between 20 and 30km. This broadly supports the comments in the Iliad that Troy was a long way from the ships.

8. The ford
The cart track from Troy to the ships crosses the Skamander somewhere near the middle of the plain.

9. The Tomb of Ilus

Just upstream of the ford will be a large mound. In the Iliad this is called the Tomb of Ilus, and it lies on the right hand side of the river as we look downstream from Troy.

10. The bend in the river

Upstream of the ford we should find a large bend in the river. This was the bend in which many Trojans were trapped when fleeing from Achilles. Even if the course of the river has changed since Trojan times, evidence that a bend was once there should be available.

11. The tomb of Old Aesyetes

A tomb mound should be found in the plain quite close to Troy. This may be the mound of Old Aesyetes, the lookout for Priam's son Polites.

12. The Tomb of Myrine

Also quite close to Troy we may find another tomb mound, with steep sides, and far out in plain with space all around it.

Concluding comments

From our reconstructed layout of the rivers and hills, it should now be possible to compare the lower valleys of the Mendere, the Bakir Cay, and other rivers if necessary, in order to see which best fits the Trojan landscape. We will now use the twelve features as listed above to help us find the real Trojan plain, and the first place we will look is at Hisarlik.

CHAPTER 5

LOOKING FOR THE TROJAN
PLAIN AT HISARLIK

Introduction A map of the region around Hisarlik. Troy at Hisarlik in 2005.
Looking for the plain of Troy.
Case A. With the Greek camp at Besik Bay (after 1982).
Case B. With the Greek camp at the river mouth (before 1982). Conclusions.

Introduction

In this chapter we return to the landscape of Hisarlik to look for the Trojan plain. This time we have before us a notional sketch map showing in outline the layout of the main features of the landscape as deduced from the Iliad. We also have a list of 12 key features, which we will try to locate and identify as we journey from the coast towards Troy. First we will look at an early map showing the location of Hisarlik. [1]

A map of the region around Hisarlik

This map shows the site of Hisarlik, bearing the name 'Troia', near the mouth of the Mendere. I have added a dashed line to show the approximate outline of the large bay at the mouth of the river, as discovered in 1980-82. For convenience I call this the Bay of Hestiaia, after Hestiaia of Alexandria. This lady was mentioned by Strabo as claiming, with remarkable perspicacity, that the plain presently before Ilion in her day was 'a deposit of the rivers' [2]. Until

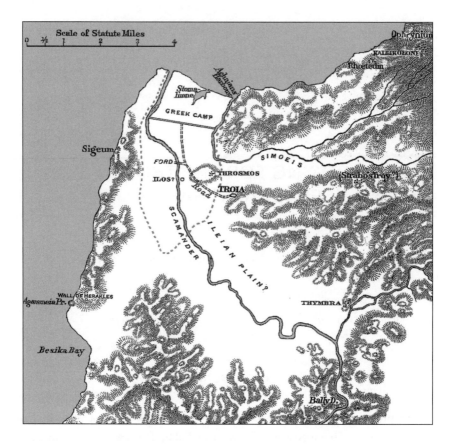

Fig. 5.1. Map of the region of Hisarlik.

the discovery that this bay existed in Trojan times, it was assumed that the Greek camp was at the mouth of the river. The Scamander or Mendere was then thought to have flowed on the eastern side of the plain close to Troy. Otherwise there would have been no 'watersmeet', and no need to cross the ford when going from Troy to the camp. As already mentioned, the discovery of this large bay has led to the claim that the Greek camp must instead have been at Besik Bay, some 9km south west of Hisarlik.

Troy at Hisarlik in 2005

Before we look for the Trojan plain, let me give you an impression of what

Troy looked like from a few photographs of Troy taken in 2005. Figure 5.2 (see colour plate section) is a general view of the site entrance, showing the famous model of Homer's Trojan horse. The site, looking generally rather flat, lies behind the horse. The road leading to the site from the Izmir to Cannakale road runs either on the level or slightly down hill across the plateau until it reaches the site on the edge of the valley.

The site itself is rather confusing for the average visitor. It is impossible to imagine what the site once looked like at any one period in time. Walls appear and disappear without serving any apparent purpose, and the differences in the details of their construction are not immediately apparent to the untrained eye. Most of the walls on display are from the Roman and Hellenistic periods. A section of the great wall of Troy level 6 is perhaps the centrepiece of the site, along with the sloping ramp that led, apparently un-gated, into the walled fortress of Troy level 2. The gap caused by Schliemann's great trench is another useful reference point. The early walls, of rougher stonework and with no mortar, can be seen in several places. The earliest of these were of more roughly shaped stones of varying sizes, not laid in even courses that are pleasing to the eye. In some walls the stones were selected or shaped to sit next to the stone that has already been placed, and may have more than four shaped sides. This type is commonly called 'polygonal' walling, and was a favoured type of wall in the Mycenaean era. It is also found occasionally in some later periods.

Fig. 5.3 (see colour plate section) shows the ramp leading up to the entrance to Troy 2, presently dated c2500-2200 BC. A section of walls of the Troy 2 settlement, with no clear courses of stonework, is visible on either side of the ramp. It was at the foot of this wall that Schliemann found what later became known as Priam's treasure.

Fig. 5.4 shows a section of the sloping wall of Troy 6, c1800-1275 BC. This is fine quality ancient stonework, built without using mortar, with the courses fairly well defined and an even face to the wall. On the top would have been a vertical section of clay brick wall to make it harder to climb. The plain of the lower Mendere between Hisarlik and the sea is flat and lacks any prominent features, as can be seen in the next figure.

Fig. 5.4 A section of wall of Troy 6, of the Mycenaean era.

Fig. 5.5 (see colour plate section) is a view across the plain of the Mendere to the Straits, looking west from the walls of Troy. This gives an impression of the height of Troy above the river plain, and the views it commanded of the river valley. A ship can be seen passing north through the Straits. Unlike the Trojan plain of the Iliad, there are no significant hills to be seen in this flood plain.

Fig. 5.6 shows part of the great trench dug by Schliemann in his haste to reach the lowest settlement layer. The foundations of some houses dating to Troy Level 1 can be seen in the bottom of the trench. In the distance across the flat plain we can see the Straits, and the encroaching outskirts of the town of Canakkale.

Overall, despite the best efforts of the site organisers, Troy today remains a rather confusing and disappointing site for the average visitor. As I climbed

Fig. 5.6. Looking north from Troy along the great trench
dug in 1872-3 by Schliemann.

back on the tour bus I found myself wondering how anyone could imagine
that this was the place that Zeus, king among the gods, said was his favourite
city among all of the ancient cities built by man.

Looking for the plain of Troy

We will now look separately and in more detail for the twelve selected features
in the alternative Trojan plains: a) the more recent one with the camp at Besik
Bay, and b) the earlier one with the Greek camp at the river mouth.

In accepting Hisarlik as Troy, scholars and the general public had to accept
that any features of the Trojan plain not found there must have been either
lost in transmission, or imagined by the poet. Now we have reconstructed

a sketch map of the layout of the Trojan plain, we will see what is missing here, or in the wrong place. We will look first at the Trojan plain with the ships at Besik Bay, and then with the Greek camp by the mouth of the Mendere. Although now known to have been impossible, the second case is worth looking at briefly, since the view that this was the plain of Troy held sway for over 2,000 years. Both case studies reveal how, for believers in Troy at Hisarlik, the distant view of Samothrace was sufficiently powerful to outweigh all their concerns about the many other missing features in the Trojan landscape.

Case A. With the Greek camp at Besik Bay (after 1982)

With the Greek camp relocated to Besik Bay, the character of the post-1982 Trojan plain was quite different to the previous one. Instead of travelling up-river from the camp to Troy, the journey involved crossing the river at right angles some two thirds of the way across the plain. With this layout the Dombrek, supposedly the Simois, lies beyond Troy, so there was no watersmeet anywhere near the ships.

We will run quickly through the selected landscape features to see how well this newly proposed 'Trojan plain' compares with the Iliad.

1. The bay and beach
Besik Bay, with only one 'headland', would provide a possible landing place, although the current flowing from north to south in the Straits would make this landing place far from ideal. It would not make a good site for a harbour. It is far from the Scamander, so does not match the Iliad's requirements.

2. The rising in the plain
There is an area of somewhat higher ground between Besik Bay and the plain of the Mendere.

3. The watersmeet
There is no watersmeet near the camp at Besik Bay.

4. The Simois

There is no river to match the Simois on the left hand side of the plain as we travel towards Troy.

5. Kallikolone

There is no beautiful hill in the plain with a distinctive brow, and with the Simois running beside it.

6. The Wall of Herakles

There is no hill deserving the description 'wall-shaped' opposite Kallikolone in this plain. However, fig 5.1 shows a flat-topped circular hill near Besik Bay labelled the 'Wall of Hercules'.

7. The distance between the camp and Troy

Besik Bay is only some 9km from Hisarlik. This is too close to match the Trojan plain in the Iliad.

8. The ford

There is no obvious place for a ford across the Mendere on the line between Besik Bay and Hisarlik, nor any convincing evidence that significant traffic once existed between the two places.

9. The Tomb of Ilus

There is no trace of a large mound on the Troy side of the river along the supposed route.

10. The bend in the river

There is no evidence that a large bend in the river existed just upstream of the ford, such as might have trapped many Trojans who were fleeing from Achilles.

11. The tomb of Old Aesyetes

There is no convincing evidence that a tomb mound once existed where the tomb of Old Aesyetes stood in the Trojan plain. If there had been such a tomb, it would have been given its Homeric name long ago. The best and safest lookout point from which to see an attack was coming would have been on the walls of Troy.

12. The Tomb of Myrine

No steep sided tomb mound has been found 'far out in the plain' before Troy, with clear space all around, to match the description of the tomb of Myrine.

Verdict on Case A

Our brief appraisal of the so-called 'Trojan plain' with the Greek camp at Besik Bay suggests that it is nothing like that described in the Iliad. Firstly the river layout is all wrong. The Scamander is not found near both the Greek camp and Troy. There is no Simois flowing in one place on the other side of the battlefield, with its watersmeet not far from the camp. While one might argue that there is a possible 'throsmos', there are no convincing candidates for Kallikolone, the Wall of Herakles, the Tomb of Ilus, the ford, or the tombs of Old Aesyetes and Myrine in the plain before Troy.

Case B. With the Greek camp at the river mouth (Pre-1982)

As already mentioned, it was assumed, with little geological support, that the river in Trojan times flowed down the eastern side of the plain, passing close to Troy. The Greek camp must have been roughly as shown on Walter Leaf's map, Fig. 5.1. If so, its defensive wall was scarcely 4km from Troy. We have already seen that the walled fort at Hisarlik was much too small to be Troy. Now it is equally apparent that this Trojan plain is also much too small to match the descriptions in the Iliad.

Here there is no need to run through all twelve features separately in order to list what is absent in the landscape. Clearly there is no bay between two headlands suitable for use by the Achaean ships on the west side of the river mouth. Since there is no suitable bay, the Achaean's beach is also missing.

The area of higher ground labelled 'throsmos' is marked on the map some 2km from the Greek camp. This is broadly in the right position in relation to the Greek camp, but is too close to Troy to match the 'throsmos' of the Iliad. To suppose the Trojans camped here instead of behind their walls seems absurd.

If in Trojan times the Scamander was on the eastern edge of the plain valley, the Dombrek (Simois) would have flowed into the Scamander close to the Greek camp, so a watersmeet there becomes possible. However, the Dombrek is a tributary draining a separate valley on the left hand side of the plain when looking towards Troy, so does not match the Simois of the Iliad. And if the Scamander was on the east side of the plain, the battlefield did not lie between the two rivers.

There is no beautiful hill in the plain with a distinctive brow. There is a hill labelled 'Kallikolone' near the coast some 6km east of the river mouth, but this location is too far from the Trojan plain to be credible. There is also no hill deserving the description 'wall-shaped' on the other side of the plain and the cart track between Troy and the camp. There is a hill labelled the 'Wall of Herakles' on the map, but while it overlooks the supposed battlefield, neither its location nor appearance are convincing.

If the Mendere was on the eastern edge of the plain in Trojan times, then the cart track would have crossed the Mendere at a ford on its way to the camp, so a cart track and ford become plausible. However, here there is no trace of a large mound on the Troy side of the ford that might have been the Tomb of Ilus. Other notable absentees are the great bend in the river, the lookout tomb of Old Aesyetes, and the steep sided mound with clear space all around to match the description of the tomb of Myrine.

Verdict on Case B

To summarise, our brief look at Case B shows that the following landscape features are either missing, or have been identified in an unconvincing location: the bay and beach, Kallikolone, the Wall of Herakles, the Tomb of Ilus, the bend in the river, the Tomb of old Aesyetes, and the tomb of Myrine.

Conclusions

With the Greek camp at either the river mouth or Besik Bay, the plain between the camp and Hisarlik bears little or no resemblance to the Trojan plain of the

Iliad. Although my own visit to Hisarlik was all too brief, I consoled myself with the knowledge that Lascelles had spent a day exploring the plain between Hisarlik and the river mouth. There he had satisfied himself that it was almost entirely flat. He wrote, 'There were no tumuli in it. Certainly there were none near the 'Troy' citadel. The only tumuli to be seen from Hisarlik are located on the skyline of the ridge over against the sea.' Hisarlik itself, with its small size and lack of a natural acropolis, is also quite unlike Troy. It is remarkable, therefore, that so much was put down to the imaginings of the poet, and that no serious attempt was made to look elsewhere. The power of the view from Samothrace and the proximity to the Straits, assumed to be the poet's Hellespont, blinded all to the possibility of finding an alternative site. So long as it is assumed and believed that no alternative could have existed, this problem cannot be resolved. This is another example where, by adopting a false assumption, no logical argument can solve the problem. As the next chapter shows, a credible alternative site does exist. Not only does it exist, it may be found exactly where Achilles tells us to look, between Lesbos and Phrygia 'in the uplands'.

CHAPTER 6

CAN TROY BE SOMEWHERE ELSE?

Introduction. Offsite signposts pointing towards Troy.
'Hellespont' in the Iliad. Naming the Hellespont. Naming the Aegean. The extent of the Hellespont.
The view from Samothrace. The verdict of Walter Leaf.
Interim conclusions about Samothrace, Tenedos and Imbros.
The view from Gargarus. Locating the Trojan allies. Comments on the Trojan allies.
The places captured by Achilles. The Achaeans at Teuthrania in Mysia.
Troy between Lesbos and Phrygia, Il. 24.543-6. The journey to Troy by Iphidamas.
Summary of evidence about the general location of Troy. Conclusions.

Introduction

So far in this book we have learned about the history of the discovery of the site of Classical Ilion at Hisarlik, and why this has come to be commonly regarded as Troy. We have looked at the sources of the Troy-related legends, and studied the Iliad for clues about the Trojan landscape. These clues enabled me to draw a sketch map showing the river layout and main features in the Trojan plain. This map shows that the plain at Hisarlik compares very poorly with the Trojan plain of the Iliad, wherever the Greek camp might have been.

This brings us to the next question. What stops us looking for Troy somewhere else? Why should we not look in the great valley of the Bakir Çayi, since this lies between Lesbos and Phrygia, where Achilles placed the realm of Priam? The answer is simple. The Iliad tells us that Troy must be visible from the top

73

of Samothrace, and near Tenedos and Imbros. This is not possible with Troy at Teuthrania or Pergamon. The problem is insoluble. If we assume, as everyone does, that these clues as to the whereabouts of Troy were part of the original story of the Trojan War, and if, within sight of Samothrace there is no site like the Troy of the Iliad, we have reached an impasse. We have no option but to say that all that is described in the Iliad and not found at Hisarlik must simply have been lost in oral transmission or imagined by the poet.

Yet there is another solution to this impasse which does not seem to have been seriously considered. This is that if Achilles is right, and if the Trojan lands lay in the Kaikos valley between Lesbos and Phrygia, could the mention of Samothrace, Tenedos and Imbros be deliberate red herrings? At first sight this may seem a far fetched idea, but it does at least have a certain statistical appeal. There are many more lines which must otherwise be explained as poetic imaginings than there are lines which place Troy at Hisarlik. For example, the name 'Samothrace' occurs only once in the Iliad, but 'Ilios' occurs 106 times. So why should 'Samothrace' be believed genuine, while the great natural acropolis of 'Ilios', non-existent at Hisarlik, is believed a poetic invention? This fact alone makes the 'red herring' theory worth pursuing. Yet why would anyone want to change the Iliad to show that Troy was at Hisarlik rather than at Bergama? We will set this important question to one side for the present, and answer it in some detail in Volume 2. Here we will use geography to explore the red herring idea, and see where it leads.

Offsite signposts pointing towards Troy

The mentions of Samothrace, Tenedos and Imbros are what I earlier called 'offsite signposts'. They point towards Troy. If we wish to challenge the integrity of these signposts, we must see if they are consistent. If they all point in the same direction, the 'red herring' theory will lack evidential support. The more obvious offsite signposts in the Iliad and Odyssey appear as descriptions of journeys to Troy and as references to various places nearby. Once gathered together, if they turn out to be inconsistent this will lend support to my suggestion that some of these lines are later interpolations.

'Hellespont' in the Iliad

The first offsite signpost we will look at is that Troy lay beside the Hellespont. This name is Greek, and means 'The Sea of Helle' or 'Helle's waters'. It was used for the Straits by Herodotus when he described the Persian invasions. He told how the Hellespont was crossed in an expedition against Scythia by the Persian king Darius, and again later by his son Xerxes on his way to invade Greece. We can therefore conclude that the name was in general use as meaning the Straits by the fifth century. The important question to ask is did this name in the Iliad apply to a wider area of the northern Aegean, or only to the Straits?

My first approach, as always where possible, is to allow Homer to illuminate Homer. So what does the poet of the Iliad tell us about the Hellespont? Looking at the use of this name, it is found ten times. Where it has a descriptive epithet, these are as follows:
'Strong stream of', or 'swift flowing' (2:845, and 12:30)
'fishy' (Strabo's translation, Book 7 Frag. 58), or 'teeming' (9:360)
'Broad' or 'wide' (7:86, 17:432)
'Boundless' (24:545) or 'endless' (Strabo's translation, 13:1:7)
The epithet 'broad' is also used in the Odyssey's only mention of the Hellespont. (Od.24.82)

Of these instances, the epithets 'broad' and 'boundless', used in total (including the Odyssey reference) four times, are not at all appropriate to the Straits. And yet Homer is famed for the general aptness of his epithets, and for his ability to use them to capture the most essential qualities of what he is describing. The epithet 'swift flowing' is apparently the only one that suggests a confined channel, but nowhere does the Iliad call the Hellespont either 'a channel' or 'narrow'. All could equally or better be applied to the whole of the northern Aegean.

Naming the Hellespont
My next question is how did the 'Hellespont' get its name? For the answer we must turn again to the ancient Greek myths and legends, this time to the story

of Phrixus and Helle. They were the son and daughter of Athamas, king of Orchomenos in Boeotia and his first wife Nephele. What happened to Nephele is not known, but later Athamas married Ino, a daughter of Cadmus. She resented the existence of her stepchildren and plotted to kill them. Cutting a long story short, they were rescued from death by a wondrous talking and flying ram with a golden fleece, sent by the god Hermes. At the ram's command, Phrixus and Helle leapt on its back and it flew away eastwards to Colchis. But as the ram flew over the Hellespont dividing Europe and Asia, Helle fell from its back and drowned in the sea below. The ram continued on its journey and eventually put Phrixus down in Colchis at the south eastern corner of the Black Sea. There, we are told, he became the founder of Phrygia. To recover the golden fleece of this ram was said to have been the motive behind Jason's epic voyage with the Argonauts to Colchis.

This legend evidently pre-dates the Trojan War and, as with most very early legends, there are some different versions of the story. [1] Yet a glance at the map shows us that from Boeotia, a direct flight to Colchis would not pass over the Straits, but over Lesbos and the Elaiatic Gulf, much further south. It would therefore fit the story better if Helle fell into what is now known as the northern Aegean Sea between Europe and Asia.

Naming the Aegean

If you are wondering how the Aegean Sea got its name, this is explained in another well known legend. This concerns Theseus, son of Aegeus king of Athens, and the Minotaur belonging to the great King Minos on Crete. Once upon a time a son of Minos had been killed in Attica, and as punishment, Minos decreed that Athens should send as tribute seven youths and seven maidens once every nine years, to be sacrificed to the Minotaur. On one occasion shortly before this tribute became due, the young prince Theseus happened to return to Athens from his heroic travels. Learning what was about to happen, and wishing to prevent it, he elected to go to Crete with the other sacrificial youths and maidens. His father, the aged king Aegus, feared that he would never see his son again. So he agreed that if and when the ship carrying the fourteen intended victims returned, it would carry a white sail if Theseus was coming home safely, instead of the black ones the ship usually carried. In due course, and after many adventures, Theseus succeeded in killing the Minotaur, and sailed home safely with the intended victims unharmed. Sadly, however, he forgot to hoist the promised white sails. Aegeus, who had long kept watch from a cliff top, spotted the black sails as the ship came into view. Believing his son was dead, in his anguish he cast himself from the cliffs into the sea below and drowned. Henceforth the sea in this region was named the Aegean after him.

These two legends suggest a common very early tradition of naming a sea after someone who drowned in it. There is nothing in these legends to oppose the suggestion that, in earliest times, today's Aegean Sea was once divided into two or more separately named seas. Perhaps the Aegean was the original name for the southern Aegean, named after King Aegus, and the Hellespont was the earlier name for the northern Aegean, named after Helle.

The Extent of the Hellespont

If I am right that in Trojan times the name 'Hellespont' applied to the northern Aegean, then when and how did it come to be applied solely to the Straits? Herodotus, as already noted, used the Hellespont as another name for the Straits when recording the crossings of the Persian kings Darius and Xerxes. Had this become its name by then? Fortunately for us, Strabo discussed this very question.[2] He said that in his time, some 400 years after Herodotus, there was still no general agreement on the definition of the term Hellespont. Some writers applied the name to all or part of the Propontos, the ancient name for the Sea of Marmara. Others applied it to the sea which faces the Melas gulf north of the Chersonese peninsular, and the open waters of the Aegean Sea. Others argued that it should apply to the whole of the Aegean Sea as far west as the sea off the shores of Thessaly and Macedonia, 'invoking Homer also as witness, for Homer (Il. 9:359) says 'thou shalt see, if thou dost wish and hast a care therefore, my ships sailing o'er the fishy Hellespont at very early morn'. Others dispute this from Homer (2:844 and 4:519), saying of the Thracians that they were 'shut in by strong-flowing Hellespont.' So it seems from Strabo that some among the ancients believed that the term

Hellespont, as well as applying to the Straits, once also applied to a much wider area of the northern Aegean. And they quoted Homer in their support.

Moving forward some 2,000 years, the problem has re-emerged. In the last chapter, we saw that after the discovery of the Bay of Hestiaia, Korfmann decided that Besik Bay must have been the site of the Greek Camp.[3] Some critics immediately objected, saying that this was not on the Hellespont as required by Homer. In response, Korfmann agreed that Besik Bay lay outside the Straits, but he cited [4] an earlier scholar who had pointed out that 'the concept of the 'Sea of Helle' before the fifth century B.C. was not restricted to the Strait, but included as well the Thracian Sea to the west and the Propontis to the east.'

Professor Luce, in his book 'Celebrating Homer's Landscapes', was one of those scholars who objected to the Greek Camp at Besik Bay on these grounds. He chose instead a site within the Bay of Hestiaia. But in discussing the problem he also noted that a leading Homeric scholar, Professor R. Janko, [5] had argued that the term Hellespont originally applied to the whole of the Northern Aegean. Learning of this support for my theory from such a leading Homeric scholar was most encouraging.

To summarise, the epithets in the Iliad describing the Hellespont, when taken collectively, do not justify the conclusion that the poet was referring exclusively to the Straits. The area of sea meant by 'the Hellespont' was not agreed 2,000 years ago in Strabo's day, and still is not agreed today. It seems equally likely that it referred to the whole of the northern Aegean. It is therefore reasonable to accept that our search for a different site for Troy may now extend beyond the confines of the Straits.

The view from Samothrace

We now come to the most important signpost anchoring Troy to the lower Mendere valley. This is its visibility from Samothrace, and its proximity to Imbros and Tenedos. This is such an important and revealing issue that I have devoted a separate chapter to it. Here I will set the mentions of Tenedos and Imbros to one side, and briefly introduce the Samothrace problem.

As already explained in Chapter 1, the Iliad tells us that Poseidon was watching the battle by the Greek ships from the topmost peak of Samothrace. And it is a fact that Mount Fengari on Samothrace is clearly seen in the distance on a clear day from Hisarlik, rising above the island of Imbros in the foreground. For pro-Hisarlik supporters, Troy can therefore be nowhere else. End of story. Yet, as this book will show, far from being the end of the story, it is just the beginning, but of a rather different story. Here I will tell you briefly what the Iliad says about Samothrace, and discuss the text in more detail in the next chapter.

Book 13 opens with Zeus watching the battle from the top of Gargarus, the highest peak of the mountain range of Ida. Then, confident that the gods would heed his warnings and not interfere again in the fighting, he looked away at some tribes who lived well to the north west of Gargarus. In lines 10-16 we read that Poseidon was also watching the battle from 'high on the topmost peak of well-wooded Samothrace', and that he 'had pity on the Achaeans that they were being overcome by the Trojans, and against Zeus he was mightily indignant'. In lines 17-23 Poseidon went down from the rugged mountain, and with his fourth stride 'he reached his goal, Aigai, where his famous palace was built in the depths of the sea, golden and gleaming, imperishable for ever.' Then in the next few lines we learn that from Aigai he crossed over the waves by golden chariot to 'a wide cavern in the depths of the sea between Tenedos and Imbros.' There Poseidon left his chariot and horses, and made his way to the army of the Achaeans.

As you can see, the evidence of the mentions of Samothrace, Tenedos and Imbros being near Troy seems incontrovertible. Poseidon, watching from Samothrace, waited until Zeus looked away then seized his opportunity, and came to Troy unseen to help the Achaeans. However, there are some problems here that are not immediately obvious.

The verdict of Walter Leaf

Many Homeric scholars have had difficulties understanding this passage. In 1892 Leaf wrote about lines Il.13.12-13. [6] He said 'This is perhaps the most striking instance in the Iliad of personal knowledge of the neighbourhood of the Troad on the poet's part; for, as a fact, the plain is visible in its whole extent from the summit of Samothrace. As the island is at a considerable distance, and Imbros lies directly between it and Troy, it would naturally be supposed by anyone not well acquainted with the country that this was not the case. But the mountains of Samothrace are so high as to look well over the top of Imbros.'

So far so good, but then he finds a difficulty. Of the journey to Troy, Leaf writes 'This journey of Poseidon is not easy to understand. There were two [coastal] cities of the name of Aegae, both seats of Poseidon worship, one in Achaia, the other in Euboia. There is also said to have been a small island of this name between Chios and Tenos, but this is not certain. In any case, why should Poseidon go to Aegae to get his chariot? At Samothrace he is quite close to Troy; so to go to Aegae, wherever it was, he had a far longer journey to make, just for the sake of coming back again. The difficulty will be removed if we suppose the allusion to Samothrace to be a later addition, and cut out lines 11-16, from 'who sat' to 'against Zeus'.'

Leaf appears to be saying on the one hand that the view from Samothrace shows Homer's striking personal knowledge of the area, and on the other that the mention of Samothrace was a later addition, because Poseidon's journey to the ships from there makes no sense. The problem is insoluble. If we leave these lines in, the journey makes no sense. If we cut them out as Leaf suggests, we find Poseidon watching from an unspecified mountain with a forested slope, from which he then goes to Troy via Aegae unseen by Zeus. Leaf implies rather lamely that perhaps Poseidon was watching from Mt. Olympus in Greece, where he was last heard of.

Interim conclusions about Samothrace, Tenedos and Imbros

My study is partly based on the belief, from Strabo, that the poet of the Iliad had a good knowledge of geography. The view from Samothrace leads us to conclude that Troy was somewhere in the lower Mendere valley. But, as Leaf pointed out, there is something odd about the journey of Poseidon from Samothrace to Troy. He found this so incomprehensible that he suggested that the mention of Samothrace was a later addition. Now we will leave further study of this offsite signpost until the next chapter, noting that its authenticity has been challenged by at least one leading Homeric scholar.

The view from Gargarus

While Poseidon was watching the battle from Samothrace, the Iliad tells us that Zeus was watching it from Gargarus. So here is another possible offsite signpost. From the maps, the highest peak of Ida is named Gargarus, and is found some 16km northwest of Edremit, with a height shown as 1766m. So, providing this is not also another later addition, Homer's Troy and the Trojan plain were visible, at least to Zeus, from Gargarus.

Locating the Trojan allies

Another approach to finding the general location of Troy is to look at the list of Trojan allies provided in the Iliad Book 2. In our search for Troy, we can at least be sure that it was not where any of her allies came from.

The Trojan catalogue lists the following allies:

1. Dardanians.
2. Zeleians from the valley of the river Aesepus.
3. Those from Adresteia and the land of Apaesus, Pityeia and the steep slopes of Tereia.
4. Men from Perkote, Practicus, Sestus, Abydus and holy Arisbe.
5. Pelasgians from deep soiled Larisa.
6. Thracians, bordering the Hellespont, and the warlike Circones.
7. Paeonians from afar, from Amydon and the river Axius.
8. Paphlagonians from the lands of Eneti, by the river Parthenius…
9. Mysians, led by Chromis and Ennomus.
10. Phrygians, from remote Ascania.
11. Maeonians, from under Tmolus. These were later referred to as Lydians,

from the adjacent river valleys of the Hermus and the Cayster, immediately south of the Kaikos valley.

12. Carians from Miletus.
13. Lycians from distant Lycia.

Many of these places are well known from historical times, their names having been passed down unchanged by historians and on ancient texts from earliest antiquity. The list has been much discussed by Homeric scholars, and I will not discuss it in any detail here. It appears to name the allies roughly in geographical order from north to south. A map indicating these places is shown below as Fig.6.1.

This sketch map shows the homelands of the Trojan allies according to Page's interpretation of the Homeric Catalogue. [7] Assuming these are placed correctly, they seem to include all the countries of Western Anatolia, as well as the Thracians, Circones and Paeones lying to the west of the Sea of Marmara.

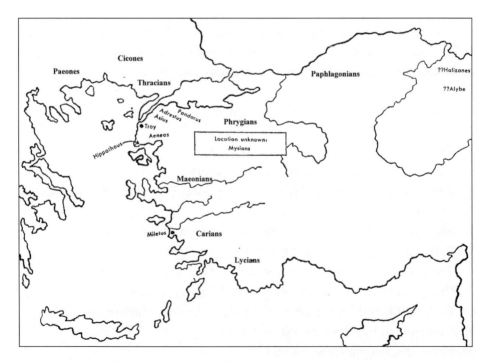

Fig. 6.1. Location of Trojan allies, from Page (1959).

Looking at the north of the Troad, the locations of Abydus, Sestus and Perkote are known. Abydus in the Troad is opposite Sestus, at its narrowest point roughly halfway up the Straits. It has the only natural harbour in the Straits. Perkote is on the Asian side of the Straits some 20km north of Abydus, and Adrestus lies just north of Perkote. Larisa, home to the Pelasgians led by Hippothous, is placed to the south of Hisarlik near Lekton Point. Page does not name the Dardanians on this map, but we may assume from Strabo that they dwelt with their leader, Aeneas, in the middle and upper valleys of the Mendere.

Further south, Page seems uncertain about the home of the Mysians. Yet according to Strabo and other ancient authorities they occupied the Kaikos valley opposite Lesbos, which for some reason is not shown on the map. Teuthrania was in this valley, and was destroyed by the Achaeans according to the Mysian war story discussed below, so we will assume Mysia was here. The areas still further south are mostly well known and are well away from Ida, so do not affect our search for Troy.

To the east of Troy lay Phrygia, which reached across the plateau as far as the banks of the Halys River. It probably occupied much of the western lands of the Hittite Empire before it collapsed around 1200. If we assume the Trojan War is dated to around 1250BC, then we must also assume that Homer's several references to Phrygia adjoining Priam's territory must refer to a period nearer his own time, when perhaps the Hittites themselves were forgotten. According to a leading Turkish archaeologist, Ekrem Akurgal, no Phrygian remains can be found that date from before around 800. This suggests that western Turkey, much like Greece, was engulfed in a 400 year Dark Age between c1200 and c800. Scholars therefore have to conclude that the mention of Phrygia by Homer is anachronistic.

Comments on the Trojan allies

Since the territory of Troy must be separate from those of its allies, Troy seems to occupy a region that barely extends beyond the boundaries of the lower Mendere valley. The Troad here appears to have become overcrowded. Yet the large and fertile valley of the Kaikos appears largely unoccupied. Leaf [8] explained the situation in the Troad in more detail. Strabo, quoting the earlier authority of Demetrios, said there were a total of eight Trojan dynasties all with their own territories in the Troad. As is seen, with Troy at Hisarlik, these territorial divisions seem to leave Priam with direct rule over a very small region around Novum Ilium. This apparent overcrowding in the Troad supports our theory that the rich and powerful country of Troy does not fit into the Troad, and did not belong there.

The catalogue of Trojan allies gives no clearly identified army from the large and fertile region of the Bakir Çayi valley. The Mysians are named as being led by Chromis and Ennomus, yet neither seem to have any family history, and the Mysians have no named king or capital city. Could this entry have been a later interpolation? One or two later scholars have commented on this problem. One asked 'Why do not peoples from the fertile middle coast district of Asia Minor appear?' [9] If they were Greeks, he said, they should have appeared among the foes of Troy; if not, then why were they not among the Trojan allies?

The evidence from the location of the Trojan allies may be summed up by saying that, with Troy at Hisarlik, the western Troad has become overcrowded. This is exactly the result expected if ancient Troy, originally at Bergama, was for some as yet unexplained reason, later relocated to Ilion at Hisarlik. This leaves the comparatively vast area of the Kaikos catchment without an identified major occupant or capital city, effectively a country without a kingdom. The rather vague mention of the Mysians in the list seems to me to suggest some tampering with the Iliad's original text. There is clearly space in the Trojan catalogue for Priam's kingdom to be moved back to the Kaikos valley. Overall, the evidence from the location of Troy's allies offers little support for Troy at Hisarlik. A location in the Kaikos valley would be more plausible.

The places captured by Achilles

Another approach to finding the general location of Troy is to consider the places captured and sacked by Achilles. Several of Troy's allies came from the Troad, and those on the coast and within reach of the Greek Camp will have been vulnerable to attacks by Achilles. So it seems reasonable to expect that the places raided and captured by Achilles should lie roughly at equal distances on either side of the Greek camp.

So what do we find? A list of Achilles' conquests is given by the ancient Greek historian Apollodorus of Athens c180-120. [(10)] The places, captured while the Trojans stayed behind their walls, are given (Epitome, III. 32-34) as Lesbos, Phocaea, Colophon, Smyrna, Clazomenaea, Cyme, Aegialus, Tenos, the so-called Hundred Cities, Adramyttium, Side, Endium, Linaeum, Colone, Hypoplacian Thebes, Lyrnessus, Antandrus, 'and many other cities'. Philoctetes was left behind on Lemnos, so perhaps Lemnos was not raided by Achilles because it was already Greek. In addition, the Kypria, another minor epic in the Trojan War cycle of poems, gives Pedasus, and the Iliad (11.625) gives Tenedos. If this mention of Tenedos is not a later addition, this makes a total of 18 named towns sacked by Achilles. This compares with Achilles' statement (Il 9:325-330) that he 'captured twelve towns from the sea, besides eleven that I took by land in the deep soiled realm of Troy', giving a total of twenty-three places. Fig. 6.2 is a map showing the approximate location of these places, where known.

Although Tenedos is included in this list, our suspicion is that other mentions of Tenedos are later additions. This casts doubt on the authenticity of this reference. From the evidence of these places, they generally lie roughly equally on either side of the coast opposite Lesbos. This is well south of Hisarlik. And if Troy was at Hisarlik, we should ask why did Achilles not take Abydos, Sestos and Perkote? Perkote, in particular, seems to have been a landing place, since it was used by Iphidamas to bring reinforcements from Thrace to Troy.

To summarise, the evidence of the location of the places sacked by Achilles, centred around Lesbos, does not support Troy being at Hisarlik. Instead it suggests that Troy was more probably in Mysia.

The Achaeans at Teuthrania in Mysia

The Mysian War story has led to speculation that perhaps the Achaeans really

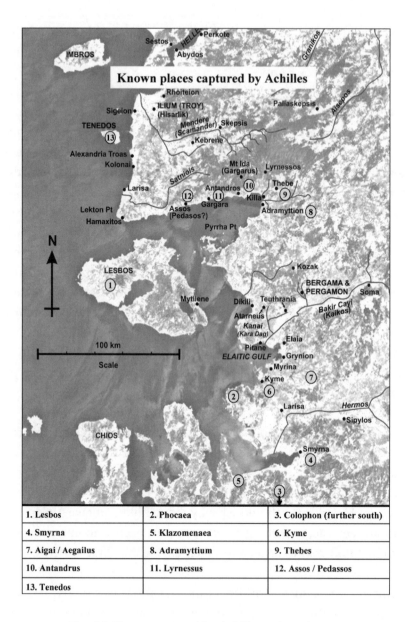

1. Lesbos	2. Phocaea	3. Colophon (further south)
4. Smyrna	5. Klazomenaea	6. Kyme
7. Aigai / Aegailus	8. Adramyttium	9. Thebes
10. Antandrus	11. Lyrnessus	12. Assos / Pedassos
13. Tenedos		

Fig. 6.2 Places captured by Achilles, where known.

did once fight a war in Mysia. In 1946, Professor Rhys Carpenter, in a study of all the sources mentioning the Mysian War, noted several parallels and similarities between the Trojan and Mysian War stories [11]. These include:

a) The Achaean fleet sailed from Aulis in Boeotia on both occasions.
b) After landing they were at first repulsed.
c) Patroclos came to the rescue and repulsed the enemy. For his efforts he was wounded, not fatally in the Mysian War, but fatally in the Iliad.
d) This motivated Achilles to fight. He singled out and pursued the native champion.
e) He could not overtake his adversary until a divine stratagem was used. In the Iliad Athena, disguised as Deiphobos, persuaded Hector to stand and fight. In the Mysian War, Dionysus magically causes a vine to trip Telephos.
f) Achilles overtakes and sorely wounds Telephos. In the Iliad he overtook and killed Hector.
g) After the decision is taken to depart, as the fleet sets sail a storm overtakes and scatters them, so many who survived the war never returned home.
h) Telephos' wound must be healed by the weapon which smote him, since he is fated to show the Achaeans the way to Troy. In the Iliad, Philoctetes is bitten by a snake and abandoned on Lemnos, but he must be brought to Troy and healed for the sake of his weapons before the city can fall.

Carpenter's verdict was that, from such far-reaching duplication, it was obvious there were not two stories but one. The same story was told of two different places, Teuthrania in Mysia, and Ilion at Hisarlik. For some story-tellers, Teuthrania may in truth have been Troy. This, he added, finds some confirmation; an ancient text (Ox Pap. xi.1359) sets the birth of Telephos at Troy. As Telephos cannot be uprooted from Teuthranian Pergamon, then Pergamon for the author of this text must have been Troy. He also speculates that this Pergamon may be an intruder into Homer's Troy, where it designates the highest quarter of the town where temples stand. 'In Teuthrania it is a place name in its own right c15 miles from river mouth, well suited to play the role of Troy for this broad river valley…'

He concludes by posing the question: 'Given the Iliad has two or three names for the river and the town, were there two stories? An Aeolic version attaching Troy and its river [Skamander] to Teuthrania at Pergamon, and an Ionic version attaching Troy to Ilios / Hisarlik and the Scamander /Mendere?' If so, he deduced that the Aeolic version, with Troy at Pergamon, was earlier than the Ionic version.

Recently, another senior scholar, Professor R. S. P. Beekes, of Leiden University, reached a similar conclusion. He noted, as did Carpenter, that the conquests of Achilles appear centred around Lesbos. He also realized that, in the Mysian war story, Achilles and Patroclos had the same roles as in the Iliad. Thinking it improbable that after the Iliad a second story was created which largely imitates it, and was presented as an error, he concluded that perhaps the earliest Trojan War story was about Greeks going to Teuthrania. This was then later transferred to Ilios at Hisarlik, which he regarded as 'a much greater undertaking.' [12]

To summarise, both Carpenter and Beekes argue, using sources outside the Iliad, that there were two 'Trojan War' stories, one set in Mysia, the other at Hisarlik. Both also agree that the Mysian or 'Aeolic' version, in which the Achaeans fought at Teuthrania, was the earlier. This was subsequently replaced by a later, possibly Ionic, story of the Achaeans going to Ilion at Hisarlik. However, neither scholar took the next step and deduced that it was the original poet of 'The Wrath of Achilles', whom the ancients knew as Homer, who set his Trojan War epic in the great plain below Pergamon.

Troy between Lesbos and Phrygia, Il. 24.543-546

I have already mentioned that in Book 24, the poet placed Priam's realm between Lesbos and Phrygia 'in the upland'. Now we will look at this in more detail. Starting as always with the poet's words, we find that in Book 24 Achilles was feeling sorry for king Priam, who has bravely come alone to the Achaean's camp to negotiate the ransom of Hector's body. Murray gives lines 24.543-546 as

'And of you, old sir, we hear that once you were happy; how of all that towards the sea Lesbos, the seat of Macar [13], encloses, and Phrygia in the upland, and the boundless Hellespont, over all these people, men say, you, old sir, were pre-eminent because of your wealth and your sons.'

In my view, a natural reading of these lines would be that Priam's kingdom lay between the island of Lesbos and Phrygia in the upland. In simple terms, Priam's lands occupied a lowland plain on the mainland opposite Lesbos, which extended inland as far as 'the upland'. This 'upland', i.e. the central Anatolian plateau, was once part of Phrygia, which had its capital at Gordion, some 500km east of Lesbos. Also due east of Lesbos is the valley of the Sangarius river, which according to the Poet (16.719) lies within Phrygia. Following our earlier debate about the 'Hellespont', it is reasonable to suggest that the name 'Hellespont' here refers to the northern Aegean Sea around Lesbos, as well as the Straits. If we look at the map to see if there are any large, low lying, horse-breeding areas opposite Lesbos, we can only find one. The great valley of the river Kaikos, later home of the Attalid kingdom of Pergamon. And Strabo included the great fertile plain of the lower Kaikos valley within his study of Troy-land, or the Troad as he called it.

But was Achilles implying that Priam held sway over all the land which lay opposite the coast of Lesbos, including the land to the north? If so this would have also included most of the Troad, such as Dardania, Skepsis, and the Pelasgian territories along the southern coast of the Troad from Thebe to Lekton Point. Much of the Troad over which Priam was 'pre-eminent' was ruled by members of his extended family, a dynasty of King Tros, as distinct from a dynasty of King Ilus. It is possible therefore that the Priam's realm meant by Achilles could be extended to include the whole of the Troad, as well as the Bakir Çayi valley, even though the Sea of Marmara, not Phrygia, lay to the north of the Troad.

By contrast, those who believe in Troy at Hisarlık must find a different interpretation for this passage. Professor Latacz [14] claims effectively to have proved that Troy was at Hisarlik. The significance of this passage did not escape him, and he dealt with it by adopting his own translation.

'And you old sir, we are told you prospered once; for as much as Lesbos... confines to the north above it and Phrygia from the north confines, and enormous Hellespont, of these old sir, you were lord once in your wealth and children.'

The difference in the translations of Murray and Latacz is surprising. This arises partly from the fact that the Iliad is written using words that had to fit into a rigid rhythmical pattern for each line, in a form called the 'hexameter'.

The constraints of meter and line at times forced the poet to use words in unusual ways. He may have had to lengthen, shorten, or even invent words to suit his intended meaning. His vocabulary was also augmented by the use of local words and dialects not always familiar to today's scholars of ancient Greek. So extracting the real meaning behind the poet's lines often gives rise to difficulties. It can sometimes come down simply to a matter of the translator's opinion. For example, Leaf believed that the word meaning 'north' that Latacz uses in his translation to make his point, is not the meaning intended by the poet.

My second comment is that Achilles clearly states that Phrygia is in the uplands. By implication, Troy is not. The topographical evidence from Homer makes it clear that the harbour of the Achaeans was between two headlands. Beyond the beach lay a great plain, with Troy out of sight in the distance. As anyone knows who has taken the bus journey from Dikili to Hisarlik, no such harbour or plain exists along the land opposite the north coast of Lesbos. The hills of Ida reach to the shore all along this coast, so the Trojan plain cannot have existed here.

There are other difficulties with Latacz's version. Homer tells us specifically that the Phrygians, led by Ascanius, came 'from afar', yet this description hardly applies if Phrygia, a large and powerful nation, was the land directly to the north of Hisarlik. If Latacz places Phrygia north of Lesbos, how does he explain that Achilles in this speech makes no mention of the other tribes that we have already mentioned as occupying the Troad? After years of warfare, Achilles must have been well aware of these tribes and where they came from, but here he makes no mention of them. To the north of the territories of Abydos and Perkote lies Lampsakos, and the northern entrance to the Straits from the Sea of Marmara. The territory of the Zeleians, led by Pandarus, son of Lycaon, lay to the east of Lampsakos, in a region watered by the Aesepus, a large river flowing north into the Sea of Marmara some 90 km east of the mouth of the Straits. Phrygia must therefore lie a long way to the east of Lesbos, on the central plateau. There seems no evidence from the Iliad to support a translation that places Phrygia north of Hisarlik in Trojan times.

To summarise, lines Il. 24.543-6 strongly suggest that Troy and the Trojan plain lay in the Kaikos Valley opposite the island of Lesbos. Strabo included the lower Kaikos valley within the Troad. It is unlikely that a region as large as Troy would have its capital city tucked far away to the northwest at Hisarlik. Any translation of this passage placing Troy to the north of Lesbos lacks convincing supporting evidence from both the Iliad and from the local geography. The Phrygia of the Iliad evidently lay far to the east. It included the valley of the Sangarius river, where Priam once fought alongside the Phrygians against the Amazons from the north.

The journey to Troy via Perkote by Iphidamas

Another signpost to Troy comes from a journey there made from Thrace by Iphidamas. Although this does not tell us where Troy is, at least it may provide indirect evidence against Troy at Hisarlik.

In Il. 11:221ff we are told that Iphidamas, son of Antenor, left Thrace with twelve beaked ships to aid King Priam when he heard of the coming of the Achaeans to Troy. He left these ships at Perkote, which is some 20km north of Abydos, and from there went on foot to Troy. This route from Thrace to Troy is interesting. The larger fertile plains of Thrace lie in the lower valleys of its largest rivers, which drain southwards into the Aegean. Its ancient capitals would therefore use the sea ports on the Aegean coast, rather than those on the Sea of Marmara. Thus these twelve ships, if they were going to Hisarlik, would have sailed from the northern Aegean, past the entrance to the Bay of Hestiaia, and then up the Straits to Perkote. There they anchored, and Iphidamas with his reinforcements would have continued on foot, journeying south to Troy at Hisarlik.

Now I think this all seems rather implausible. Firstly, in deciding which route to take, Iphidamas would have wanted to minimise the risk of being attacked by the Achaeans. If the Achaeans were camped at Besik Bay near the mouth of the Straits, the ships of Iphidamas would have been in full view as they sailed past the camp. They would also be going very slowly against the current in the Hellespont all the way to Perkote. We will assume that, on this occasion, they did not have to use the holding port at Besik Bay while waiting for a favourable wind to sail up the Straits. It seems highly unlikely that they could have sailed slowly past the Greek camp at Besik Bay unnoticed. Once seen, the Achaeans would surely have watched their progress from the shore. They may have attacked them using fast rowing ships, either at sea or when they landed at Perkote. Otherwise, they may have sent a force overland to attack them wherever they landed. If Iphidamas really was heading to Hisarlik with reinforcements, it would have been much safer for him to travel by foot across the Thracian Chersonese, cross the Straits at Perkote by ferry, perhaps by night, then come south to Hisarlik on foot. On the other hand, if Troy was at Bergama, and if the Achaeans were known to have sent only occasional raiding parties by ship to the coastal towns west of Thebe, then it would be quite sensible for Iphidamas, when the two sides were engaged in battle, to risk taking his ships up the Straits as far as Perkote. From there he would have travelled overland to Troy through the friendly territories of Dardania and Skepsis, and arrived there unseen and unmolested at the Dardanian Gate. Why did he land at Perkote in preference to Abydos or Sigeum? Perhaps here in the Straits, at that time, was one of the very few places on the eastern side where ships could be beached in relative safety.

In summary therefore, the evidence of this journey by Iphidamas suggests that Troy is unlikely to have been at Hisarlik.

Summary of evidence about the general location of Troy

We have examined the offsite signposts in the Iliad which point in the direction of Troy. Eight different lines of evidence concerning these have been discussed.

These are:

- Troy was visible to Poseidon from the top of Mt Fengari on Samothrace.
- Troy was not far from Tenedos and Imbros.
- Troy was visible to Zeus from Gargarus, the highest peak of Mt. Ida.
- The harbour of Troy was beside the Hellespont.
- The location of Troy among its allies.
- Troy's location in relation to the places raided by Achilles.

- Troy lay between Lesbos and Phrygia.
- The location of Troy from the journey there by Iphidamas from Thrace.

From these eight examples, what is at once abundantly clear is that the off-site signposts are not all pointing in the same direction. The first two lines of evidence suggest that Troy was at or near Hisarlik. The third signpost could have applied to Troy at both places, although humans cannot see Gargarus from Bergama. The fourth line of evidence could support Troy at either Hisarlik or Bergama, depending on what the poet of the Iliad meant by the name 'Hellespont'. The last four lines of evidence lead to the conclusion that Troy probably did not lie at Hisarlik. They suggest instead that Troy should be more probably found in Mysia.

In short, the evidence in the Iliad about the general location of Troy is inconsistent. Its integrity is therefore suspect.

In addition to the eight signposts above, two further points may be made. Firstly, the little we know of the Mysian War story, which tells of the Achaeans fighting at Teuthrania, suggests that this may be the same as the story of the Trojan War, but set at Teuthrania in Mysia rather than at Hisarlik. This in turn suggests that, in the minds of the earliest bards who told this story, Troy was at Teuthrania, and the Pergamos of Ilios may originally have been at Pergamon.

Secondly, we may also ask how Troy at Hisarlik can really be accepted as the capital city of a region which, according to Strabo, included the lower Kaikos valley to the south west of Mt. Ida. Surely a capital is much more likely to have been located more centrally, in a more defensible position, and to enjoy the benefit of a fine natural acropolis?

Conclusions

The inconsistencies between these offsite signposts have been exposed and discussed. If we believe that the poet's geographical evidence would have been consistent, we must conclude that some of these offsite signposts have been inserted by a different hand.

The strongest argument for Troy at Hisarlik comes from Poseidon's view from Samothrace. However, doubts have been raised regarding the authenticity of this evidence. If the Hisarlik supporters accept point 4 above, that the Hellespont could refer to the northern Aegean Sea, it is apparent that the balance of the conflicting evidence from the offsite signposts weighs against Troy at Hisarlik.

From a study of the remnants of the Mysian War story, it may be argued that the earliest Trojan War story concerned the Achaeans fighting at Teuthrania, not at Hisarlik. This literary evidence suggests that, if the Troy of the Iliad was not at Hisarlik, it may well have been in Mysia. Troy's general location at Ilion (Hisarlik) has remained unchallenged since the time of Strabo some 2,000 years ago. Given the evidence uncovered so far, this situation is about to change.

CHAPTER 7

SEVERING THE SAMOTHRACE CONNECTION

Introduction

In this chapter I will attempt to demolish the last, and most influential, pillar which supports Troy at Hisarlik. This is Poseidon's view of the Trojan plain from Samothrace, along with associated mentions of Tenedos and Imbros. I will try to show that this pillar is an illusion based on a later interpolation. While this evidence irrefutably fixes Troy in the lower Mendere valley, it is only valid if these lines were in the earliest version of the Iliad. But we learnt in the last chapter that the great Homeric scholar, Walter Leaf, suggested that we should not take this for granted. He detected signs in the opening lines of Book 13 that this reference may have been added in by a later poet.

In Chapter 6 we discovered that the offsite signposts in the Iliad were not all consistent. Some pointed towards Hisarlik, and others towards Bergama and Pergamon. Troy cannot be in both places. So the question arises – was the geography in the earliest poems confused, or has the text of the Iliad been altered in places so as to indicate a different location for Troy? We know that Leaf thought this reference to Samothrace may have been added in later. And I happen to share Strabo's high regard for Homer's knowledge of geography. So in this chapter I will investigate Leaf's suggestion of some tampering with the text, and study the Samothrace connection in more detail.

First, as always throughout this study, we will study the text of the Iliad. To try to unravel the poet's true meaning we must now set down and study exactly what is written. I have divided the text into two blocks, relying in general on Murray's translation. The text from lines 17 to 33, which refer to Poseidon's journey to the Greek Camp, will be dealt with in the next chapter.

The opening of Book 13

At this point in the story, Achilles is still refusing to fight, and the resurgent Trojans have managed to push the Achaeans back to their camp by the beach.

1. Lines 1-9: 'Now Zeus, when he had brought the Trojans and Hector to the ships, left the combatants there to have toil and woe unceasingly, but he turned away his gleaming eyes, and looked afar over the lands of the Thracian horsemen, and of the Mysians who fight in close combat, and of the lordly Hippemolgi who drink the milk of mares, and of the Abii, the most just of men. [1] To Troy he no longer turned his gleaming eyes at all, for he did not expect in his heart that any of the immortals would go and assist either Trojans or Danaans.'

2. Lines 10-16: 'But no blind watch did the lord, the Shaker of the Earth keep, for he sat marvelling at the war and the battle, high on the topmost peak of well wooded Samothrace, for from there all Ida was plain to see; and plain to see were the city of Priam, and the ships of the Achaeans. There he sat, having come out of the sea, and he had pity on the Achaeans that they were being overcome by the Trojans, and against Zeus he was mightily indignant.'

A timeless theatrical cliché

We will start by examining lines 1-9. The first thing we should bear in mind is that the poet, in recounting his story, is entertaining an audience. As an epic poet, his choice of words and phrases is designed primarily to inform, but also to retain the interest of his audience and excite their imagination. The second thing to remember is that, as well as being a poetic genius, the poet was a master of drama. It was Aristotle, according to Rhys Carpenter [2], who observed '...that the Iliad's structural type form is that of Attic drama and that its unity consequently is to be judged by the standards of fifth-century dramatic art...Many a page of the Iliad could be edited for Attic stage presentation with a minimum of alteration.' Once these two key points are appreciated, the difficulties in the text melt away.

What we have at the start of Book 13 is one of the simplest, most common, and most effective of all theatrical clichés. It is as popular today as it was over 2,500 years ago, as anyone will know who has been to a pantomime and listened to the children shouting excitedly 'Look behind you!' It works very simply. The first actor turns his back, allowing a second actor on stage to perform a deed, be it mischief or magic, unseen by the first actor. But there are four important rules which must be followed if this little piece of drama is to work:

1. The first actor must make it clear to the audience, by turning round so that his back faces the scene that is about to unfold, that he cannot see what is about to follow.
2. The second actor, if he is already on stage, must be seen to watch the first actor carefully, so he knows exactly when the other's back is turned.
3. As soon as he is sure he will not be seen, the second actor enacts his part as quickly as possible. The excitement builds because the audience does not know when the first actor will turn round and discover what has been happening behind his back.
4. The audience must be able to see both actors and appreciate all that is happening on the stage.

Now, bearing these rules in mind, let us look at the words in their theatrical context, and see exactly how our master dramatist has applied them. The scene opens with Zeus watching the battle from the top of Gargarus. We know he has used this vantage point before, so we have no reason to doubt this stage direction. The poet then tells his audience what Zeus is thinking. Having earlier expressly forbidden the other gods to interfere in the battle, and threatened them with dire consequences if they did, Zeus is sure none will dare disobey him. So he stops looking at the battle, and instead looks away at the more peaceful tribes which dwell in the lands of northern Thrace and beyond. This gives Poseidon his chance to come to Troy unseen to help the Achaeans. The audience is riveted. Will Poseidon have enough time to help their heroes before Zeus turns round and sees him? And if Zeus does, what will he do to Poseidon? From this timeless theatrical cliché, it should be perfectly clear that Troy lies in the opposite direction to that faced by Zeus when he looked at the northern tribes. Since Zeus looked away towards the north and north-west, both Troy and the watching Poseidon must be placed behind him, to the south and south east. And to the south and south east of Gargarus lie Bergama, Pergamon and Samos. Surely here, as any theatre lover will appreciate, we have uncovered another clear off-site signpost pointing towards Troy in the Kaikos valley.

The turning of Zeus

For those claiming that Troy was at Hisarlik, this passage is a serious obstacle. Hisarlik lies roughly north-west of Gargarus, in the same general direction as Samothrace, Thrace, the northern tribes. The problem is immediately obvious. For Poseidon to come from Samothrace to Troy unseen, as required by the drama of the story, Zeus would have had to turn away and look south or south-east. Our first stage direction rule has been broken. Something is seriously wrong. Unfortunately, nearly every scholar commentating on Homer has, over the last hundred years, been constrained in translating these few lines by the need to follow the consensus view that Troy was at Hisarlik. In doing so, they have failed to acknowledge the simple drama implicit in the story. But in the days before Schliemann came to Hisarlik, some early commentators did at least acknowledge this problem. It was raised in the late 18th century, at a time when the possible location of Troy was being hotly debated. Bryant, a Cambridge scholar writing a century before Leaf, appreciated that Troy could not lie to the south of Gargarus yet remain visible from Samothrace. [3] Confused by the mixed directional messages in the Iliad, he maintained that '...the War of Troy was a fiction, grounded on some obscure event in the history of Egypt, that the city of Troy had never existed, and that, if Homer had a particular situation in Phrygia in his eye when he wrote, it must have been on the south-western part of Ida...about six or seven miles south of Alexander Troas.'

This shows that apparent inconsistencies in the geography in the Iliad led some early scholars to seek different and sometimes inconsistent explanations of his meaning. None of these explanations sit comfortably alongside Homer's reputation as a great geographer and historian. Yet I can find no evidence that Bryant or Homeric scholars before Leaf even considered the possibility that the reference to Samothrace was a later addition. By assuming it was by Homer, this false premise was used to reach different but flawed conclusions about Zeus's turn, and about the location of Troy. Yet any theatre director would instinctively understand Homer's intention. Zeus must turn his back on Troy to allow Poseidon to go there unseen. Equally, Poseidon must see Zeus turn away. I would like to think that this piece of theatre was not lost on Homer's audience, particularly any younger ones who were hearing the story for the first time.

Why, the reader may ask, is an argument that took place some two centuries ago relevant to the case being presented in this book? The answer is that Bryant is the earliest scholar that I have discovered, with apparently an open mind as to where Troy might be, who took this passage to mean that Troy may lie to the south of Gargarus. Yet for well over the last century, scholars have followed the consensus view that Troy, because of the view from Samothrace, was at Hisarlik and therefore north of Gargarus. This has forced them to interpret the turning of Zeus differently, and thus to ignore the poet's theatrical intent. My next step was to look at the way in which three more recent leading Homeric scholars recognised, and tried to come to terms with, Homer's stage directions for Zeus on Gargarus.

As noted earlier, in 1892 Leaf, a firm believer in Troy at Hisarlik, chose not to refer to Zeus's turn on Gargarus at all. However, being unhappy with the introduction of Samothrace into the poem because of the unlikely journey from there to Troy, he condemned this passage as an interpolation. [4] Murray, in his 1924 translation quoted above, seems to have avoided any confrontation with the consensus view of Troy at Hisarlik. He translates Homer as saying that Zeus '...*turned away his gleaming eyes* and looked afar over the land of Thracian horsemen...' And in the next sentence, '*To Troy he no longer turned his gleaming eyes at all...*'. Murray thus interprets Homer as intending Zeus to turn away his eyes, but seems to leaves us to presume that his body remained facing in the same direction. There is no hint from Murray that Homer intended Zeus to turn his back on both Troy and Poseidon. Perhaps Homer, with his usual economy, did not bother to spell out that which he assumed would be self-evident to his audience.

More recently Janko, in his 1992 Commentary, [5] showed he was well aware of the importance of this point. In Book 13 line 3, the Greek word translated as 'back' is 'palin'. However, Janko simply states, without qualification, that the Greek word 'palin' means 'away', not 'back'. For him, Zeus did not 'turn his eyes back' from the battle to look at the northern tribes, he 'turned his eyes away'. This again, as with Murray's translation, leaves us to imagine that Zeus looked in a different direction without turning his body. Again, the poet's theatrical intent here was overlooked by Janko, as it must be by all who believe in Troy at Hisarlik.

Conclusions from Book 13, Lines 1 to 9

The evidence from these lines supports the view that Homer here was using a simple theatrical device whereby Zeus, on Gargarus, turned his back upon the war and allowed Poseidon to come swiftly to Troy unseen behind his back. It is also clear that when Zeus turned his back on Troy, he looked away at the tribes to the northwest. The conclusions of our understanding of this piece of theatre are as simple as they are devastating. Troy lay to the south of Gargarus, as also did Poseidon's mountain lookout post. And Troy, lying south of the mountain range of Ida, could not have been visible from Samothrace. So Poseidon did not watch the battle from Samothrace. He must have watched it from somewhere beyond Troy, and also well to the south of Gargarus. The last pillar supporting Troy at Hisarlik has disappeared. It was just an illusion.

By applying simple theatrical logic to the opening of Book 13, we have uncovered one more of the Iliad's off-site signposts pointing towards Troy lying to the southeast of Gargarus. And here, beyond the Plain of Thebe, we find the great plain of the Bakir Çayi, and the magnificent acropolis of Pergamon.

Poseidon's vantage point, Samothrace or Samos?

Our next task is to identify where Poseidon was sitting while he watched the battle near the Greek camp. From our second theatrical rule, Poseidon must have been watching Zeus, as well as the battle, from a peak well to the south of both Gargarus and the Greek camp. To discover where he was we must look for clues in the lines of the Iliad that refer to Samothrace. The critical lines in Book 13 are lines 10-16, as set out above. And if there is anything suspicious about or within these lines, Leaf did not mention it. Unfortunately I have no knowledge of the Greek language, ancient or modern, so I attempted, as Lascelles had already done, to check this for myself by looking, with the help of a Greek dictionary, at the actual Greek text. The Greek is given alongside Murray's translation in the Loeb edition, so here the Greek and English may be directly compared. When I looked specifically at the word used for Samothrace, I agreed with Lascelles that here was a cause for suspicion.

The word for Samothrace, actually written 'Samos of Thraken' (Thraken meaning Thrace), was split so that it actually spans lines 12 and 13. Since this is Lascelles' discovery, I will quote his words on this subject. [6]

'Let us look closely at Homer's words in the Iliad Book 13 and change the Greek letters to their approximate English equivalents. The Greek lines are as follows:

Line 12:   ...akrotatis korufis Samou uliessis
Line 13:   Thrinkis, enthen ghar efaineto pasa men Idi

In line 12, the second last word ('Samou') means 'of Samos'. The Greek-English Lexicon gives the last word, 'uliessis' as 'well-wooded'. Samothrace in the Iliad is Samou Thrinkis' spread over two lines. So here is the English translation of both lines:

Line 12:   …high on the topmost peak of Samos well-wooded
Line 13:   of Thrace. For from thence all Ida was plain to see.'

As Lascelles points out, all the words that place Poseidon on Samothrace are contained in one line, line 13. Was the adjective 'well-wooded' stuck in the middle of the name Samos-of-Thrace for poetic reasons, perhaps to fit the requirements of the hexameter? Or could line 12 have been written by Homer, and line 13, 'of Thrace, for from there all Ida was plain to see', have been added later by someone intent upon moving Troy to Hisarlik? Certainly, line 12 seems to offer a wonderful opportunity for some later poet to change the name of Poseidon's lookout from Samos to Samothrace. I have no certain answer to this question, but one thing is clear. Without lines 13 and 14, Homer placed Poseidon on the top of a well-wooded mountain on the island of Samos, not Samothrace.

The possible alternative positions of Poseidon, on Samothrace or Samos, are shown in Fig. 7.1 below.

Looking for more clues from the Iliad

If the poet placed Poseidon on Samos instead of Samothrace, this solves our theatrical dilemma. While Zeus on Gargarus was looking north-west at the northern tribes, Poseidon can come to Troy at Bergama unseen from Samos, far to the south. The poet must also have assumed that, from the top of Mt. Kerkis on Samos, Poseidon could have seen Zeus on top of Gargarus. And, as an inescapable conclusion from these findings, it is clear that, as Leaf suspected over a century ago, the text here has been tampered with.

Let me now quote to you some words from the Oxford scholar Hilda Lorimer, to my mind one of the most perceptive of British Homeric scholars. I was lucky in 2004, while browsing in a second-hand book shop in Norwich, to find a copy of her famous book, published in 1950, 'Homer and the

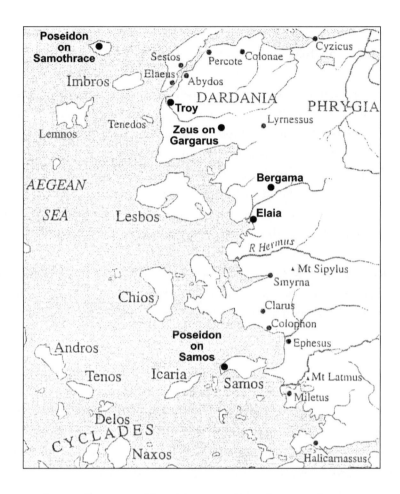

Fig. 7.1 The seat of Poseidon – on Samothrace or Samos

Monuments'. This book was her own personal monument to Homer. From her lifelong study of his epics she was well aware of many places in the Iliad where text had been added in by a later hand. I will mention her again in later chapters, but this is what she had to say about interpolations in general. 'Interpolation, like other crimes, will out as a general rule, because the criminal has forgotten to remove some important clue...' [7]. If, as Leaf suggested, 'Samothrace' is an interpolation, then my task was now clear. If I wished to find more evidence to support this argument, I must look closely at Homer's words for further possible clues left behind by some ancient 'criminal'.

Samos of Thrace or Thracian Samos?

Firstly, I wondered if it was normal for Homer, or any other early Greek writer, to write the name Samothrace as 'Samos of Thrace'. So I looked through the rest of the poems attributed to Homer for the name 'Samothrace'. If found, I could then compare the way it was written with the way it is written in the Iliad. The name is not found in the Odyssey, but it does occur once in the Hymn to the Delian Apollo [8]. In this Hymn we find Samothrace written as 'Thrace of (or by) Samos'. This is the opposite way round to the way it is written in The Iliad. Is this significant? Having found Samothrace written differently in the Iliad and the Hymn, all we can say at this stage is that 'Samos of Thrace' was not the only way to write the name of this island in ancient Greek. But if 'Thrace-of-Samos' was the more usual written form, 'Samos of Thrace' could have been a form contrived by Lorimer's 'criminal' to suit his deception.

How Samothrace got its name

Next I needed to know how Samothrace got its name. From the way the Greeks wrote the name 'Samos-of-Thrace' or 'Thracian Samos', perhaps there was an early link between Samothrace and Samos. To learn more I turned to Pausanias, my trusty guide to ancient Greece. [9] Levi's marvellously informative translation of Pausanias, although considered unreliable in places by some scholars, proved a goldmine of information. I already knew, according to one Troy foundation legend, that Samothrace was once named Dardania. This was after Dardanus, the original founder of Troy (according to the Athenian version of the legend), had settled there on his way over to Phrygia. Pausanias (7.4.1-3) tells of an early Achaean legend about Prokles, a man descended from Ion, son of Xouthos. Simplifying the story somewhat, it seems that Prokles went from Argos to Ionia, where his son Leogoros became king of Samos. While he was king, the people of Ephesos attacked and defeated him, and drove the Samians off the island. 'Some of the Samian refugees settled the island off Thrace earlier called Dardania, called it Samos-of-Thrace after that settlement; others under Leogoros put a wall round Anaia on the mainland opposite, and ten years later they crossed over to Samos, threw out the Ephesians, and recovered the island.' The translator, P. Levi, suggests in a footnote that a possible date for the foundation of Samothrace was c690.

Strabo (13.3.9) tells us that Samothrace was earlier called Melites. This could have been its name before Dardania arrived there, if the Athenian story is to be believed. And, as we have just seen, from Pausanias we learn that its name was changed from Dardania to Samothrace after being settled by refugees from Samos, perhaps around 690. These legends could suggest that, in Trojan times, Samothrace was called either Dardania or Melites. The name Samothrace dates from somewhere near the death of Homer. It therefore seems most unlikely that this name was handed down from the time of the Trojan War to Homer through bardic tradition. And if Homer did not hear of it from earlier bards, then we have another reason to doubt that he would have used this name in his epic. Could this be another clue? Perhaps this was one of the reasons why Leaf thought it may have been a later interpolation.

Poseidon's view from Samothrace

Now let us look more closely at what the Iliad tells us about Poseidon's look-out. This specifically says that Poseidon was 'on the topmost peak' of Samothrace. Yet from Hisarlik it is clear that Poseidon could have seen the battle perfectly well by going little more than half way up Mt. Fengari. So why did Homer use the phrase 'the topmost peak', as if he was striving to place Poseidon as high as possible? Perhaps I am being pedantic, but again it seems that the poet's words do not quite seem to fit perfectly with Poseidon on Samothrace.

Samothrace has only one mountain

Another small point of detail about Poseidon's look-out emerges when we read the description of him leaving his look-out and heading for Troy. The poet (Il. 13.17-19) says that, once Zeus had looked away, Poseidon went down the mountainside 'striding with swift footsteps, and the high mountains and the woodland trembled beneath the immortal feet of Poseidon as he went.' The word to notice here is 'mountains'. On Samothrace there is only one main mountain, Mount Fengari. So why would Homer tell of trembling 'mountains', implying more than one? Scholars may throw up their hands up in horror at my attempting to take Homer's words so literally, but in my search for clues to establish Homer's credibility, I must follow every possible lead, however irrelevant it may seem. In this case, it is easy to see on a map that Samos has two mountain peaks, Mt Kerkis in the west and Mt.Karvouni in the centre. So again we find that on Samos, the poet's words do fit perfectly. If Poseidon was on Samos, not Samothrace, and if Poseidon's hasty footsteps caused the whole island to tremble, then not one, but both mountains would have trembled as he hurried down the forested slopes.

Well-wooded Samothrace or Samos?

The next clue to investigate is the epithet 'well-wooded' used to describe Samothrace. How appropriate is this epithet? On Samothrace, Fengari rises to about 1600m. But photographs and descriptions in tourist guides show clearly that the mountain is a protrusion of eroded granite. Being both steep and windswept, and with heavy seasonal rains, it can retain little top soil, so few trees could grow on its upper slopes. I have found no evidence to support the notion that these hills would ever have had sufficient soil cover to support extensive forests. Here, the epithet 'well-wooded' seems quite inappropriate.

On Samos, however, the situation and the climate are both quite different. If any Greek island deserved the epithet 'well-wooded' it would be Samos. The name Samos is said to derive from a Phoenician word meaning 'high'. The higher of its two peaks is Mount Kerkis, which rises to 1433m. The forests of Samos are still of commercial importance today. The Blue Guide informs us that one of the island's main products is timber for ship-building. During my visit to Turkey in March 2005 I tried to visit Samos, but the ferry from Selçuk did not start sailing until April. However, I was told that a few years earlier there was a great fire on the island, and the flames from the burning forests were seen from the Turkish coast for five days and nights. In archaic times, it seems likely that Samos, under its famous tyrant Polykrates, was one of the first Greek islands to have a fleet of triremes. It seems probable that these were made from local timber. I conclude therefore that Homer, famous for the aptness of his epithets, meant his epithet 'well-wooded' to apply to Samos, and not to Samothrace.

The test of economy

There is one further point that occurs to me about this opening passage. Lines 13 and 14 seem, in my view, to fail the test of Homer's economy. As his story unfolds, I do not think that he would allow attention to be diverted away from the action by superfluous information. A great epic poet would not be inclined to swell his epic unnecessarily by dwelling on matters that were irrelevant to the story he was telling. He would not feel the need to state what he believes his audience already knows, such as Troy and Ilios being separate but adjacent walled cities. As we have already noted, when he tells us that Zeus turned away his eyes to look at the northern tribes, he felt no need to tell us what was already obvious; that he would, as part of this action, turn his back on Troy. And here, regarding lines 13 and 14, we note that Homer has already told us that Poseidon was sitting and marvelling at the action on the battlefield. Having done so, was it really necessary to spend a further two lines saying, in effect, that he could see the action at which he was marvelling? This point may or may not deserve the status of a clue, but it seems reasonable to ask whether or not the apparent superfluous nature of these lines is perhaps yet another indication that they were not by Homer?

The view from Samos

Having commented on Poseidon's view of the battle from Samothrace, I must now try to establish whether or not Poseidon could see this battle from 'the topmost peak' of Mt. Kerkis on Samos. Lascelles [10] made a heroic attempt to do this. He argued that his calculations show that, in conditions of perfect visibility such as existed before industry brought with it a layer of haze over Izmir, it may have been possible to see the ships on the beach at

Elaea from the top of Mt. Kerkis. Certainly Poseidon, had he only a mortal's vision, would have strained to see so far. The poet seemed to realize this when he placed Poseidon on the 'topmost peak', not halfway down.

My approach is rather different. The most important consideration is not whether the view is actually possible for a human, but whether or not such a view seemed plausible to the audience. I think the answer is yes, it did. The actual possibility of this view for humans depends upon the height of the land in the two places along this line of sight. As was the case for the view from Samothrace looking across Imbros, this possibility is not immediately obvious from the map. But it is not obviously implausible. There is no significant mountain range between the two places that would prevent it. I have already argued that the possibility of the view for humans is not strictly relevant to the unfolding drama. At the beginning of Book 5, Zeus was watching the battle from his home on Mt. Olympus. In Il. 7.17-22, when Athene saw the Trojans killing the Argives, she came down from the heights of Mt. Olympos and rushed towards holy Ilios. And Apollo, looking out from Pergamos, rose to confront her, wishing victory for the Trojans. If the poet tells us that Athene could see the battle from Mt. Olympos in northern Greece, we must accept that Poseidon could see it from Samos. We should not constrain our interpretation of the Iliad by imposing the limitations of human eyesight upon the gods. To the poet the gods were all-seeing. We should also appreciate that a youthful Homer, if brought up around Smyrna and Chios as the ancients believed, would have been familiar with the view of the top of Mt. Kerkis on the horizon far to the south. As a child he may even have been told that, from there, Hera was keeping an eye on him. She had a sanctuary there dating back to Mycenaean times. [11] All things considered, I think it reasonable to assume that Homer was well aware of the relative positions of 'the topmost peak' of Mt. Kerkis on Samos to the south, of the harbour of the Achaeans to the north, and of Gargarus still further north. Knowing this we can see why the poet placed Zeus and Poseidon where he did, and why he made Zeus turn to look to the north-west. On the other hand, we have no reason to believe that he ever went to Hisarlik, or that he knew of the view of Samothrace from there.

Summary of the case against Samothrace

Our study of the opening lines of Book 13 have so far yielded a surprising number of possible clues as evidence that the poet placed Poseidon on Samos, not on Samothrace. These are summarised as follows:

a) When Zeus on Gargarus looked away at the northern tribes, we would expect Poseidon, if he wished to arrive at Troy behind Zeus's back, to have come to Troy from the south or south-east, not from the north-west.

b) The name Samothrace or Samos-of-Thrace in the text could easily have been changed from Samos by the opportunistic insertion of lines 13 and 14.

c) The Greek name for Samothrace is written 'Samos of Thrace' across lines 12-13, but is written 'Thracian Samos' in a Homeric Hymn. This shows that 'Samos of Thrace' was not necessarily the only way that the ancient Greeks wrote the name Samothrace, nor necessarily the most common.

d) Samothrace may not have had this name until the early 7th century, and in Trojan times it was called Dardania. The name Samothrace was surely not included within the traditional stories handed down about the Trojan War. It seems unlikely therefore that the poet, who was familiar with the Trojan legends, would have used this name.

e) Hisarlik was visible from half way up Mt. Fengari on Samothrace, so why did Homer make a point of placing Poseidon on its 'topmost peak'?

f) Homer tells us that when Poseidon left his lookout to go to Troy, the mountains trembled beneath his feet. On Samothrace there is only one mountain, so Homer's use of the plural 'mountains' is not appropriate. Yet it does apply on Samos, where there are two mountains.

g) There is no evidence that Samothrace was ever well-wooded, so Homer's use of this epithet for Samothrace is inexplicable. Samos, however, fully deserves the epithet well-wooded. It was forested and famous for shipbuilding in ancient times, and remains so to this day.

h) The two lines 13 and 14 are arguably surplus to the action of the epic, and may possibly therefore not have been written by Homer.

There is no doubt that arguments may, and probably will, be levelled individually against many, if not all, of these pieces of evidence. However, I believe that taken collectively, they make a strong case for claiming that lines 13 and 14 at the start of Book 13 were not by the original poet of 'The wrath of Achilles', but by a later poet. It appears that Lorimer's 'criminal' did indeed leave several clues behind as evidence of his misdeeds. This being the case, we must assume that the purpose of the Samothrace interpolation was to make the reader believe that Troy was visible from Samothrace, thereby deliberately disguising Troy's real location. This deception was so successful that it has kept the true site of Troy a secret for over 2,500 years. Who practised this deception, and why, are very interesting questions which I will explore further in Volume 2.

I must also add here that, having no knowledge of ancient Greek, I am at the mercy of the whim of the translator in my search for clues that suggest Homer meant Samos, not Samothrace. It is quite possible that experts in Homeric Greek may find some more supportive evidence, or additional clues, by studying the spellings and dialects used in these lines, which also suggest the hand of an interpolator.

Imbros and Tenedos

Having shown that the name Samothrace was possibly a later addition, can we do the same for the mentions of Imbros and Tenedos? Samos-of-Thrace is mentioned only once in the Iliad. However, in Book 24 there is a mention of the name Samos with the implication that this is near Imbros. In Il. 24.78, Iris went with a message from Zeus to find Thetis '...and midway between Samos and rugged Imbros she leapt into the dark sea, ...and there she found Thetis in the hollow cave, and around her other goddesses of the sea gathered together...' These lines remind us that Poseidon, as we saw earlier, was also supposed to have had an underwater cavern in the sea near Imbros. For this reason, and because Samos is nowhere near Imbros, Murray, in his translation, assumed that the poet, or one of his copyists, made a mistake here in writing 'Samos' instead of 'Samothrace'. He therefore included this Samos in his index, but under 'Samothrace'. The suggestion of a copyist's mistake is often a last resort, so raises question marks. Is this another clue that could reveal the hand of an interpolator? [12]

References in Books 13 and 24 to the island of Imbros are the only ones which suggest that it was near Troy. Of these, the one in Book 13, near the cave of Poseidon, is the most important. Clearly, if my collective evidence that Troy was at Bergama is accepted, then these mentions of Imbros and Tenedos are, like the insertion of Samothrace, the work of a later hand. Here, when looking at the passage in Il. 24.78, where Imbros is named as close to Samos, I am reminded of Lorimer's words about clues being left behind. This, I suspect, is just such an example. The original Samos has been left in place, either because it was overlooked, or because, having added 'Imbros', a change of Samos to Samos-of-Thrace would not have fitted the hexameter. Or even because here the 'criminal' thought that it did not matter. So I would agree with Murray that, in the present Iliad, Samos here should mean Samothrace. In future, this 'Samos', really meaning 'Samos', may deserve is own place in the index of the Iliad.

In the Iliad, Tenedos is mentioned only once as being, by implication, near Troy. That is in Book 13 line 33, where Poseidon ends his chariot ride to the Greek Camp at a cave between Imbros and Tenedos. Tenedos is also named in the Odyssey as the place Odysseus arrived at first on his way home. But the most famous mention of Tenedos in the Trojan War story is when the Greek ships sail away and hide behind Tenedos, making the Trojans believe they had gone home. But this story was not mentioned in either the Iliad or the Odyssey. It is an embellishment, mentioned first in 'The Little Iliad', believed to have been written by a later author.

Conclusions

At the end of Chapter 6, we concluded that the mentions of Tenedos, Imbros and Samothrace all lead to the inescapable conclusion that Troy must be found somewhere in the lower Mendere valley. This conclusion is based upon the assumption that these places were named by the original poet of the Iliad. Yet the evidence of this chapter strongly suggests that this is a false assumption. It supports Leaf's comment that the passage concerning Samothrace was a later interpolation. The drama of the situation at the start of Book 13 demands that Zeus turned his back on Troy, so that when Poseidon saw this, he was able to come quickly to the camp unseen behind Zeus's back. This places both Troy and Poseidon to the south of Gargarus. Poseidon therefore cannot have been sitting on Samothrace. The epithet 'well-wooded' does not apply to Samothrace but applies well to Samos. The text implies that there was more than one mountain on Samothrace, which is untrue of Samothrace, but true of Samos. The text of Book 13, lines 13-14 fails a law of Homer's economy. The text as originally composed by Homer has allowed Poseidon's lookout to be easily changed from Samos to Samos-of-Thrace by starting a new line 13 with the word 'Thraken'. It appears that this was done by a later interpolator. There seems nothing in the mentions of Imbros and Tenedos in the Iliad to oppose the suggestion that these were also added in by a later hand.

If Poseidon went to help the Achaeans from Samos, not Samothrace his route there will have been quite different. In the next chapter we will look at this journey that so troubled Walter Leaf, and see if a new and better sense can be made of it.

CHAPTER 8

POSEIDON'S JOURNEY TO THE SHIPS

Introduction. The journey to the ships. Leaf's Aigai in Euboea. Luce's Aigai on the Chersonese.
Janko's Aigai, a fairy-tale palace. The 'Aiga' of Sappho from Strabo.
The 'Aigai' of Alkaios from Huxley. Finding Homer's Aigai/Aiga.
A speculative restoration of Homer.
A real underwater cavern at Aiga? Conclusions.

Introduction

In this chapter I will continue where I left off in the last chapter, with my study of the opening lines of the Iliad, Book 13. There I found evidence that Troy was in the Bakir Çayi valley, and that Poseidon was watching the battle near the ships from Samos, not Samothrace. Now we will look at Poseidon's journey, behind Zeus's back, to the Greek camp near the mouth of the Bakir Çayi. Walter Leaf, believing that Troy was at Hisarlik, had concluded that Poseidon's very indirect journey from Samothrace to Hisarlik via Aigai, wherever that was, was a nonsense. Can we now make better sense of this journey assuming he went from Samos to Elaia? And can we explain where we might expect to find Poseidon's underwater palace at Aigai?

The journey to the ships

We will start as usual with our trusted poet, who describes the journey as follows:

'Immediately he went down from the rugged mountain, striding with swift footsteps, and the high mountains and the woodland trembled beneath the immortal feet of Poseidon as he went. Three strides he took as he went, and with the fourth stride he reached his goal, Aegae, where his famous palace was built in the depths of the sea, golden and gleaming, imperishable for ever.' (Il. 13.18-23) Once at his palace, he harnessed his horses to his golden chariot, and then rode out across the waves in magnificent splendour. His destination was a 'wide cavern in the depths of the deep sea midway between Tenedos and rugged Imbros.' There he un-harnessed his horses, fed them, and hobbled their feet so they would await his return. Then 'he himself went to the army of the Achaeans.' (Il. 13.24-38)

Poseidon therefore makes this trip in three stages, by foot, by chariot across the waves, then finally, although Homer does not specifically say so, by foot to the Greek camp. We now have a lot of useful information, but we must read his lines with a new caution. Having exposed the hand of a deceiver in the earlier lines about Samothrace, surely we should not be surprised to find the same hand at work here. This deceiver has made us think that Poseidon's starting point was Samothrace, and his destination was Ilion/Hisarlik. So, if he changed the starting and finishing points, it is likely that he also changed the description of the journey. We must therefore watch out for false information and red herrings as we proceed with our study.

The journey starts, as required by the drama, as soon as Poseidon sees that Zeus has turned and looked away. The action demands that he goes to the ships as quickly as possible, before Zeus turns round and sees him. He will remain unseen if he is coming to the Greek camp from the south, but only while Zeus remains looking north. The scene now unfolds. He starts his journey with some urgency. He comes quickly down from the top of the mountain in three giant steps. His fourth step is the problem. Did he really get to Aegae (Aigai) in one step? And, if this was Homer's intent, where was this Aigai?

Leaf's Aigai in Euboea

Being in a hurry, Poseidon would take a direct route to the Greek Camp. So why should he make a long detour to Aigai, wherever that was, before arriving at Elaia? As stated in Chapter 6 where this problem was introduced, Leaf explained his concern saying there were only two certain coastal cities of the name Aigai, both seats of Poseidon worship – one in Achaia, the other in Euboia. 'So this journey was not easy to understand.'[1]

There is also an Aigai well inland in the Hermus valley, but from the Iliad it is clear that Poseidon's Aigai should be on the coast. So how did Leaf resolve this problem? He suggested that Poseidon was actually watching the battle from Mount Olympos on mainland Greece. From here he could collect his carriage from Aigai in Boeotia rather more naturally. But, we may well ask, why would Homer place Poseidon somewhere so far away, and so obviously out of sight of the ships? And, if we read Homer's stage directions correctly, Olympos is not behind Zeus's back when he looks to the north-west. We must try to find a better explanation.

Luce's Aigai on the Chersonese

Professor Luce, who claims to have found Homer's Trojan landscape at Hisarlik, was well aware of this problem. He had some interesting words to say as he tried to resolve it. [2] 'Zeus's gaze,' he wrote, 'has wandered far afield, but not so Poseidon, to whom Homer turns next…Poseidon is waiting for a chance to intervene on the Greek side, and his line of sight, like his intention, is diametrically opposed to that of Zeus.' Then, 'Having viewed the battlefield, Poseidon feels intense anger against Zeus and decides to intervene at once on the Achaean side. Now Homer 'zooms in' as it were on Troy and its immediate surroundings. He brings Poseidon rushing down from the craggy summit of the mountain, shaking the long ridges and the woodland as he goes. With four gigantic strides he reaches Aigai and his glittering palace in the depths of the sea (Il. 13.17-22)'.

Luce now tells us where he thinks Homer's Aigai was. He rejects the journey from Samothrace via Aigai in Euboea as being too indirect. He prefers [3] instead an Aigai on the Thracian Chersonese peninsular. Thus Luce has, without explanation, placed an Aigai close to Troy. Since the Chersonese has a long coastline, and since no more recent authority has found an Aigai on this peninsular, Luce's Aigai here seems only a guess. But an Aigai here, says Luce, 'would suit the context well because the Chersonese, better known to some as the Gallipoli Peninsular, lies between Samothrace and the Troad, and is also close to Imbros and Tenedos, which are the next places mentioned by Homer.' Luce's suggestion demands that Poseidon covered the 80km between Samothrace and Hisarlik by (i) four long steps taking him some 65km over the sea to reach Aigai, then (ii) a 40km chariot trip over the waves at right angles to his intended direction, then (iii) a 30km walk over or under the sea to the Greek camp. The total distance covered is about 135km.

This explanation is very hard to swallow. Although Luce sees drama here, it is drama without any geographical logic, and therefore not Homeric. He does not explain how Poseidon could see that Zeus had allowed his gaze to wander. He does not explain how Poseidon could make his ostentatious carriage trip, from Aigai to the under-sea cavern unseen, without entering Zeus's field of vision. And he does not explain why Poseidon should waste time getting into his chariot at Aigai and racing off in a different direction to another under-sea cavern, instead of simply taking one more step to get from Aigai to the camp? I think that this journey is just as indirect and implausible as the one via Euboea rejected by Walter Leaf.

Janko's Aigai, a fairy-tale palace

Janko, in his Oxford Commentary, gives us some more useful information. He says that Homer making Zeus avert his gaze is 'a neat device'. He explains, as already noted, that Zeus looked 'away', not 'back'. But Janko admits that he cannot understand the journey from Samothrace. [4] He asks 'Why, in such a crisis, does he deviate from the direct route for a stately entrance which only his sea creatures notice?'

But where does Janko place Homer's Aigai? When discussing Poseidon's cult at Aigai, Janko says that 'a fragment of a poem by Alkaios (frag. 298.6) places the Greek's shipwreck there; Huxley convincingly equates this with a headland called "Aiga" opposite the SE corner of Lesbos (cf. Strabo 13.68).' Alkaios (or

Alcaeus) was a Lesbian poet, floruit c600. Then he says 'there were places called Aigai in Euboea, Achaea, and Macedonia (now Vergina)…clearly it is not on the coast of Samothrake! The fact that the god's fairy-tale palace is under the sea suggests that we should not seek its location too seriously.' Thus Janko gives up on any further attempt to locate Homer's Aigai. He is dissatisfied with all the possible suggestions raised so far, and suggests that any further enquiries would be fruitless; such a fairy-tale palace did not really exist. But can we really assume that Homer's audience did not know of a palace of Poseidon at 'Aigai' or 'Aiga', perhaps one not so far away from the Greek Camp at Elaia?

The 'Aiga' of Sappho from Strabo

Strabo (13.68) tells us that the hilly region by the coast to the west of Bergama, known today as the Kara Dag, was in earliest times called Aiga, a name almost identical to Aigai. There is a conspicuous cape jutting out into the Aegean Sea to the north west of Kara Dag, close to the modern town of Bademli. According to Strabo, this 'some people call Aiga, making it identical with the word 'goat'.' Strabo explained this name, saying '… the second syllable ought to be long, Aiga (ah). This was the name that used to be given to the mountain mass now called Kane or Kanai.' He added that Sappho, the famous early 6C lyric poetess from Lesbos, used this name [i.e. Aiga] for the cape, and the rest of this hilly region was called Kane or Kanai.

Unfortunately, only a few fragments of Sappho's poems have survived, and this reference to Aiga or Aigai is not found among them. An Aigai on the coast of the Kara Dag opposite Lesbos would fit quite well with our new geographical understanding of Homer. It lies due south of Gargarus, and is quite close to the Greek camp at the mouth of the Kaikos. I am therefore suggesting that this cape, later called Kane or Kanai by the Greeks, could be the Aigai or Aiga that Poseidon arrived at from Samos.

The 'Aigai' of Alkaios from Huxley

Now we return to Professor Huxley, mentioned earlier by Luce and Janko. [5]

He had found what he thought was an ancient reference to an Aiga in a fragment of a poem by Alkaios. Janko believed that Huxley had convincingly equated the Aigai named by Alkaios with the headland, called 'Aiga', opposite the SE corner of Lesbos. This was the same headland later called Kanai, now Kara Dag, mentioned by Strabo (13.615).

Finding Homer's Aigai/Aiga.

We have now learnt that two leading scholars, Strabo quoting Sappho and Huxley quoting Alcaeus, have revealed the presence of an Aiga or Aigai on the coast of the Kara Dag peninsula. Yet the possibility that this was where Poseidon had his palace and coach house seems not to have been considered. Janko did not pursue this Aiga or Aigai any further, saying we should not seek Homer's underwater Aigai too seriously. Huxley also did not consider it as possibly the Aigai of Poseidon's journey to Troy. This presumably was because it was too far from Hisarlik, and he had a better candidate, from Stephanos of Byzantium, on the Chersonese. However, with these two independent references confirming its existence, I think it now becomes Poseidon's most likely destination. Since both Sappho and Alcaeus were early poets from Lesbos, it is possible that, within their work, we may have some original survivals from stories known to Homer. Then another possibility dawns. If this Aigai was a home of Poseidon known to Homer, surely it would have been remembered in antiquity from its link to Homer's poem. The fact that its location is at best uncertain or unknown may be evidence that this name was not Homer's. Could Homer have originally written Aiga as Poseidon's destination, a place not far from Elaia, and probably well known to his audience? And did Lorimer's 'criminal' change this to Aigai? Perhaps here is the red herring I said earlier we should be on the look out for, a change made to help disguise both the true starting and finishing points of Poseidon's journey.

My tentative conclusion therefore is that the place called Aigai in Book 13 was the place known to Homer, and later to Alcaeus and Sappho, as Aiga. Today this is known as, or is somewhere on, the Kara Dag peninsula. It seems quite possible that, if this was once called Aiga, it was amended later to Aigai without any disturbance to the hexameter as a necessary part of the Samothrace deception.

A speculative restoration of Homer

Our studies so far have, I hope, shown convincingly that Poseidon's look-out was on Samos not Samothrace. He came from there, behind Zeus's back, to the Greek camp near Elaia while Zeus looked at the northern tribes. We have found evidence for an Aiga or Aigai as the ancient name for, or on, the Kanai (now Kara Dag) peninsular, adjacent to the lower Kaikos valley, precisely where Homer's signposts direct us to look for Troy. This could plausibly have been the place where Homer intended Poseidon to have his underwater palace. From here he could easily have made his way on foot to the camp.

However, there remains the unsolved problem of Poseidon's fourth step. From this Aiga, so near to the ships, Homer would never have suggested that Poseidon delayed assisting the Achaeans while taking a pleasure trip over the waves on his golden chariot. Remember that we are expecting to find that some changes have been made in the journey itself. So, with our newly found Aigai/Aiga, let us return to the Iliad and try and make better sense of what is left of the vandalised text. Poseidon's journey comprises four key stages: a) the three tree-trembling steps down the mountain, b) his fourth step by which he arrived at his underground palace at Aiga, c) the sea-skimming golden chariot ride that carries him towards the ships, and d) his walk to the ships disguised as Chalcas. Set out like this, what happened 2,500 years ago now seems clear. The interpolator has simply reversed the order of steps b) and c). In this scene Poseidon, second only to Zeus, is racing from Samos to help the Achaeans in their hour of greatest need, and the poet will want to make the most of this long sea journey for the benefit of his audience. So, after his three giant steps down the mountain, his fourth must have been into his golden chariot, which was waiting for him on the beach. (6) Then he enjoyed a long ride in splendour across the waves to Aiga, perhaps passing between Chios and the Erythrai peninsula on his way to the coast near Elaia. There he left his chariot at his underwater palace and went on foot to the army of the Achaeans.

This reconstruction is, I think, much more plausible than the ideas we have been offered to date. It seems to resonate well with some words of Leaf that stuck in my mind when I first read them six years ago. In his comments on the opening of Book 13, he discussed the interruptions caused by interpolations in the story known to scholars as the 'Deceiving of Zeus'. [7] This tells how Zeus was distracted from looking closely at the battle by the wiles of Hera, which allowed Poseidon to help the Achaeans. Then Leaf wrote 'The later interpolators, anxious to keep as much as possible of the original lines of Homer, found it difficult to fit the brilliantly written chariot ride into the revised geography, but decided to retain it. They did their best, hoped there were enough Aigais to confuse their largely illiterate audiences, and left it at that.' This was a brilliant insight. What Leaf meant by 'revised geography' was the change he believed the interpolators had made when they moved Poseidon's starting point from Mt Olympus to Samothrace. Apart from Poseidon's starting point being Samos, not Mt. Olympus, I think his explanation is right. I would only add that Homer perhaps wrote Aiga, not Aigai, and that the Samothrace deception was completed when Leaf's interpolator, or Lorimer's 'criminal', changed 'Aiga' to 'Aigai'. The fact that a convincing 'Aigai' has never been found, yet we would expect the poet to have named a place well known to his audience, makes it even more likely that Homer wrote 'Aiga', not 'Aigai'.

A real underwater cavern or palace at Aiga?

To complete the story, we may ask one more question. We now understand that the lines which tell us that Poseidon left his chariot in a wide cavern in the depths of the sea between Imbros and Tenedos, were a necessary invention by the interpolator. He had used Homer's intended destination for Poseidon, his palace at Aiga, as the new starting point for the chariot ride, and called it 'Aigai'. So he also had to invent a new finishing point, not too far from the ships.

Now we can ask, did Homer have a particular place in mind for Poseidon's underwater palace? If the name Aiga applied to the whole broad peninsular, then such a place could be anywhere from near the mouth of the Bakir Çayi, westwards around the headland, and northwards up towards Bademli. The poet, according to our present text, tells us that '...and to the ships of the Achaeans did the prancing steeds bring him.' From these words, if they are Homer's as I believe, we may hope to find this palace somewhere near Elaia. Alternatively he may have chosen a well known local shrine to Poseidon somewhere along this stretch of coast. Perhaps the answer to this question may one day be revealed in a local legend, by a local fisherman, or by a full detailed survey of the coastline.

It may be relevant here to mention that, according to Page [8], Lesbos was home to one of the very few cult centres of the Nereids. We are told that Thetis heard Achilles' cry of anguish upon being told of the death of Patroclos. No messengers were sent. This suggests that these daughters of Poseidon may have been in an underwater cave within immortal earshot of the Greek camp. So did Homer, and his audience, know of a home of the Nereids nearby?

During my brief visit to the coast of the Kara Dag, I was shown the site of a hot spring, anciently built into the shore directly opposite the SE tip of Lesbos, not far from the promontory south of Bademli mentioned by Strabo. [9] Here I saw hot spring water bubbling up to the surface in the sea in the narrow strait between the Aginussai islands and the shore. Although this particular hot spring was quite a long way from Elaia, it would be easy to imagine the ancients here believing that such activity was the work of Poseidon. And hot springs in limestone can cause large caverns to be hollowed out in the rock. The region around the Kara Dag, proposed for Poseidon's cavern does, I think, make it at least possible that a large undersea cavern might one day be found there.

Conclusions

In this chapter we have finally been able to make sense of Poseidon's journey to the Greek Camp. With Poseidon on Samos, the dramatic action of the opening lines of Book 13 is fully sustained by both the revised geography, and by a suggested restoration of the text. An Aiga is found near the Greek camp at Elaia that fits this revised geography. The name Aiga may have been changed to Aigai as part of the Samothrace deception.

In short, the dramatic action of the opening lines requires that Homer's Troy lay to the south-west of Gargarus. Thus Homer here has given us a previously unrecognised signpost that points towards Troy being in the Bakir Çayi valley. A coherent case has now been made that Homer intended Poseidon to have been watching the battle from the topmost peak of Samos, not from Samothrace. The elegant simplicity of Homer's poetic description of Poseidon's journey to the Trojan camp from Samos can now, for the first time in over 2,500 years, be properly understood and appreciated.

Now it is time to look more closely at the Bakir Çayi valley, Bergama and Pergamon. In this valley we can feel reasonably confident that, with most of the offsite signposts now pointing there, we will at last find Homer's Trojan plain. And, if we find this plain, it will lead us to the immortal city of Troy, and the holy acropolis of Ilios.

PART 2

FINDING THE PLAIN OF TROY OF THE ILIAD

CHAPTER 9

COMPARING THE MAPS

Introduction. A look at the map. Comparing this map with our reconstructed Trojan plain. Initial conclusions.

Introduction

It is now time to look for the plain of Troy in the Bakir Çayi valley opposite Lesbos. It was here, according to the Mysian war and Telephos legends, that the Achaeans first did battle on Asian soil, capturing Teuthrania when they thought they were at Troy. Could the Mysian war battlefield be the one which is described in the Iliad?

In Part 1 I have shown that the Trojan plain, as reconstructed from the landscape of the Iliad, is very different to the landscape found at Hisarlik. When we studied the geographical clues pointing in the direction of Troy, we found that they are not consistent. Some pointed to Troy at Hisarlik, but others pointed to Troy in the Bakir Çayi valley. The most influential feature of the landscape at Hisarlik is the view from there of Samothrace. This view, above all other considerations, has discouraged any serious attempts to find an alternative site for Troy. But when we studied the passage in which the name 'Samothrace' occurs, we found good evidence that this name could have been a later addition. It appears more likely that, in the original version of the epic, Poseidon was watching the battle at the ships from a mountain on Samos, not Samothrace. Part 1 ends with a study of Poseidon's journey to Troy. In the context of the story, this journey makes better sense if he went from Samos to Elaia, rather than from Samothrace to Besik Bay.

We will start our study of the lower Bakir Çayi valley by looking at a map. Having reconstructed the landscape of the Trojan plain from the Iliad, we must compare this with the landscape features we find there.

A look at the map

The general location of Pergamon and Bergama in relation to Hisarlik and Lesbos has already been shown on the sketch map Fig.1. on page 4. This shows the Bakir Çayi flowing roughly from north-east to south-west, past Bergama and Pergamon on the north side of the valley, and discharging into the Elaitic Gulf near ancient Pitane, now the port of Candarli. What I now wanted was a detailed map of the Bergama region in the lower Bakir Çayi valley showing the roads, rivers, and small hills. But such a map, similar to our Ordnance Survey maps, proved hard to find. Eventually the Bodleian Library of Oxford University came to my rescue. There I was fortunate to discover an old military map (1). This was dated to 1941, but was based on a survey made in 1936. And in one of those coincidences with which my study has been blessed, the day of my search there coincided with a letter arriving at the library confirming that this map was now out of copyright. This meant they were able to make a copy of the relevant part of this map for me to take away. Unfortunately it was not in colour, and seemed at first sight an impenetrable maze of black lines. But it was very important for my purposes. So with apologies for its poor quality, I have included the central part of it here as Fig.9.1.

Here we see Bergama in the top right-hand (north-east) corner, and due west we find Dikili on the coast at the left-hand edge of the map. Candarli, ancient Pitane, is on the coast of the Eleatic Gulf to the south of Dikili, a little west of the mouth of the Bakir Çayi. To the north-west of Candarli lies the hilly peninsular known as the Kara Dag (Black Hill). This was earlier known as the Kanai peninsular, and may have been known in the time of Alcaeus as Aiga. The scale of the original map was given as 1:200,000, but it may be more helpful to know that the distance from Bergama to Candarli is about 30 kilometres.

The main coastal road northwards from Izmir to Canakkale is shown as a heavy black line. It passes the site of Elaia, then goes up the valley towards Bergama.

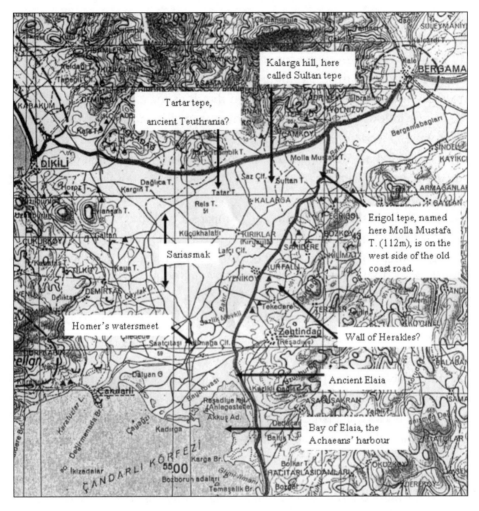

Fig. 9.1 The lower Bakir Çayi valley and the Kara Dag peninsular

But then, after crossing the river by Erigol tepe and joining the Bergama-Dikili road, instead of continuing to Bergama it turns west and heads towards Dikili, Edremit and Canakkale. However, this road junction is just a short taxi ride from Bergama. Tourist coaches from Izmir to Dikili, Edremit and 'Troy' will stop here to pick up passengers coming from, or going to, Bergama and Pergamon. The Bergama to Dikili road runs roughly from east to west along the southern edge of Mount Ida. These hills are called the Madradag. Unfortunately Bergama is not on any main through transport route, either by road or rail.

Comparing this map with our reconstructed Trojan plain

Let us now look at this map more closely. Firstly, with Bergama some 28km from the sea, we ask is this too far from the ships for it to be Homer's Troy? When we followed Priam on his journey from Ilios to collect the body of Hector, we estimated that the distance between Troy and the ships was of the order of 20-30km. We conclude therefore that Troy in this valley cannot be ruled out because Bergama and Pergamon are too far from the sea.

Now we look at the river layout, and compare it with the river layout on our reconstructed plan, Fig. 4.1. We are looking for a main river which, viewed from the bay, swings from the left side of the valley at its mouth to the right side near Troy. It must also have a main tributary which drains the north side of the valley joining it somewhere not far from the ships. What we find is a good match. This can be seen more easily if we turn the reconstructed map through 45 degrees, so the river runs from NE to SW. If we start at the river mouth, we find that to the east, or right, side of the mouth there is a large bay with two headlands. This is the Bay of Elaia, once the port of the Attalid kings of Pergamon. It seems reasonable therefore to expect that the Trojans may also have used it as their harbour. It is also quite large enough to be a prime candidate for the harbour of the Achaeans. The river is to the left-hand side of the bay when viewed by Achilles on the beach. We remember that Hector, pushing the Achaeans back towards their walls, was fighting by the river on the far left of the battlefield. So here, with the river on the left when looking towards Troy, the river layout matches Homer's descriptions. This is an encouraging start. Perhaps near here we should expect to find possible remains of a defensive wall.

Not far from the sea the Bakir Çayi is joined on its left side, still looking from the beach towards Troy, by a tributary. This as I later discovered, was called the Sariasmak Dere. Along with smaller tributaries, this drains a large part of the western and northern sides of the lower plain. We remember that Homer's Skamander and Simois met not far from the beached ships, and the Bakir Çayi and Sariasmak do the same. Here could be the 'watersmeet' of the Iliad. So far so good.

In our reconstruction, we would hope to find that the old coast road crossed the river at the site of an old ford and close to a prominent mound and a large bend in the river. Surely the odds against finding these three features all in one place are heavily stacked against us? But amazingly our good fortune continues. Today the main road between Elaia and Bergama crosses the river courtesy of a wide new bridge near the prominent hill called Erigol tepe. Our map gives the height of this hill, marked as Molla Mustafa, as 112 meters. Subsequent research revealed that earlier scholars had called this hill Erigol Tepe, after a nearby village to the south, and I have retained this name in my study. In pre-Attalid times the road from Bergama to the coast would have crossed the river at a ford, perhaps not far from this bridge.

Next we notice that there is a large bend in the river just above this bridge. Could this be the site of the bend above a ford where Achilles trapped the Trojans, killing many of them as they tried to flee towards Troy? Is it possible that the course of the river has remained unchanged here for some 3,000 years, and that this bend could still be in the same place today? Our first thought is probably not. This seems too good to be true. The Mendere at Hisarlik was thought to have changed its channel in the plain, so we should expect the same to have happened here. But when we come to look at the site more closely we will understand, from the local geology, why this bend may indeed be a very ancient one.

At Bergama, the river is on the right-hand side of the valley as we look upstream from the beach. Since we have crossed the river only once, this is again is as expected of the Skamander near Troy.

Another feature shown on this map could be important. Just south of the Bergama to Dikili road, near the village of Kalarga, is a hill marked as Sultan Tepe. Could this be a candidate for the beautiful hill Kallikolone? Does the name 'Kalarga' carry a distant echo of the name Kallikolone? It would be in about the right place, overlooking the middle of the plain to the south. But there is no sign here of a river, the Simois of the Iliad, running along it's foot on the side facing the battlefield. Unfortunately the exact location of this hill is not marked on the map, so we must examine this hill more closely when we visit the site. However, the omens so far are extremely favourable.

Before putting this map to one side, there are three further points to notice:

i) Bergama has a natural access northwards through a river valley to other regions, including the Troad. Reinforcements and supplies could reach Troy down this route unseen and unhindered by the Greeks in their camp by the ships.

ii) Beside Bergama stands the truly magnificent acropolis of Pergamon, home to the Attalid kings. This is a worthy candidate for holy Ilios. Pergamos was the name in the Iliad of the topmost precinct of Apollo, so the hill even retains its Trojan name. In every way, Pergamon is much more suitable than Hisarlik to receive immortality as 'holy Ilios' from the words of Homer.

iii) The hill immediately to the west of Sultan tepe (Kalarga Hill) is named as Tartar tepe. As we will see later, this hill is roughly where Leaf thought the site of ancient Teuthrania should be found. Again it seems possible that the name 'Tartar' could derive from the earlier name 'Teuthrania'. Certainly we know from historical records that Teuthrania was once in this valley, and a site here would not be implausible.

Initial conclusions

From an initial study of the maps, the lower Bakir Çayi valley offers an almost perfect match with the sketch map of the Trojan plain derived from the Iliad. We have already found on this map some of the most important features of the Trojan landscape. To have found these, as and where he describes them, certainly makes it seem more likely that the poet of the Iliad used the Bakir Çayi valley as the backdrop to his Trojan War epic. It is now time to visit this valley and explore this possible Trojan landscape for ourselves.

CHAPTER 10

THE GREEK CAMP AND ITS ENVIRONS

The bay and ancient harbour of Elaia. The defensive wall.
The rising in the plain, Homer's 'throsmos'. Thymbra in the Trojan plain. Conclusions.

Our site visit begins

We will start our search for the Trojan landscape at the beach, as we did at Hisarlik, and travel slowly up river towards Bergama and Pergamon. So initially we are looking for a large bay between two headlands, and the obvious place to start is at the Bay of Elaia, the ancient harbour of the Attalid kings.

The bay and ancient harbour of Elaia

The beach described in the Iliad was wide, sandy and flat, and beyond it lay grassy meadows. 'For the beach itself, wide as it was, had proved unable to hold all the ships, and the Achaeans, cramped for room, had drawn them up in tiers, covering the whole seaboard from headland to headland.' (Il.14:30-37). Arriving near Elaia, we see a large expanse of sandy flats which back onto meadows where wild flowers would grow in the spring. This bay is now heavily silted up, but it is clear that once there was room here for the ships of the Achaeans to be drawn up along the beach in long curved lines, three ships deep.

Troy had a harbour and a boat building yard where six ships were made to carry Paris on his fateful trading mission to the house of King Menelaus at

Sparta. These ships would have brought Helen back here, along with the treasures she brought with her from her royal home. This would also have been the natural place for the Achaean fleet to land when, according to the Kypria, they landed by mistake in the Kaikos valley and captured Teuthrania, thinking it was Troy. Fig. 10.1 (see colour plate section) shows a view of this old harbour as seen by John Lascelles in 1980.

What looks possibly like a defensive earthwork embankment is seen on the far side of the bay. Long after the Trojans, the harbour here would have been greatly enlarged to serve the needs of the rich Attalid kings. It would have provided anchorage and berths for the Pergamene fleet, which at that time included triremes and the larger quinqueremes. In 190 a Seleucid army tried unsuccessfully to capture Elaia, and went on to besiege Pergamon. So we would expect Elaia to have been well fortified in those days.

Near the shore we can still see blocks of the old Attalid harbour walls. Fig. 10.2 shows the tops of these still in position. The wedge-shaped depression seen on these blocks would have been filled with lead to help keep them in position. Despite the build up of silt, the shape of much of it in earlier times is apparent from the surrounding higher ground.

Perhaps we may also place the ship of Achilles at the end of the line of ships on the western side of the bay. Here, from the stern of his ship, he could see how the battle at the ships was progressing, his view apparently being unimpaired by the defensive wall (Il. 11.596-601).

The well known Homeric scholar, Maurice Bowra, [1] thought the total number of ships in Homer's Catalogue must have been exaggerated, because the Harbour of the Achaeans at Hisarlik was too small to accommodate over a thousand ships. Although I think he was right about the numbers, here we are not forced to this conclusion.

The defensive wall

In Chapter 3 I discussed the defensive wall and the confusion caused by

Fig 5.2 The wooden horse at the entrance to the site of Troy

Fig 5.3 The entrance ramp to Troy Level 2, looking north-east

Fig 5.5 Looking west to the Straits of the Dardanelles

Fig 10.1 The bay and ancient harbour of Elaia

Fig 10.3 The defensive embankment of Elaia viewed from the 'throsmos'

Fig 11.1 Erigol tepe from the main Izmir to Bergama road bridge

Fig 11.3 Looking NE towards Pergamon from Erigol tepe

Fig 11.6 Probable location of Priam's Ford, south of Erigol tepe

Fig 12.3 Kalarga Hill, Homer's Kallikolone.

Fig 12.4 Kalarga Hill from the north.

Fig 12.8 Looking south over the plain from Kalarga Hill

Fig 12.9 Homer's Wall of Heracles?

Fig 13.3 The view from a possible tomb of Aesyetes

Fig 13.10 Tavsan tepe, possibly the Tomb of Hector, from the NW

Fig 14.1 Mardalich Adasi (Island) off the south coast of the Kara Dag

Fig.10.2. Top of the ancient harbour wall at Elaia, with keyed blocks of stonework.

various references to it in the Iliad. These were summed up rather well by Bowra [2]. He pointed out that in Book 16 it was built at the beginning of the war, then built again in Book 7. In Books 14 and 15 it is sometimes present and sometimes absent. In Book 15 it is destroyed by Apollo, but in Book 12 it remains intact until the end of the war before eventually being demolished by Poseidon. I cannot believe that there was such confusion about this wall in the original epic. Leaf must be right to explain it as the result of one or more later interpolators. If the war was historical, we would expect that, unless it was demolished later by man, evidence for such a wall near the shore may still be found.

In Fig.10.1 above we saw that there was a large earth embankment protecting the east side of the bay, set well back from the water's edge. In Fig.10.3 (see colour section) we see a view of this wall from inland, where its full length and defensive significance can better be appreciated. Elaia lies near the far end of this embankment where it runs into the eastern hills. [3] Lascelles also found similar embankments on the western side of the river mouth. When he walked along these in 1981, he found that the landward slope was steeper than the seaward slope. This, in his view, confirmed that it was constructed as a defensive fortification against people from inland who might try to attack any established beachhead. On its surface he found a large number of broken pieces of Roman period pottery, c2C BC to 2C AD. Perhaps these were built originally by the Romans in 191BCE to protect their fleet from possible attack by Antiochus while it was beached there over the winter. [4]

Only excavation will tell us if the core of this wall was originally built by the Greeks at the time of the Trojan War, or whether what we see today was a later defensive construction. Homer tells us that beyond the defensive wall a trench was dug as an added obstruction to chariots. Will archaeologists one day find evidence for a man-made trench behind this embankment?

The 'rising in the plain', Homer's 'throsmos'

On the night that the Trojans camped near the ships, their camp was on an area of higher ground, above the level of the meadows by the beach. From here they looked down on the Greek camp and their ships. In the Iliad, this part of the plain was called the 'throsmos'. This word, translated by Murray as the 'rising in the plain', was discussed in Chapter 3. Our conclusion from Homer's use of it was that it did not mean a hill as such, but an area in the plain of generally higher ground that was on the same side of the Scamander as the Greek camp, and near the ships. Here, not far to the north and west of the ancient port of Elaia, we find just such a feature.

From where the photograph Fig.10.3. was taken, I was standing on a wide, generally flat, elevated part of the plain not much more than a kilometre from the bay. Homer tells us (Il. 8.553ff.) that the Trojans 'stayed the whole night through along the lines of war... a thousand fires were burning in the plain and by each sat fifty men in the glow of the blazing fire.' Although we should not take these round numbers too literally, from the Achaean camp by the bay, such fires here would have been clearly visible. Their proximity to the ships must have made the enemy seem very threatening.

The wide flat area between the rising in the plain and the shoreline is clearly seen. There would have been plenty of room here for the funeral games of Patroclus, as described in the Iliad Book 23. These games required a reasonably flat area close to the ships large enough to hold a chariot race. Such a space is not available at either of the sites proposed for the Greek camp at Hisarlik.

The 'rising in the plain' is in effect a long low flat ridge that runs out towards the mouth of the river from the foothills on the eastern side of the plain. For Fig.10.4 I stood on this low ridge and looked north across the eastern side of the plain. This ridge appears to match perfectly with the Iliad's description of the 'throsmos', and with its translation as 'the rising in the plain.' The main Izmir-Bergama road is visible before it bends to the right and heads towards Bergama. To the left of this a line of low trees can be seen which marks the banks of the Bakir Çayi. On the horizon are the foothills of Ida. Far back in the plain, some 13 kilometres away through the haze, we can just make out the distinctive shape of the brow of Kalarga Hill.

Thymbre in the Trojan plain

There is one further piece of geographical evidence concerning the 'throsmos' that should be mentioned here. In Il. 10.426ff, when the Trojan spy Dolon was captured at night by Odysseus and Diomedes while the Trojans were camped on the 'throsmos', he told them where the Trojan allies were lying. Five groups of allies, including the 'noble Pelasgi', were lying towards the sea, and another four, including the Mysians and Phrygians, were situated towards 'Thymbre'. The Thracians, 'newcomers', were lying apart, 'the outermost of all'.

With Troy at Hisarlik, the location of Thymbre has caused much controversy. It does not seem clear whether Thymbre was the name of a village, a stream, or

Line of trees on the
banks of the Bakir Cayi

Kalarga Hill

The Bergama to Izmir road

Fig.10.4. Looking north from the rising in the plain.

some other physical feature. However, Strabo (13:1:35) found a plain of Thymbre with a river Thymbrios running through it some 8km from Hisarlik, further up the valley. This was close to the Village of the Ilians, which also claimed to be the site of Troy. [5] However, a modern scholar, Cook, [6] during his study of the Troad, could find no evidence there of a town called Thymbre. And he reported that, while no coins of Thymbre were found in the plain of Troy, three have been found at Pergamon. Does this suggest that a Thymbre may have existed not far from Pergamon? Or is it possible that these coins came to Pergamon by trade from a far away place called Thymbrium, some 320km due east of Ephesos?

In the lower Bakir Çayi valley, the 'throsmos' extends from the foothills east of Elaia, and runs westwards towards the river mouth. It passes to the north of the great bay, the harbour of Elaia, and the Greek camp. While Dolon's words may be explained in different ways, he may have meant that the five groups of Trojan allies formed the front line facing the sea, while 'another four' were behind them. If so, this would place Thymbre in the plain to the north of the 'rising in the plain'. The Thracians would then perhaps be on the western end of the 'throsmos', close to the river. [7] It is also possible that the name

136

Thymbre was added in later, replacing somewhere well known not far from Elaia, in order to disguise the real location of this site. Hopefully scholars one day will be able to shed further light on this mystery.

Conclusions

Here, so far, we have found an almost perfect match with Homer's Trojan landscape. The ancient harbour at Elaia, lying in a large bay between two headlands, bordered by meadows, and overlooked by a low rising in the plain some distance inland, offers a likely site for the camp of the Achaeans. A later defensive embankment wall is also seen here, probably built during the Attalid and Roman eras. Yet perhaps a core of the Achaean wall remains within this later embankment. Nothing is found here that contradicts our proposal that Elaia was the site of the harbour of ancient Troy. Here the Achaean ships came prepared to do battle for the return of Helen. Those who told the Mysian War story will also have assumed that the Achaean ships landed in this bay.

CHAPTER 11

THE SKAMANDER, FORD AND TOMB OF ILUS

Introduction. The Bakir Çayi. The hill, ford and the river bend. Priam's ford.
The tomb of Ilus. The bend in the river, a trap for the Trojans.

Introduction

In Chapter 3 we looked at descriptions of the rivers as they appeared in various
places in the action of the Iliad. In Chapter 4 we used this information to
reconstruct the layout of these rivers. Then in Chapter 9, when looking at the
map, we found that the layout of the Bakir Çayi and Sariasmak Dere appeared
to match well with our reconstructed map. Now, as we visit the plain, we will
look at these rivers more closely, starting with the Bakir Çayi.

The Bakir Çayi

The Bakir Çayi was known earlier to the Greeks as the Kaikos and to Roman
historians as the Caicus river. It is most easily seen in the lower valley at the
place where it is crossed by the bridge carrying the main Bergama to Izmir
road, as shown in Fig.11.1 (see colour plate section).

In this photograph, taken by John Lascelles in October 1991, we are at the site
of the most recent bridge over the Bakir Çayi (abbreviated to 'cay' on the sign)
on the main Bergama-Izmir road. As we look north, the river flows from right
to left. The conical hill on the opposite bank is the hill known as Erigol tepe.
The village of Erigol lies in the foothills on the south side of the river. The

acropolis of Pergamon lies some ten kilometres away, directly behind Erigol tepe. To the left the foothills of Ida, which run along the northern edge of the plain, are seen on the horizon.

This is a modern bridge, replacing one that lies a kilometre or so further upstream, i.e. to the right of this picture. I saw no obvious evidence from the height of the river banks that here was once the site of an ancient ford. In this photograph the flow was minimal. The river bed was a series of pools of varying size and depth, with areas of the sandy river bed exposed in places. The Iliad sometimes mentions the pools of 'eddying Xanthus'.

When I visited in June 2003, the scene was different, as fig 11.2 shows.

Here the summer flow is sluggish and shallow. What is particularly striking is the profuse vegetation that flourishes on either side of the water course. This is doubtless cut down periodically by river maintenance workmen, to reduce

Fig.11.2. The Kaikos river in blossom near Erigol tepe, June 2003.

flooding by keeping the river channel free from obstructions. In earlier times many mature trees would have flourished along these river banks. Some of these, like the elm tree mentioned in the Iliad when the river attacked Achilles, would have fallen eventually into or across the watercourse. The river channel here is not much more than about 30-35 metres wide, much less than the Mendere near Hisarlik. Here it would have been quite possible for a fully grown elm tree on the bank to fall across the river and span its banks, as the poet described.

In Book 21 we read that the river god 'Xanthus' tried to help the Trojans. When Achilles was busy killing Trojans trapped beneath its banks, Xanthus rose up and attacked him. Hera, in order to quell the anger of the river, said to Hephaestus 'and you along the banks of Xanthus burn up his trees, and set about him with fire...' (Il.21:333). Hephaestus did as he was bidden. 'The elms were on fire and the willows and the tamarisks. And burning too were the celandine, rush, and galingale, herbs that grow in lush profusion by the beautiful stream of the river.' Luce [1] tells us that tamarisks 'with their handsome feathery fronds' are still found in thickets along the Mendere, and we may expect they are also found beside the Bakir Çayi. Were these lines inspired purely by the poet's imagination? I don't think so. He must surely have seen for himself the extent to which trees and vegetation flourished along this river bank.

The hill, ford and the river bend

Somewhere near the middle of the Trojan plain, there was a large bend in the river just upstream of a 'great mound' called the Tomb of Ilus. Here also was the site of a ford. Priam, on his journey to the Greek camp, passed the Tomb of Ilus before he reached the ford, so we expect this tomb mound to be on the right bank of the river when looking downstream. We have already seen that a cluster of three such features is shown on the 1941 map, and now the map comes to life. Both Fig. 11.1 and 11.2 show the prominent conical hill near the bridge on the main Izmir to Bergama road. While obviously not a man-made tomb mound, this hill is a great landmark in the plain between Pergamon and the sea, and may have once been the site of a royal burial. One sunny afternoon in March 2005 I climbed this hill. With the sun behind me I enjoyed a panoramic view of the plain to the east, with Pergamon clearly visible on the distant skyline. (Fig. 11.3, see colour plate section)

This picture gives a good view of the flat and fertile lower plain between Erigol and Bergama. On the horizon (centre) we can see the familiar shape of the Pergamon acropolis, with the town of Bergama spread out across the plain below it. On the plain we can make out the thick line of bushes along the banks of the Bakir Çayi as it flows towards Erigol tepe. It seems likely to me that the river, hugging the left or southern side of the plain as it passes Bergama, has gradually, over the millennia, been eroding its way towards the centre of the valley. Perhaps one day the relevant experts will discover how much the river channel has changed its position since Trojan times. But when it comes to the edge of the rock outcrop that forms the hill, the river must flow around it. Here it is forced to turn sharply to the south. Then, after some 2-300 metres, it turns sharply west again and flows past the southern side of

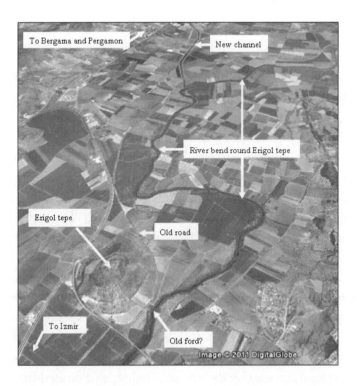

Fig. 11.4. Satellite image of Erigol tepe, river bend and site of old ford.

Erigol and on to the sea. The bend in the river, in relation to both the positions of the roads and the hill, is best understood from a satellite image made available as Fig. 11.4 (page 141) by Google Earth.

Like other natural hills on the plain, Erigol is a granite extrusion, formed by an up-swell of rock as a result of underground volcanic activity. The exposed rock in the foreground of Fig. 11.3 is andesite, the same brown stone that was used for the earliest buildings on Pergamon. Now, with this geological explanation, we can understand that the river channel must have flowed around this hill since the time it was formed thousands of years ago. From the action of the epic it is clear that the poet of the Iliad knew of this extraordinary bend. Perhaps he regarded it as the work of Poseidon.

Fig. 11.4 gives a satellite view of Erigol tepe, looking towards Bergama and Pergamon from the south west. The line of the river can be seen to meander towards the centre of the plain after it has passed Bergama. But as it approaches Erigol tepe it forms a great bend around the southern side of the hill.

The modern road, coming from Izmir in the south, sweeps round the western side of Erigol. In both Fig. 11.3 and 11.4 we can then see that it bends to the north before joining the Bergama to Dikili road, which hugs the foothills of Ida on the northern side of the valley. Passengers for Bergama from Izmir travelling on buses to Dikili, Edremit and Canakkale, must get off at this junction, and catch a local bus or waiting taxi into Bergama. Before the modern roads were built, the old road from Bergama to the coast ran between Erigol tepe and a much smaller low rocky hill on its eastern side. The line of this old road is shown on Fig. 11.3 and 11.4, and is seen from ground level in Fig. 11.5. This earlier road, now an agricultural track, may well follow the line of the ancient road from Pergamon to Elaia in Attalid and Roman times. Earlier still, this could have been the track taken by King Priam in his chariot, followed by the 'wise Ideaus' driving a wagon laden with treasure, on their way to try and ransom Hector's body from Achilles.

The photo, Fig. 11.5, was taken looking south from the bend on the main highway. Here we can see that the volcanic activity that created Erigol tepe also created a much smaller low granite hill on its eastern side. The old road ran

Fig. 11.5. Looking south along the old road past Erigol Tepe to Priam's Ford.

between the two hills. When it reached the river, it turned sharply to the right (west) for a short distance before crossing it at the most favourable place. To see if this crossing point is a possible site for Priam's Ford, we need to look at the river on the southern side of Erigol. From the 1941 map shown as Fig. 9.1., it appears that this may have been the line of the main coast road to Izmir until some time after the second world war.

Priam's Ford

We will now look south from the top of Erigol tepe, and try to locate the site of Priam's Ford.

Here we can see the tree-lined river flowing from left to right, and the earlier road crossing the river before bending away down the south side of the valley. This road and bridge must have been the main route to Izmir before a new bridge, the one seen in Fig 11.1, was built a kilometre or so further downstream. However, there are no obvious signs at either bridge to suggest they were built on the site of an ancient ford.

The history of the Pergamon to Izmir road where it crosses the Bakir Çayi now appears as follows:

- The earliest road from Pergamon to Elaia ran between Erigol and its low eastern neighbour, and crossed the river by a ford somewhere just past Erigol tepe. Perhaps the Attalids or Romans later built a bridge on this site.
- Shortly after the Second World War a new road was built around the north side of Erigol, crossing the river at the bridge seen in Fig. 11.6 (see colour plate section).
- More recently the road was again improved to carry heavier traffic by building the new wider bridge further downstream that we saw in Fig.11.1.

Looking more closely at Fig. 11.6 we notice that there are two tracks some 200m upstream of the bridge, on either side of the river, that appear to be heading towards each other. The one on the far side bends a little to the west, as if towards the line of an ancient bridge. Did Priam's ford lie in a direct line between these two tracks? An ancient ford will normally cross where the river bed is most suitable for horses and wagons, and evidence for such a crossing here may still be visible. The task of locating Priam's Ford more precisely must be left to others. Here I will simply conclude that Priam's ford lay just south of Erigol Tepe, where a rock shelf on the river bed provided a firm footing for horses and wagons. Foot soldiers, on the other hand, could have crossed in several places during the summer, when the river at times ran almost dry.

The Attalid kings and the Romans would probably have built and maintained a bridge in this general location. If so, evidence for this should not be hard to find, but no ancient bridge remains are readily visible there today.

The tomb of Ilus

With the help of these photographs, let us now consider where the Tomb of Ilus might have been. The poet, describing Priam's journey from Ilios to the Greek camp, tells us: 'Now when they (Priam and his servant Ideaus) had driven past the great mound of Ilus, they halted the mules and the horses in the river to drink, for darkness had now come down over the earth.' (Il 24.349-351). On the return journey, the Tomb of Ilus is not mentioned. We are simply told that Priam 'came to the ford of the fair flowing river, eddying Xanthus…' just as 'Dawn, the saffron-robed, was spreading all over the earth.' (Il. 24.693ff.). Here perhaps we find another example of Homer's economy. On Priam's outward journey Homer mentions the Tomb of Ilus but does not use the word 'ford', and on the return journey he names the ford but does not mention Ilus. His audience already knew that Priam returned the way he had come, and had stopped at the ford each time. So to mention both Ilus and the ford on each journey was unnecessary. Our poet rarely provides information that is superfluous to the action.

Unfortunately, on the outward journey, we are not told whether Priam passed the 'great mound' on his right or left before he reached the ford. Thus possible sites for a Tomb of Ilus are a) on Erigol tepe, on its summit or on its eastern side; b) on the lower hill between Erigol and the river bend, or c) a free-standing mound in this general area. The reference here to the 'great mound', with no separate mention of the great conical hill, made me think at first that he was referring to the hill itself, for why would he use a much smaller man-made mound as a topographical marker while ignoring the presence of such a magnificent natural hill in the same place? Perhaps this hill acquired the name of the illustrious king, because his resting place was on it or nearby. However, this view is not easy to reconcile with a passage in the Iliad where we are told that Alexander (Paris), aimed an arrow and hit Diomedes in the foot while 'supporting himself against a pillar on the mound that men's hands reared for Ilus, son of Dardanus…' (Il. 11.166-8). Was this mound on the top of Erigol? This seems unlikely as it would be difficult to take material for a large tomb mound up to the top of the hill, and from there it would be too far to shoot an arrow at someone standing near the foot of the hill. Alternatively, is it possible that Homer knew nothing of the shooting of Diomedes in this place and in this manner, and these two lines were later additions?

We must leave these questions unanswered, and hope that a future archaeological exploration in this area will one day discover its whereabouts, if it ever existed. The early 20th century German archaeologists who explored the plain discovered the remains of an ancient fort on Erigol. This was believed to have been manned in Attalid times as an early warning lookout post, when attack was threatened from the coast. If this is correct, it seems likely that any ready-made building blocks available from a nearby Trojan tomb mound would have been used in building the later fort. Given the history of the many wars in the Attalid era, any monument here, if it had survived from Trojan times, would probably have been destroyed during these wars. A famous collection of ancient monuments, collected and erected by the Attalid kings and known as the Nikephorium, stood outside the walls of Pergamon. This was destroyed at least twice when the city was besieged in Attalid times. If such a mound was thought to have contained any treasure, it may also have been excavated long ago. For the purposes of this study, therefore, I have assumed that, in Homer's day, Erigol Tepe was called the Tomb of Ilus after the famous king who was believed to have been buried on or near it.

The bend in the river, a trap for the Trojans

We saw in Figs. 11.3 and 11.4 how the river turned sharply to flow around the south side of Erigol tepe. This bend in relation to Erigol and the plain is best seen in the satellite image, Fig. 11.4. With the help of these pictures, let us now look at the account of how Achilles trapped and killed many Trojans in the river by the ford, and see if we can understand how this might have happened.

In Murray's translation we read (Il. 21.1ff) that when the fleeing Trojans 'had now come to the ford of the fair flowing river…there Achilles split them into two groups, and one he drove to the plain towards the city…but half were forced into the deep flowing river with its silver eddies…so cowered the Trojans in the streams of the dread river beneath the steep banks.'

Rieu [2] gives a slightly different translation. Here we read that, as the Trojans fled back towards Troy, 'Achilles cut the Trojan forces in two'…the first group he drove towards the city and they 'spread across the plain in wild disorder… The rest were chased into a bend in the river, where Xanthus pools ran deep… the Trojans cowered under the overhanging banks of that terrible river.'

The first point to note is that, having checked in several other translations, Rieu seems alone in using the word 'bend' in his translation. It seems that this word is not specifically used by Homer. However, it also seems clear that the poet intended that a bend was here from the mention of undercutting of the banks, and from the concept of the Trojans being trapped in the river.

Exactly where and how Achilles 'cut the Trojan forces in two' is not explained. Trying to reconstruct the scene, it seems safe to assume that the Trojans, as they approached Erigol tepe, were fleeing back to Troy on both sides of the river. Fighting had earlier been taking place on the plain between the Skamander and the Simois, so some must have crossed the river not far from the Greek camp. Traces of a Roman bridge over the river have been found between Elaia and Candarli.

Believing we now know the real layout of the Trojan plain, I can speculate as to how Achilles may have set his trap for the fleeing Trojans. In order to cut them off, Achilles and his men could have used their chariots to reach the Tomb of Ilus and the ford before many of the Trojan foot soldiers arrived there. Then Achilles set his trap. He could, for example, have tried to prevent those on the south side of the river from crossing at the ford. This would have forced them to try to cross it somewhere further up the valley nearer Troy, and some may have been trapped in the river when they did so. Another possibility, perhaps more likely, was to block off the passage on the old road between Erigol and the small hill beside it. The Trojans who had crossed at the ford would then have to decide either to go back across the ford, or to head for Troy directly. Those who headed directly towards Troy would have found themselves trapped in the great bend of the river just upstream of Erigol. Here the banks would, in some places, have been steep and overhanging. Such a possibility is illustrated in Fig. 11.7.

Although we may never know exactly how it happened, there is no doubt that the relative positions here of the bend, the ford and Erigol make the story of Achilles trapping the Trojans in the river quite plausible. Perhaps the great double bend near Troy was well known to the audience in Homer's day. Perhaps, in the same way that he did not need to mention the ford on Priam's outward journey, the poet felt no need specifically to spell out the bend's existence. Either way, his account of the battle does fit the landscape near the ford. Here it does seem possible to believe that the Iliad portrays a real historic event that happened during the Trojan War.

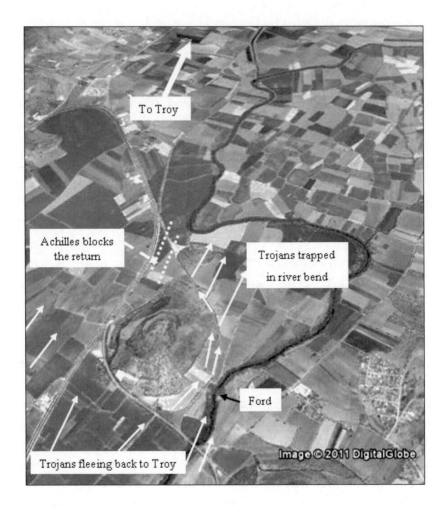

Fig. 11.7. Trapping the Trojans in the river

CHAPTER 12

THE SIMOIS, KALLIKOLONE, AND THE WALL OF HERAKLES

Introduction. The Sariasmak Dere. Homer's Simois. Kallikolone beside the Simois.
The 'watersmeet'. The vanishing Simois. The Wall of Herakles. Summary and Conclusions.

Introduction

In Chapter 11 we found that the size and layout of the Bakir Çayi in its valley below Bergama matched the descriptions in the Iliad of the Skamander in the Trojan plain very well. Particularly significant was finding a site for an ancient ford just below a large bend in the river. Here also stood Erigol tepe, a hill which could equate to the 'great mound' of the tomb of Ilus. In this chapter we will look at the Sariasmak Dere and the features associated with it, to see how they compare with the Iliad's descriptions of the Simois.

The Sariasmak Dere

It is not easy to find a map which shows this river. In 2002, the only detailed map I could find was the 1941 military map. On this I could scarcely make out a separate river that drained the western and northern sides of the lower valley and joined the Bakir Çayi near its mouth. When I visited Bergama in 2003 I was unable to find anyone who knew the name of this river. However, John Lascelles had managed to find its name on an old British Admiralty Chart. [1] A sketch map based on this chart is shown as Fig.12.1. It shows the name of this river as the Sariasmak Dere, although its position, with no tributaries, is only roughly indicated.

Fig.12.1. The Kara Dag coast and the Sariasmak Dere.

This map is very useful, since as well as naming the Sariasmak, it also gives the names of some of the small islands around the coast. We will refer to it again in a later chapter. The Sariasmak is fed by an extensive network of small streams from the Kara Dag and the northern hills, most of which dry up in the summer. One such tributary draining the northern foothills of Ida was seen where it passes under the Bergama-Dikili road. Here it was named the Tahtali (dere), as seen on the roadside signpost photograph, Fig. 12.2.

The reason for including this photograph here is to show how the trees and vegetation along the banks of the Bakir Çayi might have looked, in the days before community funding paid to keep the main river channel clear of unwanted obstructions. Unlike beside the Bakir Çayi, here the vegetation appears unrestrained, and fully grown trees are seen along its river banks.

The references in the Iliad to the 'watersmeet' of the two rivers near the Greek camp have already been mentioned. At one stage the battle swayed to and fro across the plain, 'midway between Simois and the streams of Xanthus', (Il.6.4.) before the Achaeans got the upper hand. This implied that, at some point not far from the watersmeet, the Simois flowed roughly parallel to the Skamander, and the battlefield lay between the two rivers. We can see this area on both the

150

Fig.12.2. The Bergama-Dikili road crossing the Tahtali Dere.

Admiralty Chart and our simplified sketch map. Here the Sariasmak flows west on the north side of the plain before turning to flow south into the Bakir Çayi. No such area between the Dombrek and Mendere exists at Hisarlik.

Another point to notice is that, in order for both armies to be fighting between the two rivers, they must have been able to cross the Skamander not far from the watersmeet. Perhaps such a crossing was possible only in the summer months when the river flow was low. From Il. 12.22-24 we hear that by the banks of the Simois 'many shields of bull's hide and many helmets fell in the dust...'. This confirms the extent of the battlefield between the two rivers.

Kallikolone beside the Simois

The only other mention of the Simois which will help us locate it is in lines Il. 20.51-53. Here, the poet tells us that Ares, the god of war, came to give strength and resolve to the Trojans when they needed it after they had fallen well back from the ships. He incited them to greater efforts, one moment from the top of the citadel, the next 'from the banks of the Simois, as he ran along the slopes of Kallikolone'. [2] 'Kallikolone' means 'beautiful hill' in Greek, and the poet refers to its brow as if it was a distinctive feature. We should therefore expect to find a hill in the plain with a distinctive brow, some way inland from the ships. When we do, the Simois should be running beside it on the side of the hill facing the battlefield. Should we find such a hill meeting these specific requirements, the chances that we are in Homer's Trojan plain become ever more certain.

First let us look across the plain downstream of Erigol tepe, and see if we can find a hill to meet these specifications. Standing on the main bridge over the Bakir Çayi from which he photographed Erigol tepe, but now looking west instead of east, Lascelles had no difficulty. There before him was Kalarga Hill, standing tall and proud in the middle of the plain. John Lascelles took this photograph, Fig. 12.3 (see colour plate section), in 1991.

Another view of this hill, Fig. 12.4 (see colour plate section), which I took from the foothills on the north side of the valley, shows how this hill rises majestically above the flat plain in the lower valley.

Like Erigol tepe, it was formed by an upthrust of volcanic rock. By some strange accident of geology it, like Erigol, has a much smaller neighbour on its eastern side. The Bergama to Dikili road can be seen in the foreground. On the far horizon the rising in the plain prevents a view of the sea between the two hills. Kalarga village lies in the plain on the other side of the hill. Its distinctive brow, mentioned in the Iliad, is clearly seen in this picture.

The 'watersmeet'

In 1980, John Lascelles climbed to the top of Kalarga Hill. From there he saw and photographed the Sariasmak, using a black and white film. He then walked across the plain to the point where this stream meets the Bakir Çayi, and photographed the 'watersmeet'.

Unfortunately the day was rather overcast, but in Fig.12.5. the water surface of the Sariasmak is visible where it reflects the sky, showing clearly that it flows westwards away from the southern side of this hill.

In Fig 12.6. we see the confluence of the two rivers, the 'watersmeet' of the Iliad. This is not a natural river confluence, and its shape suggests that it has been formed artificially and quite recently by land drainage contractors. The Turkish name of this stream, Sariasmak, could mean, in effect, 'yellow flood waters'. It is interesting to reflect that another name for the Skamander in the Iliad is 'Xanthus', which can also mean 'yellow'. Could it be that in today's Turkish name we find an echo of an ancient tradition that rivers here carried yellow flood waters?

Fig.12.5. The Sariasmak from Kalarga Hill.

The vanishing Simois

When I visited the south side of Kalarga Hill in March 2005, I found that the river once flowing there had now become an interconnecting series of mainly

Fig.12.6. The 'watersmeet' of the Simois and Skamander?

dry drainage ditches. This is seen in Fig 12.7. How, I wondered, could these dry ditches once have been one of Troy's two noble rivers? This, I think, can be explained by understanding the combined effect of changes that have taken place in this valley over the last 2,000 years.

In the Iliad, the Simois had banks for Ares to run beside as it flowed past Kallikolone. This suggests that the Simois probably once had its source in the foothills well to the east of this hill. But increasing demands for water for Pergamon and Bergama have robbed the upper catchment of the Sariasmak/Simois of much of its natural run-off.

From the map, and from the satellite images, it seems clear that the overflow from the springs of the Asklepion flow directly westwards, not eastwards through the town of Bergama. The stream draining the Asklepion would, in Trojan times, have collected other springs and streams along the north side of the lower valley as it flowed westwards. By the time it flowed past Kalarga Hill it would have been much larger, and known as the Simois of the Iliad.

The size of the Simois probably started being reduced in Attalid times. King Eumenes II famously built a great aqueduct to bring water to Pergamon from the northern foothills. The remains of this aqueduct are still visible today, and are illustrated in the better guidebooks. In Roman times, Pergamon and Bergama grew in size, and at one time it is thought that as many as 200,000 people lived there. The Romans dug wells and adits into the northern hills to collect spring water to meet the needs of this population. And flows in the Simois dwindled as a result. More recently, increasing demand for water, and the need to take water from the Bergama Çayi to help fill the new lake behind the dam beside Pergamon, have reduced the amount of water left in both rivers to the west of Bergama. From Fig.11.4 in the previous chapter we can see that the stream which drains the Asklepion and areas to the west of it now flows, in what looks like an artificial channel, into the Bakir Çayi, some half way between Bergama and Erigol tepe. This new channel probably carries much of the urban drainage from the rapidly expanding town.

With so much water now diverted from the headwaters of the Sariasmak into the Bergama Çayi, and with increased agricultural development and irrigation in the lower valley, it is not surprising that what was once the Simois has almost disappeared in the region to the east of Kalarga hill. Long gone are the days when this river carried warm surplus water from the Asklepion, gathering

Fig. 12.7. The headwaters of the Sariasmak. March 2005.

run-off from the northern foothills as it went along, until it flowed past Kallikolone as a noble river, and on to the watersmeet near the Greek camp.

The Wall of Herakles

Kalarga Hill, 'Kallikolone' in the Iliad, provides a panoramic view across the plain, part of which is seen in Fig. 12.8 (see colour plate section). In the foreground, the line of a drainage ditch at the head of the Sariasmak Dere is seen running across the middle of this picture. In the distance, a broken line of dark trees marks the line of the Bakir Çayi as it crosses the plain. Somewhere on the opposite side of the plain we now expect, rather than hope, to find the 'Wall of Herakles'.

The name of this hill is explained by the story of Herakles and Laomedon, told briefly in Chapter 2. In Chapter 3 we saw that in Book 20 the Iliad tells us about the 'heaped up wall of god-like Herakles, the high wall that the Trojans and Pallas Athene had built for him so that he might flee there and escape from the monster of the deep when it drove him from the sea shore to the plain' (Il 20:145ff.).

At one stage during the war, the gods supporting the Trojans and the Achaeans watched the fighting from two hills overlooking the plain. Poseidon, Hera and Athene, the Achaean supporters, sat on the 'Wall of Herakles', while '...they on the other side sat opposite on the brows of Kallikolone, around you, archer Phoebus (Apollo) and Ares, sacker of cities.' (Il.20.146-151). A few lines earlier, Poseidon said to Hera (Il. 20:135) 'But for our part let us then go apart from the track to some lookout spot and sit there, and the war will be the concern of men.'

The poet therefore gives us three clues to help us find this wall-like hill. Firstly, it lies 'opposite' Kallikolone. Secondly, it is 'apart from the track'. The only cross country track mentioned in the Iliad is the one that goes from Troy to the Greek camp via the ford, so this is likely to be the track mentioned by Poseidon. By saying it lay 'apart from the track', I think the poet is telling us that the Wall of Herakles should be found on the side of the track away from the battlefield. Thirdly, this hill is high enough to be a 'look-out spot' from which the battle could be viewed.

The directions could not be more clear. We may expect to find the Wall of Herakles in the foothills on the far side of the plain directly opposite Kallikolone. There is no need to search for a man-made hill. The poet tells us the 'Wall' was built by Athene with help from mortals, so we may assume that it was too large to have been built by men alone. At Hisarlik, the Wall of Herakles was identified as a natural hill. Here we should also look for a natural hill shaped as if by man.

On the day I went to see Kalarga Hill, I did not attempt to climb to the top. But from the side of the hill I took the photograph seen in Fig.12.8.

As you can see, the foothills opposite are rather too distant for us to be able to select the best candidate with any confidence. Looking closely at Fig. 12.8, I have indicated a possible 'Wall of Herakles'. This seems to have a fairly level top, as we would expect of a 'wall'. It is also opposite Kallikolone, and nearer the Achaean camp, making it an ideal balcony seat for the Achaean supporters. Clearly I needed to see this hill more closely from Poseidon's 'track'. The present main Izmir to Bergama road runs along this side of the valley between the edge of the foothills and the ancient flood plain, so it is reasonable to assume that Priam's 'track' followed a similar line.

Fig. 12.9 (see colour plate section) is a view from the north of this hill, which stands close to the Izmir road. Driving towards Bergama from Elaia, this was the only suitably shaped hill seen in these rolling foothills. It is roughly 7-8km north of Elaia and a little south of the village of Yenikoy. It is the only prominent hill in these foothills with a wall-like appearance. From the road it appears as a low, flat-topped hill some 2-300m long, sitting at an angle to the road so that it faces roughly north-west towards the plain.

It is only very recently, in late 2009, that good clear Google Earth images of the lower valley became available. From these we can now clearly see the relationship between this hill and Kalarga hill.

Fig. 12.10 is a Google Earth image of part of the Bakir Çayi plain including Kalarga Hill and the valley further south. Kalarga Hill is seen near the top left hand corner. The Bakir Çayi flows from north to south, and the Izmir to Bergama and Dikili road runs along beside the foothills on the eastern side of the river. If we note the axis of Kalarga hill, and look at ninety degrees directly opposite it to the foothill beyond the river and the main road, our eye is drawn to an interesting hill. This appears to have a clear track running along its top, and two access roads at each end of the hill. This seems an obvious candidate for the Wall of Herakles.

A close-up of this hill is seen in Fig. 12.11

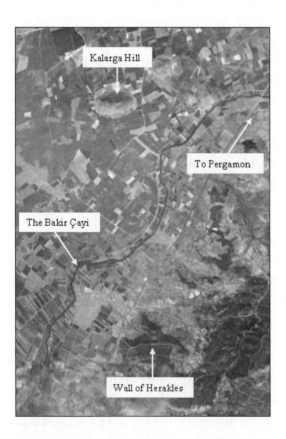

Fig. 12.10. Google Earth image of the Bakir Çayi plain below Kalarga Hill

Fig. 12.11. An aerial view of a possible Wall of Herakles (from Google Earth)

It was very satisfying to find that there is an excellent candidate for the Wall of Herakles exactly where the poet of the Iliad said it should be. If, as I like to believe, Homer travelled this way, he cannot have failed to notice it. If so, this view may have inspired him to create a mythical story to explain its origin. It certainly fits the Iliad's descriptions in size, shape and location. How clever of the poet to see these two hills as potential viewing platforms for the war going on between them, and to weave them so effortlessly into the fabric of his epic. If my guess is right, we are yet again reminded of just how well he knew this valley.

Summary and Conclusions

In summary, the Sariasmak Dere and Kalarga Hill, in both their geographical position and topographical detail, fit the descriptions of the Simois and

Kallikolone very well. The conjunction of the Sariasmak and Bakir Çayi fits well with the 'watersmeet' of the Iliad, found not far from the beach at Elaia. On the foothills opposite the southern face of Kalarga Hill we also found a wall-like hill with a level top, which fits the description of the 'Wall of Herakles'. The poet revealed his knowledge of this plain when he placed the gods supporting the Trojans and Achaeans on each side of the battlefield, behind the side they were supporting. For the first time we can explain why the gods supporting the Trojans sat on Kallikolone, and those supporting the Achaeans sat on the Wall of Herakles, rather than the other way round. This arrangement meant that, with the battle in the plain taking place between these two landmarks, the gods sat like troops held in reserve on the battlefield, well placed to join the battle if the opposing side looked like gaining the upper hand.

In Chapter 11 we found a cluster of three possible Homeric features, the bend, ford and tomb of Ilus, all together in their expected places. In this chapter we find here another cluster, this time of five such features: i) Kalarga Hill where we would expect to find Kallikolone, ii) a hill with a distinctive brow, iii) a stream at its foot, iv) the stream flowing away from the nearby main river, and v) the stream being on the side of hill facing the plain. These two clusters of features, as and where expected from the Iliad, constitute a very specific and probably unique arrangement. The discovery of a wall-like hill in the foothills orientated so that it stands directly opposite Kalarga Hill is another statistically important find. The chances of us finding all these features, as and where described in the Iliad, in any other valley draining at least part of Mount Ida, are extremely remote. Put the other way round, even at this early stage of our visit, the probability that here we have found the Trojan plain of the Iliad is already very high.

Some Homeric scholars may flatly deny that such topographical minutiae could have been transmitted accurately by oral bardic tradition across what they believe was a Dark Age of some 500 years. Yet, in apparent contradiction to this assumption, here we have found a perfect match with all the details of Homer's landscape. We can now, I think, begin to feel confident that the principal author of the Iliad really did have a good personal knowledge of this valley.

CHAPTER 13

BERGAMA AND TOMB MOUNDS

Introduction. General layout of Bergama. The unnamed tomb, the tomb of Old Aesyetes?
Maltepe. Yigma Tepe. Tavsan Tepe. Comments on the tomb mounds.
Bergama's two rivers. The Bergama Çayi. Finding Homer's Skamander.
How old is the culvert? Conclusions.

Introduction

In our journey across the plain we travelled from the ancient harbour of Elaia to the outskirts of Bergama. Along the way, we found all the landscape features that were present in the Trojan plain of the Iliad. These included the river layout, the great bend in the river, Kalarga hill in the plain, a wall-shaped hill directly opposite in the foothills, Erigol tepe beside the likely site of an old ford and a bend in the river. All these are as and where we should expect them to be from the Iliad. Equally importantly, no prominent features were found in the landscape of the war zone that, for some unexplained reason, are not mentioned by the poet. Statistically, all these facts are highly significant when calculating the probability that this really was the Iliadic Trojan plain.

In this chapter we look at Bergama's tomb mounds and rivers. Here we also find instances where the local topography fits the descriptions in the Iliad very well. Before we reach Bergama, however, we should first study its layout by looking at a map of the town.

General layout of Bergama

We saw in Fig.11.3 a distant view of the Pergamon acropolis, with Bergama at its foot spreading out across the plain on the western side of the hill. Urban sprawl has also allowed a ribbon of development along the Dikili road on the northern edge of the valley almost as far as the Dikili-Izmir road junction. From this junction, the road runs along the edge of the northern foothills towards Bergama. On my first visit I came by overnight coach from Istanbul, via Dikili. I remember being amazed that the Pergamon acropolis did not come into view until we were well into the suburbs of Bergama. Until then it was hidden behind one of the northern foothills. Suddenly it made a spectacular appearance, looming large before us in the morning sun, which glinted on the white marble columns on its summit.

I was unable to find a good up-to-date street map of the city. So I have adapted an image from Google Earth to give a view of the city and of the location of a few of the most important places mentioned in this book. This satellite image is included as Fig. 13.1 (page 163).

Shortly before the bus reached the Ottogar, the main coach station (location 12 on the map), I caught my first glimpse of the three tomb mounds in the SW suburbs of Bergama. Two are close to the main road, Izmir Caddesi (Izmir street). The third, and largest, stands further away from the road to the south (location 6 on the map). This, as you will see from my photographs, looked rather strange from a distance, having recently suffered from a grass fire on its northern side. I could appreciate how much the town has grown recently because, when Lascelles first came here in 1980, these mounds, now partly hidden behind modern blocks of flats, stood in much more open ground.

Leaving the coach station, a short walk along the main road towards the town centre brings you to the archaeological museum and the tourist information office, both on your left. The Asklepion, a famous Hellenistic and Roman spa and healing centre, is about a 2km walk from the bus station, turning left just past the information office and walking along a track past some older houses. From the bus station, visitors can take a taxi up to the acropolis. This journey of some 5km follows the main road until it crosses the Bergama Çayi by the

Fig 13.1 Satellite image of Bergama and Perganon

Key :

1.   The acropolis of Pergamon, Homer's Ilios.
2.   Musalla Mezarlik or Cemetery Hill, possible part of the site of Troy?
3.   The location of the springs in the hillside behind Musalla Mezarlik.
4.   An unnamed tomb mound, perhaps Old Aesyetes tomb.
5.   Maltepe, a Hellenistic tomb mound.
6.   Yigma tepe, identified as Homer's tomb of Myrine.
7.   Tavsan tepe, identified possibly as Hector's tomb.
8.   The Red Hall, with courtyard extending over the Bergama Çayi.
9.   The Asklepion, a warm spring in Roman times.
10.   The main road from Izmir and Dikili to the town centre, Izmir Caddesi.
11.   The Soma road, bypassing the town centre.
12.   The main bus station, or 'Ottogar'
13.   Military camp on the hill overlooking the town.
14.   The Archaeological Museum, close to the Information Centre.

Red Basilica, then winds its scenic way round the back of the hill to reach the car park near the top. Some of Pergamon's ancient ruins are clearly seen from Bergama. The best known of these is the famously steep open air theatre, with its seemingly interminable banks of stone seats. We will look more closely at Pergamon in Volume 2. In this chapter we are concerned with Bergama's existing tomb mounds, and the layout of the rivers. After looking at these mounds, and incredible as it may sound, it seems possible that three of the four may be those mentioned in the Iliad, provided they are old enough.

The un-named tomb, the tomb of Old Aesyetes?

The first mound I visited was the one which lies furthest from Pergamon, location 4 in Fig. 13.1. It is not named on the town map. In the Iliad there are two tomb mounds that lay outside Troy in the direction of the Greek camp. The first was the tomb of Old Aesyetes, which we will assume was the furthest from Troy. Here Polites, a young son of Priam, 'sat as a lookout of the Trojans, trusting in his fleetness of foot, on the topmost part of the grave mound of aged Aesyetes, watching for the time when the Achaeans should start out from their ships.' (Il. 2.791-794). In a slightly different translation, Rieu tells us that Polites, acting as lookout, was 'ready to dash home at the first sign of a sortie from the Achaean ships' [1].

Geographically, I think this is the most likely of the existing tombs to have been used as a lookout by Polites. Although not as high as Yigma tepe, it is close to the northern foothills. From here a lookout could catch an early sight of troops approaching up the middle of the plain past Erigol tepe from the ships. From here Polites had the best chance of seeing a pending attack, and he also had a safer passage back to Troy. A raiding party, however, may have tried to catch him unawares by approaching unseen along the northern foothills, or along the south side of the river while hidden by the trees lining its banks.

I walked across the clear space around the mound, taking care not to tread on a small tortoise that was basking in the sun at my feet. This reminded me of some lines about the site of Troy by Lord Byron, in his famous poem 'Don Juan':

Fig. 13.2. Looking SW at an unnamed ancient mound, possibly Old Aesyetes' tomb.

'High barrows without marble or a name,
A vast, untilled and mountain-skirted plain,
And Ida in the distance still the same,
And old Skamander (if 'tis he) remain:
The situation seems still forged for fame –
A hundred thousand men might fight again
With ease; but where I sought for Ilion's walls,
The quiet sheep feeds, and the tortoise crawls.' (Canto IV, 77)

From here I looked towards Erigol tepe and the distinctive brow of Kalarga Hill, and saw the distant view that I imagined Polites must have seen some 3,000 years ago. As you can see in the photograph Fig 13.3 (see colour plate section), this view, possibly one of the most famous in antiquity, is today sadly marred by the modern buildings in the foreground.

This picture was taken in clear early evening light in June 2003. Despite the buildings, I could make out the line of trees marking the river as it flowed towards Erigol tepe, and the flat plain as it extended into the distance towards the sea. In Homer's time this line of trees would have provided good cover for the Greeks, allowing them to approach Troy and Ilios unseen from the far side of the plain. By a strange coincidence it was another large force of Achaeans who came here in 190, to help the Attalid king Eumenes II. At that time he was besieged on the acropolis by the Seleucid king Seleucus IV and his son Antiochus, but the Achaeans managed to relieve him by reaching the acropolis at night. [2]

From here we can see that, provided the Achaean forces stayed in the middle of the plain, by the time they came into view they were already some two thirds or more across the plain. To be heroic, perhaps Polites would stay at his post for as long as possible, hoping to discover the size and make-up of the attacking force, and whether or not Achilles was among them. Then, in a few minutes, he would have run back to safety behind Priam's Gate and the walls of Troy. He may also have had some form of warning signal, such as a trumpet or a flag that he could raise if the Achaeans were sighted, that would be visible to the sentries on the acropolis.

Murray's translation of the passage naming Polites seems to imply that he could see the Achaeans' ships from his vantage point. Yet the Iliad tells us there was a 'rising in the plain' a short distance inland, as well as a possible defensive earth embankment in front of the Greek camp and their ships. Either or both of these would make a view of the ships impossible from anywhere near Bergama. If this really is the plain of Troy, then we can understand that these lines were intended to explain that Polites, from his lookout, would be the first to catch sight of an attacking force approaching Troy. Rieu's translation is therefore preferred to that of Murray. In fact, neither Erigol tepe nor this tomb mound can be seen from the northern suburbs of Bergama, since the foothill on the northern edge of the town blocks the view down the plain.

Professor Radt told me this mound has never been excavated, so its date is unknown. On its top there are at least two depressions which could mark attempts by would-be tomb robbers to try and dig up antiquities. Or perhaps this was where foundation stones may once have been placed to support some grave-top monument such as a column or stele. These shallow pits reveal the mound to have a core of rounded stones, which would have been plentiful across the flood plain, especially near the river. The Iliad mentions mounds that were built using the 'materials of the plain'.

While gazing at this view I remembered Strabo's comments (13.1.37) about the mound at Hisarlik that was claimed as Polites' lookout. He said of Polites sitting there, 'He was doing a foolish thing, for even though he sat on the topmost part of it, still he might have kept watch from the much greater height of the acropolis, at approximately the same distance, with no need of fleetness of foot for safety; for the barrow of Aesyetes now pointed out is 5 stadia (about a kilometre) distant on the road to Alexandria.' Here at Bergama, Strabo would have made no such complaint. However, until further site investigations are carried out, the identification of this mound as the tomb of Old Aesyetes must remain highly speculative.

Maltepe

The next tomb mound was a little closer to the Izmir road and some 350m nearer to the bus station. It is known locally as Maltepe, a name taken to mean 'treasure hill'.

This name implies that the locals preferred to remember valuables once buried there, not the name of its occupant. It is the best known of Bergama's ancient tombs, and George Bean [3] tells us quite a lot about it. It has a diameter of

Fig.13.4. Maltepe in 1991 from the NE, with the entrance on the left.

some 150m and was originally surrounded by a wall, of which only the filling remains in a few places. On the north side a passage about 3.15m wide and 4.45m high and about 75m long leads into the mound. It is lined with handsome ashlar masonry and roofed with a vault. It ends in a cross-passage about 17m long running right and left, off which open three grave-chambers, in which fragments of sarcophagi were found. This part is also handsomely built and vaulted. The method of construction was to erect the masonry first, then to heap the tumulus over it. On the summit stood a monument, but the architectural fragments recovered by the excavators were not enough to indicate its nature. Hansen [4] tells us that, because the walls and doors had been built with lime mortar, Dorpfeld regarded the monument as Roman. However, the use of mortar was later found in two cisterns which belong to the main period of Attalid kingdom, and therefore to the 1st half of 2C. Thus this mound could be Hellenistic, but not earlier. The remains of a structure on the top led to a local belief it belonged to Auge, mother of Telephos. Pausanias (8.4.9) said Auge's tomb could still be seen in his day at Pergamon; '…it is a tumulus of earth surrounded by a stone platform and surmounted by a naked woman in bronze.' Its owner was obviously wealthy, and if the Hellenistic date is correct, it may have belonged to one of the rulers of Pergamon, or to an honoured member of the royal family.

When John Lascelles visited Bergama in 1991 the tomb was open, but when I saw it in 2003 the entrance was barred. I was told that it would be reopened when it had been cleaned up and lights had been installed. From its location, he speculated that Maltepe was the tomb of Marina [5]. However, its attribution to the Hellenistic era militates against this suggestion.

I first came across Hansen's book 'The Attalids of Pergamon' in that wonderful facility, the Rotunda Reading Room in the British Museum. Here, all sorts of rare and out of print books were freely accessible to the general public. This facility was closed in 2007 to make way for an exhibition, but I hope it will return to the museum in due course. Since Radt's book on Pergamon is not available in English, and since my German is poor to non-existent, finding Hansen's book there was a real stroke of luck. She mentions [6] two smaller mounds to the south of Maltepe that were excavated in 1906 by Conze and

Fig.13.5. Entrance passage to Maltepe in 2003.

found to be rich Hellenistic burials of c300-200. The mounds had a base ring of stone blocks some 30m in diameter, as seen in Fig.13.6. [7] They contained stone sarcophagi with the contents undisturbed, evidently the tombs of a prominent man and his wife. Inside was a golden oak wreath with a tiny figure of Nike, two centimetres high in the front centre of it. On the left side of the man lay a long sword, on his right a short one, both of iron. His spurs were there also. Hansen added that the contents of the larger mounds must have been correspondingly richer. Here was the evidence I'd been hoping to find. It showed that, at least in these two tombs, the dead had been allowed to sleep undisturbed for over 2,000 years without being robbed by local inhabitants or foreign invaders. Surely, then, there was a good chance that the unexplored tomb mounds may contain burials still intact.

Yigma Tepe

The largest of all the tomb mounds, called Yigma tepe, stands some 700m SE

Fig. 13.6. A Hellenistic tomb mound excavated in 1906.
(From 'Pergamon' by W. Radt. 1999)

of Maltepe. Its local name is sometimes written as Yimatepe, which we were told means 'a heaped up mound'. It is about 30m high, and has a circumference of some 500m. When I saw it in 2003 it was discoloured by a recent grass fire, but a few hardy thorn bushes have survived.

This mound, seen in Fig. 13.7, is different from the other two in that it was surrounded by a wide shallow ditch that may once have been much deeper. The material dug out was probably used to build the mound. It is also located well out towards the middle of the plain, whereas both Maltepe and our 'Old Aesyetes tomb' are quite close to the northern foothills.

Another difference is that its sides appear rather steep. It has no entrance passage, and has a large depression on its northern side. This, we are told, is evidence that it was once ransacked. Hansen explained its odd appearance: 'A deep cut in the side, made in an attempt in the Byzantine era to rob the tomb, gives the mound the appearance of having a double point, and for this reason it was for some time regarded as the *heroum* (a hero's tomb) of Pergamus and Andromache.' [8]

The mound was partially investigated by German archaeologists in 1907.

Fig.13.7. Yigma tepe as seen from Maltepe.

The photograph, Fig. 13.8, shows the stonework around its base. [9] This revealed a ring of three or four courses of long blocks of stone laid round the circumference of this mound to form its base. These stones, laid without mortar, were mainly of roughly rectangular cross-section, with rounded unfinished ends. The quality of the masonry suggested that this was a royal tomb, but a tunnel driven into the mound in 1909 failed to find a grave chamber, and it was concluded that one probably did not exist. In the guidebooks, Yigma tepe is also dated to the Hellenistic or Roman periods, but the reasons for this are not explained. The blocks of stones shaped like long loaves of bread look to me as though they could be much earlier.

Who was Myrine, and how well does Yigma tepe match her tomb? Some translators refer to Myrine as 'light of step', and hence to the 'tomb of dancing Myrine'. Others believe she was called 'much-bounding', perhaps a reference to her exploits on horseback, and assume she was an Amazon. In the Iliad (2.811ff) we read: 'There is in front of the city a steep mound far out in the plain, with a clear space round it on all sides; this men call Batieia, but the immortals call it the grave mound of Myrine, light of step.' It was around this tomb that the Trojans and their allies first lined up to face each other in battle formation.

171

Fig. 13.8. Yigma Tepe as partially excavated in 1907.
(From 'Pergamon' by W. Radt. 1999)

The bus-loads of visitors who disgorge on the Pergamon acropolis, but who do not stop in the town, get a good but distant view of Yigma tepe from the coach park. Looking west across Bergama, as in Fig. 13.9, the most prominent building is the Roman Red Basilica in the foreground. Yigma tepe can just be seen in the distance, beyond and to the left of this building, standing well out in the plain and away from the northern foothills. The top of the more gently sloping Maltepe can just be made out near the foot of the hill on the right. So Yigma tepe appears an excellent match for the Tomb of Myrine. It has 'a clear space round it on all sides', since it stands on its own and well out into the plain. Here a large army could easily be drawn up around it. And we have one more clue. The only epithet used to describe this mound is 'steep', which should mark a distinctive feature of the mound. As the photographs show, this epithet also applies to Yigma tepe.

Looking at this mound from the acropolis, we remember the scene before the battle in Book 3 of the Iliad, where the ageing King Priam sat with Helen by

Fig. 13.9. Bergama from the side of the acropolis, looking SW, 2005.

the Scaean Gate. There he asked her, with her youthful eyesight, to point out to him the leading heroes of the Achaeans. Some scholars have claimed that, since the two sides had been fighting each other for some nine years, it is unlikely that such introductions would have been necessary, so the lines were probably a later addition. If our identification of this mound is correct, we would have some sympathy for old king Priam and his failing eyesight. Even with the aid of a long distance camera lens used it would be very difficult to recognise a particular hero from this distance. Was this passage a later addition? Or was it simply a poetic device used by the Poet to remind his audience of the key participants in the forthcoming battle?

Rieu translates 'Batieia' as 'Thorn Hill', 'Batieia' meaning a thorn bush. They are almost the only type of bush that will grow without watering in such exposed conditions, where the dry season can last as much as six months. A few small thorn bushes were growing on both Yigma tepe and our Old Aesyetes tomb, as perhaps they did when the poet saw them 2,700 years ago.

Tavsan Tepe

There is a fourth mound at Bergama, known locally as Tavsan tepe, meaning rabbit hill (Fig. 13.10). It lies due south of the acropolis between the Bergama Çayi and the Kestel Çayi. It is of similar size to our 'Old Aesyetes' mound. In 2003 it was within an enclosed yard for reclaimed building materials. The mound itself was planted with olive bushes. To climb onto the mound I had to find my way through an occupied cattle shed belonging to the local owner. However, when seen by Lascelles in 1991, Fig.13.11, it was still in the open plain.

Fig. 13.10. Tavsan tepe, possibly the Tomb of Hector, from the NW.

A point to notice in the foreground of Fig 13.11 is the bridge over the dry bed of the Ketios river. This river now has a dam built across it, forming a large lake to the north and east of the acropolis. The lake provides water supplies for the rapidly growing city.

Apart from the tombs of Myrine and Old Aesyetes, the only other important burial mentioned in the Iliad as being near Troy is the barrow of Hector. So can we identify Tavsan tepe as Hector's tomb? His burial is described at the very end of the Iliad. Priam had asked Achilles for a truce, so that the proper funeral rites for Hector could be observed. 'For nine days we will wail for him in our halls, and on the tenth day we will make his funeral, and the people will feast, and on the eleventh we will heap a mound over him, and on the twelfth we will do battle, if we must.' (Il. 24.664-667). As for the burial rites, we are told that Hector's body was first cremated on a large pyre, and then the fire was quenched

Fig.13.11. Tavsan tepe from the south face of the acropolis, 1991.

with wine. Then the bones were '...placed in a golden urn...the urn laid in a hollow grave, and covered it over with great close-set stones. Then they quickly heaped the mound...' (Il 24.795-800). We are not told where this barrow was, but it must have been quite close to Troy, as a keen watch was kept in case the Achaeans broke the truce and attacked without warning.

Given the circumstances, it would be understandable if time did not permit the building of an abnormally large mound. It would also be understandable if, given the Trojans' concern about being attacked, this mound was built on the far side of the Bergama Çayi. The river could form a potential defensive barrier should the Achaeans break the truce and attack. There may not have been time to ensure that its sides had a uniform slope all the way round. Notice that we can see this in Fig.13.10, where the SW slope is more convex than that on the opposite side. The 'great close-set stones' could be ones similar to those used in Yigma tepe, our Myrine's tomb, shown in Fig.13.8. From such considerations, I think that Tavsan tepe is a reasonably good candidate for Hector's barrow. Radt thought that it had never been excavated. Is it too much to hope that one day the golden urn containing Hector's ashes might be discovered, lying undisturbed below some 'great close-set stones' at the base of this mound?

General comments on these tomb mounds

A good general discussion (in German) of Bergama's tomb mounds and graves is given by Radt [10]. He says that the graves of the dead at Pergamon were not investigated systematically. Most were to the NE of the town, where lots of small rings of stone were found in the Ketios valley, but graves were found everywhere. Many were destroyed by tomb robbers in past ages, and most were found empty and by accident. Tumuli, or traces of them, large and small, were found on the lower part of the acropolis and further up. In both Hellenistic and Roman times it was common practice among the wealthy to build such mounds. Radt thought that Maltepe may have had some sort of structure on top, perhaps a shrine or temple or tomb decoration to honour the dead, such as that seen by Pausanias on the tomb of Andromache. Radt, as already explained, thought that neither Tavsan tepe nor our Old Aesyetes tomb had ever been opened.

A Google Earth image of the three tomb mounds in western Bergama is shown in Fig 13.12.

Fig. 13.12 The three tomb mounds in west Bergama

Given the uncertainties over the number and dates of tomb mounds, we can only speculate that three of the four surviving mounds here date back to Trojan times. If so, could these have belonged to Old Aesyetes, Myrine and Hector? The two Hellenistic mounds excavated near Maltepe were undisturbed, which supports Radt's suggestion that no organised or methodical programme of tomb robbing has taken place in modern times. So, however unlikely it may seem, these three tomb mounds of the Trojan era, named in the Iliad, may still be found at Bergama.

Bergama's two rivers

Two rivers flow from north to south, one on either side of the acropolis. The Bergama Çayi (Greek 'Selinos') is on the west side, and the Kestel Çayi (Greek 'Ketios', Roman 'Cetius') is to the east. They drain the upland region called Pindarsos Kozak, part of the Madradag, the SE part of the Ida massif. The rapid growth of Bergama has meant that these rivers have had to provide ever more water for the growing population. The recent water supply dam across the Kestel Çayi has already been mentioned.

Today, these two rivers are artificially controlled. Upstream, tunnels between the two river valleys allow water from the Bergama Çayi to pass into the Kestel Çayi, boosting the amount of water being stored behind the dam. But in summer, both river channels through the town are almost dry. This means that today we cannot appreciate what the natural flow in the Bergama Çayi was like in Trojan times. However, we can still get some idea of the size of ancient storm flows in the Bergama Çayi from the size of the twin culverts under the Red Hall or Basilica. Eumenes II is credited with bringing water to the city from the springs that feed these two rivers, a feat that was described as 'the mightiest (work) of its kind before the Romans.' [11]. As already mentioned, the remains of this aqueduct and its supporting piers, which filled small storage reservoirs in various places on the acropolis, are still visible today. As Pergamon expanded under Roman rule, several other aqueducts were built to sustain the city's increasing demand for water. A study of Pergamon's water supply was made by Jones [12]. He showed that a system of spring-water collection pipes was constructed westwards close to the small valley of the Teledere towards the Asklepion. This helps explain why the flow from the springs behind Musalla Mezarlik today is much less than we might have expected.

The Bergama Çayi, or Selinos

The Bergama Çayi was known to the Greeks and Romans as the Selinos. It must be crossed by all those approaching Pergamon from Bergama and the lower valley.

Fig. 13.13 shows the Bergama Çayi flowing under the Roman two-arch bridge before passing towards the twin culverts under a modern bungalow and the Roman Red Hall a further 100m down river. It provides one of four river crossing points for people and traffic crossing over to the old town on the lower slopes of the acropolis. The Athena Pension, mentioned in the Prologue as my home during my first visit, is only some 100m from this bridge, so it became a familiar landmark as I explored the town.

Fig.13.13. The Bergama Çayi flowing south, June 2003.

The second culvert on the left is obscured by a bush just in front of it. When I first walked to the top of the acropolis I crossed this bridge. I then followed a well worn path past a few rows of ancient houses, and through a large hole in the chain link fencing at the foot of the hill. Apparently this was a route used in summer by some local residents, seen early one morning, who were picking wild tobacco plants on the north side of the hill. Perhaps this explains why it is known locally as Tabak bridge.

A little way downstream there is another old bridge with three arches, Fig. 13.14. The guidebooks say it was built in the Byzantine era, and it does seem to have smaller and better faced stone blocks than those used in Tabak Bridge.

However, if you look closely you will notice that the base of the piers of both bridges appeared to be of an older type of stone construction than the more sophisticated stonework of the Roman and Byzantine arches they support. This suggests to me that these piers may be earlier than Attalid or Roman times. So again I found myself wondering if, like the tomb mounds, they could

Fig.13.14. The three arch Byzantine bridge over the Bergama Çayi.

Fig.13.15. The Bergama Çayi where it emerges from the twin culverts.

date back to the Archaic or even Trojan eras. Did these piers once support a wooden bridge?

Finding the Skamander

How can we explain the origin of the name 'Skamander'? At Hisarlik, the Mendere is the only river flowing past Hisarlik. Those believing in Troy at Hisarlik have therefore no option but to assume that the Greek name 'Mendere' was somehow derived from an older local name 'Skamander'. Although 'mander' and 'Mendere' appear similar, the initial letters 'Ska' present a difficulty for the linguistics experts. Korfmann was aware of this problem, since he started to call it the 'Kara Mendere', a name quite unknown to early explorers of the Troad. I assume that he added the name 'Kara', which means 'black', so as to make its derivation from 'Skamander' sound more plausible. However, this does not sit comfortably with the other name for the Skamander, Xanthus, which means 'yellow'. So there are good reasons for questioning the identification of the Mendere as the Skamander.

At Bergama, the chances of finding this name appear, at first sight, worse than at Hisarlik. The names 'Bakir Çayi', or 'Kaikos' are quite unlike 'Skamander'. According to Leaf, this name is probably not Greek. If he is right and it is

Anatolian, there is a chance that it may still be found once we are looking at the right river.

River names can be some of a country's most ancient words, since they are handed down by countless generations of people living beside them. Hansen [13], from late 19th century German scholars, tells us a little about the earliest people of Bergama and their languages. 'They left their record in this region in a few place names: Cetius (or Ketios), the earlier name of the Caicus, Pindarsus, Nacrasa and Cidanis, the earlier name of Elaea.' Later newcomers from Europe, who spoke a branch of Thraco-Phrygian, an Indo-European language, also left traces of their language in topographical names. 'To them have been assigned the words Caicus, Pergamos, and Teuthrania.' She then adds that when the Greek colonists arrived they either settled on the coast, or further in land on the heights that commanded the surrounding plain. [14] If such early names survive, then the name Skamander may also be found here if it really existed. Or was it possible that this name, like 'Samothrace', had been added in by a later poet? I think this unlikely. Surely the name of the river of Troy was too entwined within the story of the Iliad, and its name would have been too widely known since earliest times, for a later poet to get away with changing it?

We know from the Iliad that the Skamander carries water which comes from Mt. Ida. At Bergama, the Bergama Çayi is fed by water from the hills of Ida. We are also told (Il.22.146-7) that the two springs at Troy feed the Skamander. Overflow from the springs behind Musalla Mezarlik flow into the Bergama Çayi. On this evidence, could the Bergama Çayi also be the Skamander? The problem is that the earlier Greek name of the Bergama Çayi was the Selinos, which bears no resemblance to 'Skamander'.

Fortunately, a possible answer to this problem soon emerged. In the summer of 2002 I found a book containing a map which showed that the Bergama Çayi had an earlier local name, the 'Uç Kemer Çayi'. [15] What does this name mean? 'Uç' is Turkish for 'three'. The Turkish word 'Kemer' usually means an arch. Yet I was told by two amateur archaeologists in Bergama that it can also mean a 'belt'. We already know that 'Çayi' means 'river'. So the Turkish name 'Uç Kemer Çayi', 'three-arch-river', could derive from the fine 3-arch Byzantine bridge below the Red Hall. The word 'belt' could also apply here in the sense of a constraint. As a belt constrains a human waist, so a culvert constrains a river in its channel; a culverted river could be imagined as a belted river. Cook [16] also noted that 'Kemer' can mean 'bridge' or 'aqueduct', and suggested that the name of the Kemer Su at Hisarlik came from the arches of the Roman aqueduct carrying water over it. The word 'Kemer' was also known to Strabo, so it is an ancient pre-Turkish word. In short, 'Kemer Çayi' could suggest an 'arched-over', or 'belted' river. Professor Radt told me that in Turkey today a 1-2m wide stream is always a 'dere', but one 10m wide is either a small 'Çayi' or a large 'dere'. But 'dere' is also a good old Russian word for 'river', while the Turkish word 'Çayi' is probably more recent. So here is another clue. In pre-Turkish times the Uç Kemer Çayi could well have been called the 'Kemer dere'. Is it credible that the Iliadic name 'Skamander' derived from 'Kemer dere'? I think so, but certainty may be a bridge too far. Perhaps the poet used the same name for the river flowing past Pergamon as for the river in the plain. If so, then the main river in the middle and upper valleys would have had a different name. This could then have been the Ketios, if, as Hansen says, this was the earlier name for the Kaikos.

How old is the culvert?

Another question arises. If the Bergama Çayi was Troy's Skamander, then every passage to and from the acropolis of Ilios through the Scaean Gate must have crossed this river. Surely, when describing the fighting near Troy, any bridge over the Skamander by the Scaean Gate would have been an important strategic feature of the battlefield? Narrow bridges could have severely disrupted access to Ilios, particularly if a large army was fleeing back to the safety of the acropolis. The river itself would also have formed a natural last line of defence against an attack using chariots. Given the continuous need for the people of both the upper and lower cities to cross this river, a number of bridges would surely have been built over it. Can we explain Homer's silence on this subject by suggesting that the river was already culverted in Trojan times? Is there any evidence to support this possibility?

Today, the Bergama Çayi in summer is almost dry. This is largely because, further upstream, water is now diverted into the Kestel river and the new dam. In Trojan times, while summer flows would normally have been very low, winter flows would have been much greater. The wide banks and the two large culverts are silent witnesses to the great volume of flood water that once flowed through Pergamon. What, I wondered, gave the Romans the idea of placing such an important building on this particular site? Did this ancient culvert pre-date the arrival of the Romans? Was the Red Hall built at a time when defence of the acropolis was no longer considered a priority, when few had need to dwell there, and when the long culverted section was not needed for military or civilian purposes?

A useful description of this culvert is given by Klaus Nohlen [17]:
'The flat surface for the sanctuary [of the Red Hall] was obtained by covering the Selinus with two parallel barrel vaults running diagonally underneath the temenos to a length of c150m. They still serve their original purpose by supporting parts of the city of Bergama. With their spans of nearly 10m each, the well functioning channels were able to drain even the most enormous floods of the river. The vertical walls consist of mortared rubble with a facing of small square bricks, while the vaults themselves are radially-set boulders. In the crown of the vaults are square openings of nearly half a metre in length set at regular intervals. Whether they were closed, or originally served just for draining the water from the surface, or perhaps even had a cultic use inside the courtyard, is impossible to decide. [18] This masterpiece of Roman engineering is not only a strong construction, it is a subtle one: upstream the ashlar vault-head arches face the arriving water in identical alignment, while downstream the vaults extend just far enough to support the southern temenos wall in a very economical manner.'

This description confirms that the culvert was built, or rebuilt, in Roman times to support the Red Hall. But the possibility remains that the Romans got the idea for it from an earlier culvert on the same site. Nohlen comments on the extreme far-sightedness of the builders, in providing a culvert with a capacity of 760 cubic metres per second – sufficient to carry approximately a 1000 year storm. What better way of knowing how big such a culvert should be to avoid flooding, than by replicating an earlier one that had stood there, successfully containing the largest floods, for a thousand years?

Apart from the size of the Roman culvert, some of the stones used in the piers of both the culvert and the bridge upstream of the culvert, seen in Figs. 13.13 and

13.14, seemed very ancient. They reminded me of the large stone blocks with rounded ends used to form the base of Yigma tepe, which I have tentatively identified with the Trojan Tomb of Myrine. Professor Hertel found similar stones with rounded ends, that he described as resembling a loaf (of bread) in what he thought were the earliest walls on the acropolis, dating to the Bronze Age. [19] Is it possible that these blocks and piers were part of original bridges here that dated back to the Trojan era? Or is this just another example of old materials being reused? We must leave this for the experts to decide. But I will speculate that once Troy and its acropolis of Ilios were built, the Trojans will soon have realized that access between the two was too important to be restricted by one or two bridges. So they built a culvert for the river, with stone sides, roofed with wooden beams covered with small stones and packed earth. In due course the culvert may have been enlarged if this was found necessary, and the wooden beams would eventually have been replaced with stone arches, possible more than once.

In short, if the culverted section of the Bergama Çayi has a Trojan origin, then the name Skamander, for the 'Kemer dere', the arched-over, or 'belted', river, needs no further explanation. And, as a bonus, the site of the Scaean Gate of Ilios may also be sought on the lower slopes of Pergamon directly opposite this culvert.

Conclusions

In this chapter we have found that we can identify several more features in the plain around Bergama that are described in the Iliad. The three tomb mounds, Myrine, Old Aesyetes and Hector, may possibly still be found as and where described. The only other tomb mound still visible there today, Maltepe, is dated on archaeological grounds to the Hellenistic or Roman eras. A possible source of the name Skamander has been found in 'Kemer dere', perhaps a pre-Turkish name for the Uç Kemer Çayi, now the Bergama Çayi. It is also suggested, from the ancient construction of the bridge piers, that the culverted section may date back to Trojan times. This might then explain why the poet mentions no bridge between Ilios and the plain. Alternatively, since no such river exists beside Hisarlik, all mentions of this river and any bridges over it by the poet may have been removed by those placing Troy at Hisarlik, as part of the Troy deception.

CHAPTER 14

FURTHER EVIDENCE FROM BERGAMA AND LESBOS

Introduction. The island burial place of Achilles and Patroclus? Teuthrania in Mysia. Poseidon's underwater palace at Aigai or Aiga. Elaia and the tomb of Protesilaus. Early and Late Bronze Age settlements on Lesbos. The journey home from Troy. Summary and Conclusion.

Introduction

In Part 2 of this book, I have shown that all the descriptions of the Trojan landscape in the Iliad have been found, as and where described, in the plain of the Bakir Çayi below Bergama. This evidence, by itself, is sufficient for me to claim, beyond reasonable doubt, that at last we have found the Homeric plain of Troy. In this chapter I will introduce further supporting geographical evidence from near, but outside, the field of battle.

The island burial place of Achilles and Patroclus?

One of the best known monuments in the ancient world stands close to Sigeum near the mouth of the Hellespont. This is the burial mound of Achilles. This tomb mound, visible from far out to sea, was said to mark the final resting place of the greatest of the Greek hero warriors. It was a sacred site long before it was effectively consecrated by Alexander the Great, who is said to have danced naked around the mound during some ritual ceremony. Over a century ago Schliemann burrowed irreverently into it, and found no evidence

185

of a Mycenaean cremation burial. The finds were mostly trinkets dating from the 6th or 5th century. The integrity of this site then became suspect. Now we have shown that the Trojan plain was at Bergama, clearly this mound can be no more than a later cenotaph. Yet if Achilles was a real historical person who died at Troy, and if he was not buried near Hisarlik, where was he buried?

First, as always, we will look at what the poet has to say. Since the Iliad ends before the death of Achilles, the tale of his burial is told in the Odyssey. Here, in a scene from Hades in Book 24, we find the ghost of Agamemnon talking to the ghost of Achilles. Achilles was reassured to learn that he was buried with full honours and ceremony. He was told that his dead body had been cleansed, treated with unguents, and wrapped in immortal clothing. His funeral was attended by his mother Thetis, accompanied by nine immortal sea nymphs. After seventeen days of mourning he was placed on a pyre. 'But when the flame of Hephaestus had made an end of you, in the morning we gathered your white bones, Achilles, and laid them in unmixed wine and unguents. Your mother had given a two-handled golden urn, and said it was a gift of Dionysus, the handiwork of famed Hephaestus. In this lie your white bones, glorious Achilles, and mingled with them are the bones of the dead Patroclus… And over them we heaped up a huge and flawless tomb…on a projecting headland by the broad Hellespont, that it might be seen from far over the sea both by men that now are and that shall be born hereafter.' (Od. 24.71-84) When the mound was finished, games were held in his honour, and beautiful prizes for the winners were brought from the gods by Thetis.

Other translations differ slightly. Rieu here says Achilles was given 'a great and glorious mound', but Shewring describes it as 'a tall cairn on a jutting headland'. Is this difference significant? A tall cairn would usually be made of stones. But at Hisarlik the so-called tomb of Achilles, while being on a headland and visible from far out to sea, was apparently a huge mound built mainly of soil.

Now, having found the plain of Troy at Bergama, I must assume that whoever 'moved' the Trojan plain to beside the Hellespont had to 'move' Achilles' tomb there as well. With Troy at Hisarlik, Achilles had to be buried nearby, and a headland at Sigeum seemed as good a place as any. We know now that it is more likely that he was buried near Elaia, but here we find no obvious candidate for his tomb. One may have existed which has since been destroyed, but with other ancient tomb mounds still found in the area, this seems unlikely. So the problem remains. If Achilles was buried close to the Greek Camp near Elaia and given a suitably grand tomb mound visible from far out at sea, can I find his burial place?

Given the Greek genius for story-telling there must, from earliest times, have been many tales about the death and burial of Achilles. Fortunately, a slightly different one seems to have been handed down by tradition and recorded for us by Apollodorus. In his Epitome, Apollodorus wrote 'The death of Achilles filled the army with dismay, and they buried him with Patroclus in the White Isle, mixing the bones of the two together.'[1] Then he adds that the funeral games which followed included contests in chariot-racing, running, quoits and archery. Now why, I wondered, should Apollodorus, writing as late as the 2nd century BC, give a different description of the burial place for Achilles than that given by Homer? In the Loeb edition of Apollodorus the translator, J.G. Frazer, discusses some of the different accounts of the funeral of Achilles. He tells us that this version comes from the Aethiopis, one of the poems of the Epic Cycle. It was thought to have been written by Arctinus of Miletus, an early Greek poet who was regarded as a disciple of Homer. Frazer, assuming along with the rest of the world that Achilles was buried near Sigeum, pointed out that the statement by Apollodorus that he was buried on the White Isle 'must be regarded as erroneous'.

Now perhaps we can disagree with Frazer. With Achilles buried near Elaia, an island burial becomes a distinct possibility. The story we have from Apollodorus gains a new credibility. Perhaps it is a survival, thanks to Arctinus, from the original Homeric story. So is there a White Isle near Elaia? Did the poet's story of the burial of Achilles on the 'White Isle', possibly preserved by the Homeridae on Chios, manage to survive separately from the version in the Odyssey? Could this be a genuine ancient tradition which sailed on independently through the centuries in the work of Apollodorus, to arrive intact in the present day? I think this is quite possible.

As it happens there is an island not far from Elaia that offers a plausible site for the burial place of Achilles and Patroclus. In 2003 I was driven round the new

Kara Dag coastal road, from where I took the photograph of the island, Fig. 14.1. (see colour plate section). John Lascelles, in his unpublished book, suggested that this island could be the White Isle mentioned as the burial place of Achilles and Patroclos by Apollodorus. He visited the island, called Kiz Kulesi, in 1991 with the help of two local boatmen, and took a few photographs of it.

From my vantage point the true size and shape of the island is not apparent. It is the largest of a group of islands which, as seen on the old Admiralty Map, Fig. 12.1, was earlier known as Mardalich Adasi, 'adasi' meaning 'island'. The island is of limestone, as seen in Fig. 14.2.

If the white face of a hill was seen from the sea or the mainland in ancient times, this could explain the name 'White Island'. It may or may not be significant that the small island beside it to the east is called 'Kara Adasi' or 'Black island' on the Admiralty chart. Were these two adjacent islands once called 'Black Island' and 'White Island'? This idea does have a certain appeal.

Fig. 14.2 View looking west from Kiz Kulesi, showing a white limestone hill face.

Also clearly visible from the shore is a conspicuous watchtower on the lower hill on its western end. This is seen in Fig. 14.3. Lascelles considered that its exterior stonework was probably Byzantine, but the interior is of rounded stones, such as are commonly found all over the plain on the mainland. A number of questions spring to mind. I wondered why the builders had placed a watchtower here on the lower end of this island, rather than on the other end which is higher. Was this tower re-faced in Byzantine times? Was it built here because a large pile of stones was already found there? If so, could this earlier pile of stones have once formed a burial monument or cairn? Could this old watchtower possibly mark the burial place of Achilles, and possibly also Patroclos?

Lascelles was amazed to find that a large central grassy area existed on the island, not visible from the mainland. This is seen in Fig. 14.4. Both the Odyssey and Apollodorus tell us that after the joint burial of Achilles and Patroclus, traditional funeral games were held in honour of the dead heroes.

Fig.14.3. Ancient lookout tower on Kiz Kulesi island.

Could the Achaeans have held the funeral games of Achilles in this large open space? Is there enough room here for a chariot race? Or were the funeral remains brought here for burial, and the games, or at least the chariot race, held on the mainland? This place, well away from the eyes of the Trojans, would certainly have been safe from any surprise attack.

The sight of the prominent mound on the island beyond this open space prompts another question. Was a cairn or mound once built here on the hill shown in Fig.14.4? I hope that some day someone will be able to provide answers to these speculative questions. The modern name of this island, Kiz Kulesi, means 'Maiden's tower'. Lascelles commented that 'Because it has a tower, the island appears to be named by analogy with the famous island of Kiz Kulesi, 'Maiden's Tower' or 'Tower of Leander', at the junction of the Bosphorus and the Sea of Marmara.' I have been unable to discover an obvious Turkish meaning for the earlier name 'Mardalic', and can only wonder if perhaps this name may have come from an ancient local official or owner.

Fig.14.4. The surprising large open space on the island in front of the old watchtower.

Whether or not this was the case, it remains possible that its earlier name could have been 'White Island'. [2]

To summarise, I am speculating that all stories about the tomb of Achilles being built on a headland at Sigeum derive from a time after Troy was moved to Hisarlik. This is supported by archaeological evidence from the tomb mounds. A more likely burial place of Achilles, perhaps as originally told by the poet and later by Arctinus and Apollodorus, was the White Isle. This island may tentatively be identified as the island known today as Kiz Kulesi, off the coast not far from Elaia. Perhaps it was anciently called 'White Island' from exposed limestone faces, such as that seen in Fig. 14.2.

Teuthrania in Mysia

As mentioned in Chapter 1, in historical times Teuthrania, the ancient city of the Teucrians, was in the lower Kaikos valley. Pausanias (1.4.5.) said it was the earlier name for Pergamon, although modern scholars do not agree with him. Perhaps Pausanias was referring to the territory ruled from both places, rather

Fig. 14.5. A possible site of Teuthrania – Tartar tepe?

than to the cities themselves. Strabo (13.1.69) located Teuthrania to the north of the Kaikos, between Elaia, Pitane, Atarneus and Pergamon, not more than 70 stades (c. 15km) from any of them.

In recent times archaeologists have tried to locate its site. German archaeologists in the days of Dorpfeld thought it was at Kalarga Hill. But Walter Leaf, when he visited the region in 1911, found no evidence there of Bronze Age occupation. He preferred instead to suggest that Teuthrania was on a mound to the west of Kalarga Hill, where he found some Bronze Age material. There are a number of mounds in the plain here, most of which look as if they were formed by volcanic extrusion, the same geological process that formed Kalarga Hill and Erigol tepe. The site preferred by Leaf is, I think, the one shown in Fig. 14.5. This photo was taken looking south-east from the Dikili-Bergama road, at a mound some 2 km west of Kallikolone. This may be the tepe shown on the 1941 Military map, Fig 9.1., as Tatar tepe, a name which could carry a faint echo of the name 'Teuthrania'. It may not have been mentioned by the poet, since it lies well to the west of the Trojan battle field, and away from the action now reported in the Iliad. Alternatively, as suggested earlier, any mention of Teuthrania in the Trojan plain by the poet would have been deleted when Troy was 'moved' to Hisarlik.

When I met him in 2003, Professor Radt told me that Bronze Age remains have subsequently been found at Kalarga Hill. He considered the site chosen by Leaf to be too small for such an important ancient city. So he preferred to join Thramer, Humann and Conze in placing Teuthrania at Kalarga hill, which he said is also known as Prophet Elias.

The possible relationship between Teuthrania and Troy has been mentioned in Chapters 1 and 2. From the Troy foundation legends it appears that Teuthrania, whether here, at Kalarga hill, or somewhere as yet to be identified, was the original home of the pre-Trojan kings and the first Trojans. Later, king Tros moved his town further inland to a much safer site, beside hot and cold springs and a great acropolis, and called it Troy. His son Ilus later built a fortified city on this acropolis which was called Ilios. Any residents who remained at Teuthrania would probably have vacated it rapidly after the Achaeans landed at Elaia, to seek safety behind the walls of Troy.

Teuthrania survived as a town on the plain long after Troy was destroyed. It was mentioned by the later Cyclic poets as the home of Telephos in a region they called Mysia, and by Xenophon in 399. We can now guess that its growth was always limited by the lack of a good water supply. I suggest that the Mysian war and Telephos myths were post-Homeric inventions, designed to obscure the fact that Teuthrania was the original home of the Teucrians or Trojans. If this fact had become widely recognised, it would have been very hard to convince anyone that Homer's Troy was far away from Teuthrania, on the site of Novum Ilium at Hisarlik.

Poseidon's underwater palace at Aegae or Aiga

We have already shown that Poseidon probably came to the Greek camp from Samos, not Samothrace, to help the Achaeans in their battle against the Trojans. When he did so, our reconstruction of the journey suggests that he left his chariot in a subterranean cave near the Greek camp. As discussed in Chapter 8, I concluded that Homer's 'Aigai' may actually have been the 'Aiga' of Strabo and Alcaeus, and that it was changed from Aiga to Aigai as part of 'moving' Troy to Hisarlik. Today this is called the Kara Dag peninsula.

In Fig. 14.6 we see the southern ends of the two islands off the west coast of Kara Dag. The southern tip of Lesbos is just visible on the horizon. Leaf [3] referred to these islands as the Aginussai Islands. They are clearly shown on the map, Fig.12.1, which names the nearer one as Kalemadasi and the far one as Garipadasi. The two islands here are also of limestone, and this white stone is seen along their shorelines. Leaf [4] tells us that these islands 'attained a sinister fame for the defeat of the Spartan fleet here by the Athenians in 406. The bank between them is only some 2-4ft deep.'

Between Kalemadasi and the mainland is a narrow stretch of water about 2km long. Here my taxi driver showed me some hot springs which were bubbling up into the sea just offshore. He then took me to his favourite swimming place nearby. Built into the side of the shallow cliff was an old hot-spring collection chamber. What appear to be large stone blocks nearby suggest that this site was known and enjoyed in ancient times.

Fig.14.6. The two islands off the west coast of Kara Dag.

Fig.14.7 shows a small stone building over the collecting chamber. Fig. 14.8 shows the inside of this chamber, which seems to have a lower step for easy access to the water at the far end. The water temperature, at a guess, was somewhere around 25-30 degrees C. Sites of hot springs like this, which may possibly be found in other places around the shores of the Kara Dag, could well have been special places to the earliest Greeks. Perhaps this spring was considered a gift from the gods, a place favoured by Poseidon, lord of the seas. Certainly Lesbos was one of the very few early cult centres of the Nereids, those beautiful daughters of Poseidon and sisters of Thetis. Did the poet give them a home in a cave near here? Perhaps some local fisherman may know of a large subterranean cavern on these shores, not far from the mouth of the Bakir Çayi, which may have been scoured out of the limestone by hot spring waters.

Elaia and the tomb of Protesilaus

Let us look a little more closely at what is known about Elaia. Strabo, (13:4:1-4), when he recounted its history, said that it was founded by the Athenians.

194

Fig.14.7. (Left) Looking south at the old collection chamber of a hot spring.
Fig 14.8. (Right) Interior of the collecting chamber.

Leaf visited Elaia, which has never been excavated, during his study tour of the Troad in 1911. He said [5] that the ancient harbour was then about 1km from the shore, and the level surface of the silted harbour was being used as a saltpan to dry seawater for salt. Two curving moles with towers once formed the harbour. Nearby was a small oval hill, 15m high and 300 paces in length, now called mal-tepe (treasure-hill), which was the acropolis. The oldest Elaia covered only some 15 acres but the Roman town was larger. He said it was once an Aeolic town, but wondered why an Aeolic town could have been founded by Athenians. However, coins from Roman Imperial times showed that it claimed Menestheus, king of Athens, as its founder. Herodotus did not include it in his list as one of the original Aeolic towns, but from its location it was politically Aeolian. Leaf thought it may originally have been Mysian and, like Adramyttion, became Hellenised in the 5th century. It first appeared in the Delian league, paying 1000 drachmas in 452-440. Coins from Elaia are known dating to c450, and the town became important with the rise of Pergamon. In earlier times, the territory of Pergamon did not include the towns on the coast. The 'barbarian' origins of Pergamon kept it apart from the Hellenic colonies, despite the long reigns there of Demaratos and his family, and the Attalid dynasty. This, Leaf added, may explain why Strabo treated Elaia separately from Pergamon.

Pausanias (9.5.7.) also mentions Elaia. He recounts the legend that one of the Attic heroes, Thersander, son of Polyneikes and grandson of Theseus, was killed by Telephos after some heroic fighting in the Kaikos valley. This was claimed to have happened during the Mysian war. His memorial was in Elaia, a stone standing in the market place, and local people sacrificed to him as a divine hero. If not Athenian propaganda, this suggests that a settlement at Elaia may have been founded before the start of the Trojan War, which is what we would expect from our study. It even appears possible that Telephos, possibly the Hittite name 'Telepinus', was the name of a real leader of the Teucrians who was known to the early Greeks, and who took part in the Trojan War. Is it possible that he really did kill Thersander here in the early stages of the Trojan War? Alas, as with so much else, we can only speculate as to what might have happened.

Protesilaus was said to have been the first Achaean to leap from his ship when the fleet landed at Troy, and the first Achaean to die there. As already mentioned, a 'tomb of Protesilaus' is one of those so-called 'Homeric' tomb mounds that are found not far from Hisarlik. Herodotus (9.14) tells us that it was situated at a place called Elaeus on the coast of the Chersonese, almost directly opposite Ilion. Now we have good reason to believe that the fleet landed in Mysia, perhaps his tomb may be found near Mysian Elaia. Provided, of course, that there is any truth in this story. Was the name Elaia/Elaeus taken to the Chersonese from the harbour at Elaia as part of the Troy deception? Professor Radt, at my meeting with him in 2003, said there were several tomb mounds at Elaia, the largest of which he had investigated. This one, like Maltepe at Bergama, had been opened long ago, and was from the Hellenistic or Roman period, not earlier. The acropolis at Elaia has never been excavated, so a tomb of Protesilaus may possibly be one of the unexplored tomb mounds remaining there.

In summary, Leaf speculated that, since Elaia could not claim any Aeolic title deeds, a respectable Homeric ancestry for it was invented as an Attic colony. With the Trojan plain now found here, then whether or not Elaia was a Cretan or an Attic foundation, it seems that it actually did have a good Homeric ancestry all along.

The journey home from Troy

The discovery of the Trojan plain in Mysia should help to shed light on some other Troy-related problems. One of these concerns the Achaeans' return home from Troy. From the Odyssey we learn that, after the sack of Troy, Agamemnon and Menelaus quarrelled over their departure plans. Agamemnon (Od.3.145ff) wanted to stay with the army until they had appeased 'the dread wrath of Athene'. Menelaus, however, wanted to leave without delay. So half the army stayed with Agamemnon, while the other half, which included Menelaus, Odysseus, Nestor and Diomedes, sailed away to Tenedos. There they sacrificed to the gods. Odysseus then decided to go back and join Agamemnon, but Diomedes, Nestor and Menelaus, anxious to get home, sailed on to Lesbos. Here they discussed whether to sail to the east or west of Chios. They 'asked the god to show us a sign, and he showed it us, and bade us cleave through the midst of the sea to Euboea, that we might soonest escape from the misery.'

There is another passing mention of the Achaeans' sojourn on Lesbos in a poem by Sappho. The poems of both Sappho, and her contemporary Alcaeus, were analysed in some detail by Professor Page. [6] He explained that Sappho's poem, in a few important points, portrays a different version from the story told in the Odyssey:

a) Sappho tells us that Agamemnon and Menelaus are both together in Lesbos, but in the Odyssey the two had parted company long ago.
b) Sappho appears to know nothing of any quarrel between them.
c) In Sappho the brothers pray to the Lesbian trinity of Zeus, Hera and Dionysus, but in the Odyssey they pray only to Zeus. The same Lesbian trinity is mentioned in a poem by Alcaeus, where he calls Hera the 'illustrious goddess of Aeolians, mother of all...' [7]
d) In the Odyssey they pray for guidance on the choice of route. But in Sappho, the implication is that they pray to be able to do something that they at present are prevented from doing. Page suggests that what they were prevented from doing was departing from Lesbos because of adverse weather. In the Odyssey there may be an echo of this in the line 'a shrill

fair wind began to blow'. (Od. 3.176) This implies that the wind was unfavourable until Zeus gave the sign.

I think that the difference between these two accounts may now be explained. From the Iliad (Il. 2. 718-723) we learn that the route to Troy from Euboea was via Lemnos and Tenedos. Philoctetes was left behind on Lemnos with a noxious wound from a poisonous sea snake. It would seem reasonable for them to return by the same route, unless prevented from doing so by winds or currents. However, now we know that the Greek camp was at Elaia, to go from Elaia to Lesbos via Tenedos makes no sense. This is further evidence that the mention of Tenedos here in the Odyssey is another interpolation, added as part of the Troy deception.

According to the Odyssey, from Lesbos the choice of the route home was either i) a longer journey, staying in sight of land as much as possible in case of storms. First they would have sailed south to Samos, then turned west, passing close to the islands of Icaria, Delos, Tenos, Andros and on to Euboea; or ii) to head directly west across to Scyros and Euboea. So the choices of route from Lesbos as discussed in the Odyssey make good sense.

What we learn from Sappho's poem may be a genuine reflection of the authentic Homeric tradition. It seems that there was a strong residual folk memory on Lesbos of the returning Achaeans being driven on to their island by a storm after they left Elaia. And, as with the memory of Achaeans fighting in Teuthrania, this was too strong to be ignored by those 'moving' Troy to Hisarlik. They thus had little alternative but to say that the Achaeans departed from Troy at Hisarlik, and arrived at Lesbos via Tenedos. Although to some this will have seemed highly improbable, no doubt an ill wind could have been invoked to support this explanation.

In summary, there is nothing relating to the homeward journey in either the Odyssey, or in the poems of Sappho and Alcaeus, to oppose locating the Trojan plain at Bergama. On the contrary, with the discovery of the Trojan plain now in the Bakir Çayi valley, they can be interpreted as offering significant support for this discovery.

Summary and conclusions

We have found some features in the landscape, outside the battlefield of the Trojan War, which support the theory that the Trojan plain was at Bergama. They show that this wider area is compatible with the Trojan landscape. We have identified a new possible island site for Achilles' tomb. Finding Teuthrania in the Bakir Çayi valley, whether at Tartar hill or Kalarga Hill, provides further evidence for Troy being in this valley. Perhaps the authors of the Troy deception tried to rewrite the legends to obscure such a conclusion.

We have seen the hot springs bubbling up in the sea off the Kara Dag peninsula, perhaps once called Aiga. This coast may, in early times, have been regarded as providing an underground home for Poseidon.

Finally, evidence from Sappho on Lesbos supports the story that the returning Achaeans stopped there on their way home from Troy, perhaps forced to do so by inclement weather. From these circumstances, it seems more likely that they were departing from the Greek camp at Elaia, than from the coast near Hisarlik. The story that some Achaeans went home initially via Tenedos bears the hallmarks of a later interpolation.

CHAPTER 15

MORE GEOGRAPHICAL EVIDENCE FROM STRABO AND LEAF

Introduction. Geographical studies of the Troad by Strabo and Leaf. The Larisa of Hippothous. The return of the daughter of Chryses. The flight of the Kilikes. Dardania and Skepsis. The Gergithes at Ilium. The Keteians of Eurypylus. Conclusions.

Introduction

The traditional stories about the Trojan War covered events that happened far beyond the confines of Mysia and the Iliad, and many of these were known to the bards and their audiences. Unfortunately, the deception as to the whereabouts of Troy gave rise to many later myths, invented in the 6C and later. These later inventions, created to support a new enlarged Athenian version of the Iliad with Troy at Ilion, are entwined with the earlier ones. Thus it becomes very difficult to separate genuine ancient historical legends from later myths.

Although I believe we have now effectively confirmed that the action of the Trojan War, as described in the Iliad, was set against the landscape in the lower Bakir Çayi valley, I have been careful to say that we cannot therefore automatically assume that the war was a real event. Nor can we say that Troy and Ilios were real places. We certainly cannot yet claim as fact that Ilios and Troy were at Bergama and Pergamon.

We can explain different possibilities in different ways:

i)   The landscape of the Achaean's battlefield in the Mysian war may somehow have been later applied, in epic tradition, to the story of Achaean's war against a Troy at Hisarlik. This might have been done, for example, to give added interest to the landscape at Hisarlik, and extra interest to the battle scenes.

ii) The poet of the Iliad did not know where Troy was, perhaps because by his time it had happened so long ago that no-one could remember where it took place. He therefore drew upon the traditional poems of his day to create his masterpiece of 'The wrath of Achilles'. This he set within the lower Kaikos valley, a landscape he knew well. In his story, the real acropolis of Pergamon became Ilios, imagined as the holy acropolis of Troy. In this way, his poems provided a record of this war for posterity, set within a real landscape, but not necessarily on the site of the original war.

iii) The so-called Mysian war, beside the Kaikos river in Mysia, was really the Trojan War. This war was an historical event, and Pergamon really was the acropolis of ancient Troy.

For the present, we will leave a discussion of these, and other possible scenarios until later, after we have looked in Volume 2 for Ilios on Pergamon and for Troy at Bergama. In this chapter we will uncover further evidence, from within the Troad, which supports our discovery of the plain of Troy at Teuthrania. This evidence will also provide some support for our original assumption that the Trojan War was historical.

To find this evidence we must look at the writings of some earlier authorities on Homer. One such authority already mentioned is Strabo. In his study of the geography of the Troad he brought to light a number of interesting problems. The geography of the Iliad did not always appear to agree with his findings. And some of these discrepancies, as we shall see, provide further support for our discovery of the Trojan plain at Bergama.

Geographical studies of the Troad by Strabo and Leaf

First, a word about my sources of information. Both Strabo and Walter Leaf have already received honourable mentions in earlier chapters, so need no further introduction. Strabo, acknowledging the importance of the Troad in relation to Homer and the Trojan War, devoted the whole of his Book 13 to a study of this region. But Leaf believed that Strabo never went there to check the facts on site for himself. Instead, he thought that Strabo relied for his information about its history and geography on the work of Demetrios of Skepsis. Leaf's study of Homer had made him appreciate just how important it was to have a sound knowledge of the geography of this region. So in 1911 he carried out a major study of the Troad. He toured the region with Strabo in hand, gathering vast amounts of information. This he compared with the findings of Demetrios as reported by Strabo. In 1923 he published a monumental and invaluable study entitled 'Strabo on the Troad'. [1] In it, Leaf brought an illuminated magnifying glass to bear upon Strabo's Book 13.

Strabo's study was probably written c10-20CE, while his source, Demetrios of Skepsis, wrote perhaps about 150 years earlier. Demetrios is said to have devoted his life to writing a geographical commentary in thirty separate books on Homer and the Trojan catalogue. Sadly, none of his work has survived. Lascelles wondered if the later Athenians, and other guardians of the dogma of the day, could have contributed to the non-survival of some of the earlier work that gave a non-Athenian view of the past. We will probably never know, but it does seem possible. Demetrios studied the geography of the Troad, its towns and its people, as he journeyed throughout the region. He was perhaps the first great scholar to test the Iliad's geographical data concerning the Trojans in comparison with facts as they were then known. Leaf, it seems, was the second. Strabo's study extended as far as Elaia, so he regarded the vast fertile plain of the lower Kaikos valley as bordering the Troad. But he does not explain why a region as large as the Troad should have its capital city in such an inconvenient and peripheral location as Hisarlik. In Book 13:1, Strabo wrote that Demetrios and his followers 'conjectured that the whole of this coast became subject to the Trojans and, though divided under nine dynasties, was under the sway of Priam at the time of the Trojan War and was called Troy.' He then studied each of these nine separate sub-regions in detail, using the historical and legendary information provided by Demetrios. He tried to locate the people and places mentioned in the Iliad, and to follow population movements where legendary or historical evidence allowed. Today, some of these tribes are now lost in antiquity, and many places can no longer be identified with any confidence. But much of the wider geography of the Troad in Homer's day, as inferred from the Iliad, is confirmed by the work of Demetrios, Strabo and Leaf. Evidence for the existence of people and places mentioned in the Iliad comes from a profusion of Homeric legends found embedded across the region. This cumulative evidence strongly supports the view that the Trojan War was a real and local historical event. It also confirms that the poet was familiar with the geography of this wider region. Put simply, the Trojan War left an indelible mark upon the history and geography of the Troad.

During his study, Leaf came to disagree in places with Homer's geography and topography. He also disagreed on occasions with the views of Demetrios and Strabo. Some of these disagreements stemmed from Leaf's belief that Troy was at Hisarlik. Such disagreements are to be expected if we pause and think about it for a moment. We now believe that Troy in the Iliad was not at Hisarlik, but some 150km away at Bergama on the opposite side of the Troad. So if, for example, Homer said that a place was close to Troy, while Leaf found it was far from Hisarlik, Leaf simply assumed that Homer was wrong. He put his faith in Troy at Hisarlik above his faith in Homer's knowledge of geography.

Demetrios preferred to find Troy some 8-10km south-west of Hisarlik at the Village of the Ilians. Both he and Strabo were scathing of the claims of the Ilians that they lived on the site of Troy. It seems that Strabo thought that Ilion and Troy were different and separate paces. Yet neither, so far as we can tell, considered that Troy might lie outside the Mendere Valley.

I will now draw attention to one or two parts of Leaf's study where locating the Iliad's Troy at Bergama resolves some of these disagreements. The problems Strabo and Demetrios faced in reconciling some Homer-related legends with Troy at Hisarlik can then be better understood. With Troy at Bergama, we also have an opportunity to assess the arguments for ourselves, and to discover which of the competing claims we should support.

The Larisa of Hippothous

In the Iliad, Hippothous led the Pelasgian tribes against the Achaeans at Troy. When he was killed, the poet tells us that he died 'far from his native Larisa'. This gives us the geographical clue that Homer's Larisa, wherever that was, is 'far from Troy'. This is a good example of the problems faced by Strabo and Leaf. Where was Homer's Larisa?

As with any Homer-related problem, we must first look at exactly what the Iliad has to say. The list of the Trojan allies (Il. 2:840) tells us, 'And Hippothous led the tribes of the Pelasgians that rage with the spear, them that dwelt in deep-soiled Larisa; these were ruled by Hippothous and Pylaeus, scion of Ares, the two sons of Pelasgian Lethus, son of Teutamus.' The evidence of the Iliad is therefore, in brief, that this Larisa was far from Troy, had fertile soils, and was home to Pelasgians.

Strabo tried his best to make sense of these words. In a section concerned with the area some 25km south of Elaia around Kyme (13.3.2.), he noted that there were enough Pelasgi for more than one tribe. Near Kyme was another place called Larisa, and he assumed this was the one meant by Homer. The location of the two Larisas is shown in sketch map 15.1. He said that the Larisa near Hamaxitos 'was in plain sight of Ilium and very near it, and, therefore, it could not be said with any plausibility that Hippothous fell in the fight over Patroclus 'far away from' this Larisa…'

On the other hand, the Larisa near Kyme, 'Larisa Phr' on the map, short for 'Larisa Phriconis', was some 1000 stadia further away. He also mentioned a third Larisa not far from Ephesus, but this was less well known. So, after considering all three, Strabo chose the one near Kyme as the most likely home of Hippothous. This lies beyond the Troad, in the valley of the river Hermus some 8km south east of Kyme. He ruled out the Pelasgian Larisa at Hamaxitos near Lekton since this was almost within sight of Ilium.

When Leaf came to consider the same problem, he disagreed. He said [2] that Strabo 'blundered in his comments about the home of Hippothous', by trying to stretch the kingdom of Priam much too far to the south. The Larisa near

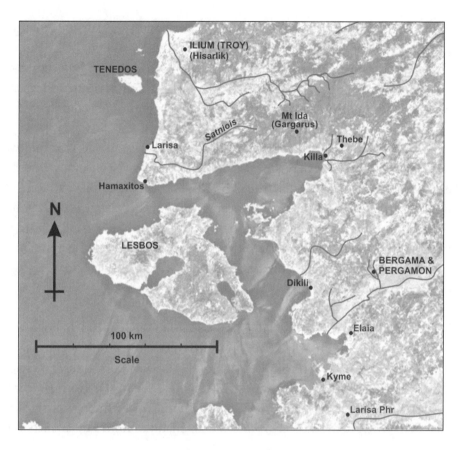

Fig. 15.1 Sketch map showing the location of the two Larisas.

Kyme was not in the Troad, where we would expect to find it. Instead Leaf preferred the historical Larisa near Hamaxitos, not far from Hisarlik. He pointed out [3] that the whole length of the southern shore of Ida, from the Lekton point to the Plain of Thebe, belonged to the Pelasgi. Here these people were divided into two tribes, the Leleges and the Kilikes. He commented [4] on the exceptional fertility of the southern slopes of Ida, which are drained in part by the Satniois. He concluded that the historical Larisa, despite being near Ilium, is clearly the one intended by Homer.

Now Homer (Il. 10.428) also mentions 'Altes, king over the war-loving Leleges, who holds steep Pedassos on the Satniois.' So we know that the Leleges were present at Troy, and that their king had survived the earlier marauding of

Achilles. We also know, since the Leleges were a tribe of Pelasgians, that the Pelasgian king Altes ruled over the territory of Pedassos beside the Satniois. This river flows westwards from Gargarus and into the sea a little north of Lekton Point, running quite close to Larisa. Leaf also identifies Homer's Pedassos with historical Assos, not far from Lekton, with some confidence.

The dilemma is intractable. From the Iliad we must conclude that the two tribes of the Pelasgi dwelt in the catchment of the river Satniois. But the Pelasgian Larisa here is not far from Hisarlik/Ilium. Strabo follows Homer's directions and finds a Larisa far away, near Kyme, but fails to convince Leaf that this is the home of Homer's Pelasgians. Leaf, on the other hand, chose to understand Homer's 'far' as a relative term, and followed the remaining evidence to show that the historic Pelasgian Larisa near Hamaxitos was obviously the one he meant.

This dilemma remains intractable only so long as scholars believe that Homer's Troy was at Hisarlik. With Troy at Bergama the problem is amicably resolved. We can now agree with Leaf that Homer was obviously referring to the historical Pelasgian Larisa near Hamaxitos. This is far from Bergama and, as it happens, quite close to Novum Ilium. And Strabo was right to insist that, when he wrote 'far from his native land', Homer meant what he said.

The return of the daughter of Chryses

The location of Chryse caused another difference of opinion between Strabo and Leaf. In the Iliad Book 1, Agamemnon has to give his prize woman, Chryseis, back to her father Chryses, a priest of Phoebus Apollo. The priest had come to Agamemnon from Chryse with a ransom for her release. When Agamemnon refused to release her, the priest prayed to Apollo for help. The archer god then wreaked such havoc among the Achaeans that Agamemnon reluctantly had to agree to give up the girl. Odysseus took command of a twenty-oar ship and returned her to her father in Chryse. The Iliad gives us a few more details. Achilles had previously sacked the town of Thebe and those in the rich plain around it, including Chryse. Chryse possessed the temple of

Sminthian Apollo, and Chryses' daughter was captured in Thebe. Briseis, the prize woman of Achilles, was captured in Lyrnessos in the same campaign. Hence we would expect Lyrnessos to be near Thebe. Leaf did find one there, but where exactly was Chryse?

Strabo tells us (13.1.63) that Chryse was a small town on the sea just below Thebe. In his day the place was deserted, and the temple had long been transferred to the modern Chryse near Hamaxitos, not far from Lekton. He said those who claimed that the modern Chryse was the Homeric one were wrong, and lists several reasons:

a) Because it has no harbour, whereas Homer says Odysseus came to a deep harbour there. (Il 1:432).
b) Homer says the temple there was by the sea, but there is none beside the sea at Hamaxitos. Nor is the modern Chryse near Thebe, as Homer implies when he says Chryses' daughter was captured at Thebe.
c) Homer also couples Chryse with Killa in Il 1:451-2: 'thou who hauntest Chryse and holy Killa'. But no place called Killa is seen in the district of Alexandria Troas, nor any temple of Killian Apollo. But in the Plain of Thebe there is a Killa to be seen close by.
d) Finally, the distance from Chryse of the Kilikes to the Naval Station at Ilium is around 700 stades. This distance would be a full day's voyage, which agrees with Homer. Odysseus sacrificed to the god on arrival, spent the rest of the day appeasing the god with songs and libations, then stayed over-night and returned the next day. But if Odysseus had only gone as far as the Chryse some 22km south of Alexandria Troas, he could have gone and returned to the Greek camp in the same day.

The locations of the old and modern Chryse are shown on Fig. 15.2.

Again, Leaf disputed most of what Strabo said. Poor Strabo was accused of abandoning fact, and theorising badly. Leaf argued that, off the Plain of Thebe, 'There is not and cannot be a natural harbour on this alluvial coast...We may safely take it for granted therefore that he had no positive evidence whatever for any Chryse in this neighbourhood...for the statement in 13.1.65 that Astyra was 20 stades from the ancient Chryse, there is no indication that

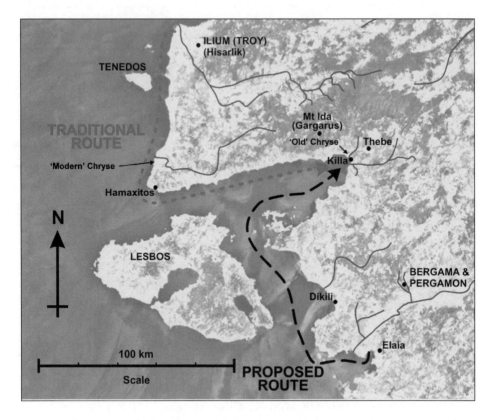

Fig. 15.2 Sketch map showing Odysseus's route to Killa from near Hisarlik or Elaia.

Strabo had any definite idea of its position…20 stades places Chryse at Ak Chai, or Killa, and it would seem that Chryse is conceived only as a temple in a grove close to Killa.'

Leaf preferred the modern Chryse. He pointed out that there is a harbour about a mile from the temple of Sminthian Apollo by the modern Chryse. Although this temple is not on the shore, Leaf said this 'does not carry much weight'. We should remember that many Mediterranean sites tended to move short distances inland for the sake of safety in times of piracy. So there may have been an older shrine of Apollo there close to the shore. Leaf agreed with Strabo's estimate of about 700 stades from Ilium to Thebe. If the ship was rowed at about 6 knots, this would take about 12 hours. But Odysseus starts out after a long debate in the assembly in Book 1, and 'something must be added for preparations for the voyage.' And, as Leaf explained, 'the return journey could certainly not be done in 12 hours against the current from the Hellespont, which sets all down the western coast of the Troad and runs at some 2 knots.'

Strabo argued that Chryse must have been close to Thebe because Chryses's daughter was captured there. Against this, Leaf said there is nothing in Homer to say she had not married and moved to live in Chryse some 80km distant from her home town. The Kypria told that she had gone to Thebe to attend a festival of Artemis. He concludes 'the argument from time is conclusively against the eastern site for Homer's Chryse.' He placed Chryse probably on or very close to the site of Hamaxitos, some 12km N of Lekton. However, he does accept that there was a Killa near Thebe.

To summarise, Strabo believed Homer's Chryse was the old Chryse, near Killa and close to Thebe, for several reasons. Leaf preferred the new Chryse near Hamaxitos partly because, from the old Chrysa, Odysseus would have taken more than a day to return by boat to the Achaean's harbour near Hisarlik.

As with Pelasgian Larisa, this problem is easily resolved with Troy at Bergama. From Elaia, Strabo's Chryse was some 100km away near Thebe. From there, the return journey in a fast ship, aided by the favourable winds as promised by Apollo, would have taken comfortably less than a day. Furthermore, we now know that Cook, in his study of the Troad, [5] found that the Chryse near Hamaxitos yielded nothing earlier than Hellenistic pottery. I conclude, therefore, that Homer's Chryse was probably the one near Thebe as suggested by Strabo, not the more modern Chryse at Hamaxitos as proposed by Leaf.

The flight of the Kilikes

The Kilikes were a Pelasgian tribe who apparently were named after their home town, Killa. This came under attack during the Trojan War from raids by the Achaeans, led by Achilles. As we have just seen, Strabo (13.1.63) tells us that Killa was a small town close to the old Chryse near Thebe. The Apollo temple at Chryse had been transferred to the modern Chryse near Hamaxitos, not far from Lekton. This may have happened when the Kilikes fled to a new home to escape the marauding Achaeans. Strabo said that some went to Hamaxitos, and some went to Pamphylia on the coast opposite western Cyprus.

But Strabo's explanation caused Leaf to scoff with incredulity. He pointed out that if the Kilikes were driven out by Achilles during his raids on Thebe, they would hardly have settled around Hamaxitos, some 80km nearer their enemy at Hisarlik.

Fig. 15.3 shows the flight of the Kilikes to a new home at Hamaxitos, further away over land from Achilles.

Yet again, much of Strabo's explanation can now be accepted and understood with Troy at Bergama. Most of Leaf's objections, valid if Troy was at Hisarlik, now disappear. The Kilikes of Killa, because of their fear of attack by Achilles,

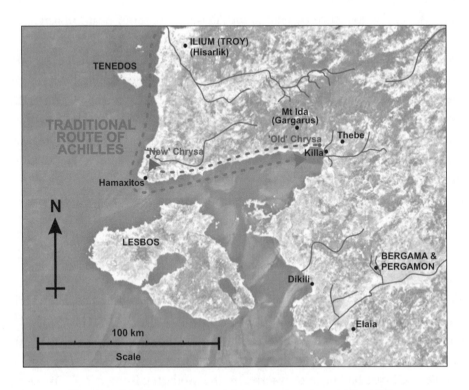

Fig. 15.3. Traditional route of Achilles when he attacked Killa.

did not move nearer to the Achaeans. Instead they actually moved some 80km further west, considerably further away by land from the Greek camp at Elaia.

Dardania and Skepsis

The legends about the founding of Dardania have already been discussed. In the Iliad (Il. 20:216) we read that 'Dardanus founded Dardania at a time when the sacred city of Ilium had not yet been built to shelter people on the plain and they still inhabited the watered slopes of Ida.' There seems no good reason to doubt the integrity of these lines. They do not contradict the Cretan version of the Troy foundation legend, in which a Teucer or Teuthras from Crete founded Teuthrania in the Kaikos valley.

Strabo tells us that Dardania included the middle and upper valleys of the Skamander. Skepsis, the home of Demetrios, lies within Dardania, and Demetrios was an expert on local history. And according to Demetrios the territory of Skepsis lay wholly on the right bank of the Skamander. The right hand bank, looking down-stream, would be its northern side.

During his study tour, Leaf found a few residual Phrygian names which supported the Homeric legend that Dardanus was given some lands from Phrygia. The Dardanian promontory lies about 12km south of Abydos, with the town of Dardanus nearby, on the other side of the mouth of the Rhodius River. The tomb of Hecuba, mother of Hector, was said to be on the opposite shore. Another local legend ties Troy to this region. This promontory is one of the reputed scenes of the rape of Ganymede, the beautiful son of Tros, taken from him by Zeus in return for a pair of immortal horses (or, in a different legend, a golden vine), to be his cupbearer on Olympus. [6] Leaf explained that Dardanus was an ancient settlement, but so insignificant that the kings have frequently transplanted it to Abydos, and back again to its ancient site. It existed till the fall of Constantinople, and had its own coins till around 300.

Skepsis and its southern neighbour Kebrene were both members of the Delian League, appearing in the Athenian tribute lists of c454-440. In the Trojan Catalogue, neither Skepsis nor any other city is named as the capital of Dardania.

The first Dardanians 'dwelt on the slopes of many fountained Ida' (Il. 20.218). At Troy, the Dardanians were led by Aeneas, 'whom fair Aphrodite conceived to Anchises among the spurs of Ida.' (Il. 2.820-821). From local legend, Skepsis was established as a city after the fall of Troy by Scamandrios, son of Hector, and Askanios, son of Aeneas. [7] Scamandrios was a Trojan, and Askanios was a Dardanian. The descendants of these two royal houses were still recognised in historical times, and enjoyed the honorary title of kings. Demetrios explained that this happened because the Troas/Trojans were already close at hand, and that Kebrenia to the SW of Skepsis belonged to them. For positive evidence he pointed to two facts; (i) Kebrene contained the tomb of Paris and his wife Oenone, and (ii) that Kebriones was eponymous with the town of Kebrene. Paris and Kebriones were both sons of Priam, hence Kebrene was Trojan not Dardanian. So Demetrios argued that Skepsis was not founded by fugitives from the fallen Troy, but earlier. Both Paris and Kebriones fell at Troy, so the Trojans must have been there long before the war.

Leaf found a problem here that was hard to explain. He said that Demetrios divides the extensive fertile plain of Bairamich between the Dardanoi on the north and the Troas on the south 'curiously'. The two tribes are supposed to have faced each other in two long strips, divided by the upper Skamander or Mendere, which was a fordable river. And according to Demetrios the whole southern, or Trojan, strip was ruled by Hector from Troy. This was what Leaf found 'curious'. He struggled to find a plausible explanation as to why Troy, far to the northwest at Hisarlik, should rule the southern side of the river here instead of the northern side. He believed that the only natural division was to give the plain of Troy to Hector and his Trojans, and the middle basin above Burnabashi to Aeneas and his Dardanians. 'This,' he said, 'was no doubt what is meant by Dardania in Homer.' [8] He did not deny, however, that Demetrios' theory of the river boundary, though inconvenient, was genuinely historical. For a long time Skepsis had owned the northern half of the plain and Kebrene the southern half, a situation that lasted till Alexandria Troas was founded and it was 'put away with by force.'

From the comments of both Strabo and Leaf, I will make two points:
(i) With Troy at Hisarlik, Leaf could not understand why Trojans should hold the southern half of the middle Skamander valley, the side furthest away from

Troy, while the Dardanians held the northern half. However, with Troy at Bergama far to the south east, this division is the natural one. This is now what we would expect to find. Crucially, as far as evidence for a historical Troy at Bergama is concerned, such a division is historical, not legendary.

(ii) There are clearly many legends in the Troad that relate directly to the Trojan War. Some of these are only explicable by accepting a) that Troy was not at Hisarlik but at Bergama, b) that the Trojan War was a real historical event, and c) that it took place in the lower Bakir Çayi valley. In other words, I would argue that here we find evidence for a historical Trojan War.

The Gergithes at Ilium

From Herodotus we learn that a people he called the Gergithes were found in the region of Ilion around the time of Xerxes' visit. He said that these people were a remnant of the ancient Teukrians, i.e. Trojans. Leaf, who had no doubt that Ilion was once Homer's Troy, would have expected to find remnants of the Trojans living there, so was happy to accept this observation by Herodotus. As we have seen in our discussion of Skepsis, 'remnants' or descendents of the Trojans were also living there, not far away from Ilion.

Strabo, however, did not let this pass without comment. He said (13.1.70) that near the source of the Kaikos is a village called Gergitha. This was where King Attalos of Pergamon settled the people from the Troad when he destroyed some of their towns. Leaf tells us that Gergitha cannot be found with any certainty. But a village called Gertza was found near Soma, where several sarcophagi were cut into the rock and covered over with slabs. 'Near here then there must have been an ancient settlement, possibly Germe, Gergitha, or Sandaina, which commanded the road from Soma to Gelembe and perhaps also from Pergamon to Magnesia'.

As a speculative suggestion, perhaps some survivors from Troy fled eastwards and settled round a place called Gergitha or similar, somewhere north of Soma. Later they migrated north and west and eventually settled at a place they called Gergithes near Novum Ilium. If so, this might explain the legend mentioned by Jebb in 1882 [9] that the inhabitants of Ilion moved more than once before settling there.

The Keteians of Eurypylus

The Keteians are a tribe that are only mentioned once by Homer, in the Odyssey (Od. 11.521). Here, possibly in an interpolated section, we learn of the death of Eurypylus, the son of Telephos, fighting against the Achaeans. Eurypylus, we are told, fell with many comrade Keteians round him, 'all for women's gifts.' Who were the Keteians and what does this mean?

Speculation about these seemingly enigmatic lines irritated Strabo. He wrote '...commentators produce silly fables more to prove their inventiveness than to solve the problem.' (13:1:70) Dismissing the mention of 'women's gifts' as a fable, he said that from Homer, Eurypylus must have ruled in the district of the Kaikos. The name of his comrade Keteians probably came from the river Ketios, which flows into the Kaikos just south of Pergamon.

Leaf [10] also tried to explain this passage. According to the fable, Priam, fearful of losing the war against the Achaeans, had called on help from Eurypylus and his Keteians. Eurypylus was willing to fight, but his mother refused to let him go. So in order to persuade her, Priam sent her a gift of a golden vine, which had been given to king Tros by Zeus in reparation for the abduction of his son Ganymede. This, he said, explains the reference in the Odyssey to the death of Eurypylus being 'all for women's gifts'. He said that Eustathios in his commentary on the Odyssey brings forth a list of variants to their story, which certainly justify Strabo's contemptuous phrase 'silly fables'. [11] Leaf pointed out that Homer never said that a son of Telephos ruled on the Kaikos, and shows no knowledge of the Telephos myth. In the Odyssey, (11.520) Eurypylus, a son of Telephos, led a people Homer called the Keteians. The river Ketios is not in the district of Elaia, but flows on the eastern side of the citadel of Pergamon. The name is attested on coins of the Imperial age, so is historical. 'So the name was local but not necessarily ancient. It may possibly have been given to form a link with Homer, and the fact that it was disputed tends to this conclusion.' Leaf also mentions that according to an early commentator on Od. 11:521, Alkaios, the Lesbian poet, 'uses the name Keteian as equivalent to Mysian.'

Collectively this evidence seems persuasive. Strabo concluded that Eurypylus must have ruled somewhere in the district of the Kaikos valley in Mysia. Very much earlier, Alkaios thought Keteian was another name for Mysian. Now that we can show that the Trojan plain was in Mysia, and the Ketios was a river in Mysia, it appears probable that the Keteians were from the region of the river Ketios. If Troy was in this valley, and if they were also present at the time of the Trojan War, it seems equally likely that they fought for Priam against the Achaeans. So with Troy in Mysia the name does have a respectable Homeric ancestry. And if further support were necessary, we saw in Chapter 13 that Hansen also concluded that Ketios was an earlier name of the Kaikos. [12]

Recently, several ancient sites have been found in this valley to the north of Pergamon, so this identification may potentially find archaeological support. Since I have earlier argued that a Telephos, or Telepinus, may have been known to the poet, it is also possible that he had a son, called Eurypylus by the Greeks, who also fought at Troy as a leader of the Keteians. Perhaps the mention of Eurypylus and his Keteians is a genuine survival from the time of Homer. Have we found here yet another fingerprint left behind by the hand of the interpolator? Or was the mention of the Keteians deliberately retained, helping to fill the void in the Kaikos valley left by moving Troy to Hisarlik?

Concluding comments

My aim in this chapter has been to offer further geographical evidence, from parts of the Troad outside the Bakir Çayi valley, that the Trojan plain was at Bergama. In addition, this evidence supports my view that the Trojan War was a real historical event. Some Troy-related legends about those living in the Troad could not be explained convincingly with Troy at Hisarlik. However, with Troy at Bergama, no such problems arise. Against all current expectations, the poet has turned out to be an extremely accurate recorder of the topography of the Trojan plain. He knew his site very well. He also had a good geographical knowledge of the wider region of the Troad. We can look again at some of the odd words, asides and little diversions found in Homer, that Bowra [13] told us we should not expect to be able to take literally. Instead, in many cases, these can be seen to confirm the accuracy of Homer's descriptions. Strabo also has come in for some unfair criticism from Leaf because Leaf mistakenly believed that Troy was at Hisarlik. The collective evidence presented in this chapter is further powerful evidence that the Trojan war was a real historical event that took place at Bergama.

CHAPTER 16

SOME ARCHAEOLOGICAL EVIDENCE

Introduction. The Hittites of Anatolia. Early and Late Bronze Age settlements on Lesbos.
Teuthrania. Candarli, ancient Pitane. A bronze Mycenaean sword from Pergamon. Conclusion

Introduction

The Trojan War, if historical, was an event which took place in the Late Bronze Age or earlier, before the fall of the Mycenaean palaces. If it took place in Mysia, we should be able to find there evidence of well established settlements at this early period. Hisarlik was only accepted as Troy after Schliemann had shown Early and Mid Bronze Age settlements existed there for hundreds of years before the Mycenaean period. Can we show that Mysia was also occupied at these early times? There is, in fact, much accumulated evidence of Bronze Age occupation in this valley. In this short chapter I will table some limited evidence from a few specific sites. However, I will leave a discussion of the archaeological evidence from Pergamon and Bergama, including the latest Bronze Age finds there, for Volume 2, in which these sites are identified as those of Ilios and Troy.

The Hittites of Anatolia

The best known civilisation living in Anatolia in the Bronze Age was the Hittites. Introducing them, Seton Lloyd wrote: 'For five centuries, then, beginning in about 1700 BC, a great nation whose rulers were of Indo-European origin, occupied an increasingly large proportion of central Anatolia, contesting its southern borders with Egypt and Assyria.' [1] Their capital for much of this time was at Hattusas in Cappadocia, and thousands of clay tablets found there tell us something of their history.

On several tablets the name Wilusa appears as a vassal state of the Great King of the Hittites. Also, 'In a Hittite document of c1420 BC the western Anatolian state of Wilusa (or Wilusiay) appears next to a place called Taruisa, which - tantalisingly - appears only this once in the Hittite archive.' [2] Many scholars now accept that these two names were probably the Hittite equivalents of the names 'Ilios' and 'Troy' found in the Iliad. 'Ilios' was spelt 'Wilios' in an early Greek dialect. Today it is assumed that the capital of Wilusa was at Troy/Ilios on the site of Hisarlik. In fact Hawkins [3] in 2002 concluded that, with no evidence either way, Wilusa was either in the Kaikos valley or at Hisarlik. He chose Troy at Hisarlik, at least partly from the archaeological evidence found there.

Early and Late Bronze Age settlements on Lesbos.

One of the places named on the Hittite texts was 'Lazpas', which, from its geographical associations, is now commonly accepted as referring to the island of Lesbos. This was later the primary base for the Aeolian settlers of western Anatolia, and Mytilene on its east coast became 'one of the greatest cities of the Aegean.' [4] Thus we have historical evidence for the occupation of Lesbos, close to the Kaikos valley, in both the Bronze and Iron Ages.

Archaeological evidence from Lesbos confirms the presence of settlements from as early as the Early Bronze Age (EBA). Nigel Spencer [5] reports finds of EBA local ceramics from sites on Lesbos similar to those found in Levels I and II at Troy. The limited excavations on the island to date have confirmed it was settled throughout the Bronze Age. Then, following a hiatus, it was also occupied throughout the Proto-Geometric, Geometric and Archaic eras. Finds include some imported as well as some locally made copies of Mycenaean ware. Some LBA burials were also found on the mainland in the region a little to the north of Dikili. Thus archaeological evidence confirms that these regions on the southern side of the Troad were occupied roughly at the same time as was the fortress at Hisarlik.

Teuthrania

The site of Teuthrania, said to have been destroyed during the Mysian War by the Achaeans before they fought at Troy, was discussed in Chapter 14. There I mentioned that, in 1911, Walter Leaf had identified a mound to the west of Kalarga Hill, perhaps as shown in Fig. 14.5, as a possible site of Teuthrania. On the 1941 Military Map, this may be the hill named Tartar tepe. He chose this mound because he found evidence of Bronze Age occupation there. He found no such evidence at Kalarga Hill.

As also mentioned in Chapter 14, Professor Radt told me that, since the time of Leaf, Bronze Age remains have now been found at Kalarga Hill. He therefore preferred to join the earlier German archaeologists in placing Teuthrania at Kalarga Hill. Here, therefore, is evidence for Bronze Age occupation at two sites in the central part of the lower Bakir Çayi valley.

Hansen, in her magnificent book on the Attalid kings of Pergamon, gives a little more information. She said that the story of the Teuthranian (Mysian) War reflected local resistance to what she called the Greek colonists. This resistance, she added, was confirmed by archaeological finds. [6]

Candarli, ancient Pitane

Candarli, on the western side of the Bakir Çayi river mouth opposite Elaia, is believed to be the site of ancient Pitane. George Bean discusses the earliest histories, with sketch maps, of both places. [7] At Elaia, which has not been excavated, he did not report finding any Bronze Age material. Pitane was a very early Greek settlement, being the northernmost member of the Aeolian League. However, Bean said it was much older than that, because 'pottery has been found there dating back to the third millennium.'

Finds from the Mycenaean era, including a stirrup jar, were unearthed in the necropolis of ancient Pitane. This jar was decorated with an octopus motif, and thought by Bittel to be dated to the Late Helladic 3C period. This suggests a settlement was there in the late Mycenaean era, very close to the Achaean's camp at Elaia.

A bronze Mycenaean sword from Pergamon

Hansen's comment quoted above implied that evidence of possible fighting in the Teuthranian War had been found. An example, cited in a reference she gave, was recorded by Bittel: 'One bronze sword found in the neighbourhood of Pergamon. Provenance not better known than this, but it is Mycenaean, although apart from the Mycenaean characteristics, there are also relevant deviations. Probably of local origin, partly derived from Mycenaean examples. Now in the Ashmolean Museum, Oxford.' [8]

Is this, I wondered, the first evidence yet to be found of the Trojan War having been fought at Bergama? Could its apparent 'local origin' mean that it was made by a Trojan for use against the heroes of the Achaeans? What an extraordinary coincidence to find that in Oxford, my home town for many years, lies an ancient, and possibly Trojan, bronze sword from the neighbourhood of Pergamon. I cannot help but muse over the possibility, however remote, that this sword, perhaps the only one of its kind in captivity, may once have been used to defend Troy against the army of Agamemnon. [9]

Conclusion

Both the historical and archaeological evidence confirm that the lower Bakir Çayi valley was occupied in the Mid to Late Bronze Ages. There is nothing here to oppose my conclusion that here was the site of the Trojan War as described in the Iliad.

CHAPTER 17

SUMMARY AND CONCLUSIONS

General summary. Summary of each chapter. Conclusions.
Possible explanations. Addressing the jury.

General summary

The main objective of my studies has been to show that Pergamon may now be indentified with Ilios, the holy citadel of ancient Troy as described in the Iliad and Odyssey. My findings are presented in two volumes. Here in Volume 1 my purpose is to show, beyond reasonable doubt, that the Trojan plain upon which the Homeric Trojan War was fought has now been found in the lower Bakir Çayi valley below Pergamon and Bergama. If we accept the findings of Volume 1, then logic demands that both Ilios and Troy must once have stood at the head of this plain. In Volume 2 I will show that the descriptions of Ilios, in both the Iliad and Odyssey, offer a near perfect match with the acropolis of Pergamon. The site of Troy should therefore be sought in the northern suburbs of Bergama just south of the Asklepion, where warm and cold springs were once found close together. In Volume 2 I will also explain the Troy deception, the ruse which led the world, for some 2,500 years, to believe that Troy was once at Ilion. This was the work of the Pisistratid tyrants of Athens, who altered the text of the Iliad to show that Troy was visible from Samothrace. This endorsed their claim that Troy once stood at Classical Ilion, beside the Straits of the Dardanelles, on the site we know today as Hisarlik. They then claimed entitlement to the lands of Troy around Ilion for a much needed new colony, saying it was awarded to them by the Achaeans as their share of the spoils of the Trojan War.

Volume 1 is divided into two parts. The first looks carefully at the site of

Hisarlik and shows that it offers a very poor match when compared to the descriptions in the Iliad. All the landscape descriptions in the Iliad are collected together, and used to produce a reconstructed plan of the Trojan plain. This plan is then compared with the plain at Hisarlik, a comparison which leads to the conclusion that Schliemann was wrong to claim that his excavations there had uncovered the site of Homer's Troy.

The second part of Volume 1 explores the possibility that the link between Troy and Samothrace could be a later insertion into the Iliad, and that Troy should be sought somewhere else. A number of off-site signposts are identified which point towards Troy lying to the east of Lesbos. These, together with the Mysian War legend, which tells of Achaeans fighting at Teuthrania in the region of the lower Bakir Çayi valley, makes this a more likely location for Troy than Hisarlik.

A site visit to the region of Pergamon and Bergama, in what was once ancient Mysia, reveals a landscape that almost perfectly matches that of the Trojan plain. Yet more supporting evidence is then found from a study of the nearby countryside, and from Walter Leaf's study of the Troad. Collectively, this evidence is, I believe, sufficient to claim, beyond reasonable doubt, that the Trojan War of the Iliad took place on the plain of the Bakir Çayi below Bergama.

Summary of each chapter

Part 1 Rejecting Troy at Hisarlik

Chapter 1
In Chapter 1 the first major doubts are expressed about Troy at Hisarlik. These include:

1. Unlike Troy, Hisarlik has no natural acropolis. Yet Troy had a magnificent and spacious acropolis, described as very steep, or 'beetling'.
2. The so-called walled 'citadel' is much too small to have been the walled acropolis of Ilios.

3. The archaeological evidence at Hisarlik shows that it was first settled much earlier than suggested by the Trojan legends. It reveals no strata which can be clearly shown to have been Priam's city. No evidence of a Greek attacking force has been found.

4. Between 1980 and 1982, a large bay was found to have existed at the Mendere river mouth in Trojan times. Troy at Hisarlik was then effectively a coastal fortress. With Troy close to the beach, there is no room for the plain of Troy between it and the Greek camp beside their ships. Yet the Iliad tells of battles surging to and fro across the great plain before Troy. The absence of this plain therefore makes a mockery of this great epic poem.

5. An alternative site for the Greek camp and the Trojan battlefield was proposed at Besik Bay. However, the resulting plain, like its predecessor, failed to match the descriptions in the Iliad.

6. The Trojans, according to Herodotus, were also known as 'Teucrians', probably the eponymous name for the citizens of Teuthrania. The legends tell us that Trojans (or Teucrians) built Troy and Ilios to give better protection to the people living on the plain. Yet Teuthrania is known to have been in Mysia, not far from Pergamon. Troy should therefore, from these legends, be in the same valley as Teuthrania, not in the Mendere valley at Hisarlik.

Did Troy exist at Hisarlik? An old debate

An old debate about whether or not Troy existed at Hisarlik, still valid today, concluded that, in the absence of positive proof, this must remain a matter of personal belief. Troy, if it ever existed, could only be somewhere else if we could show a) that the mentions of Samothrace, Tenedos and Imbros were later additions in the Iliad, not written by the original poet, and b) the term 'Hellespont' as used by the original poet of the Iliad, did not refer solely to the Straits of the Dardanelles.

The first signpost to Troy in Mysia

In Book 24 of the Iliad Achilles tells us exactly where we should look for Troy.

From a natural reading of lines 24.543-546, we learn that Priam's kingdom lay between the island of Lesbos and 'Phrygia in the uplands'. Phrygia in the Iliad included the Sangarios valley. The capital of Phrygia was Gordion, which is on the central Anatolian plateau some 600km due east of Lesbos. Bergama, Pergamon and ancient Mysia all lie due east of Lesbos, where Achilles placed Troy, whereas Hisarlik lies to the north.

Chapters 2, 3, and 4

Chapter 2 gives more background information about Homer and the Trojan War stories from the epic poems, myths and legends. In Chapters 3 and 4 details of the Trojan landscape were abstracted from the Iliad, and used to reconstruct a theoretical map of the Trojan Plain. A list was made of 12 key features of the Trojan landscape.

Chapter 5

Here the battlefield at Hisarlik was compared with the theoretical map. For comparison purposes I have assumed that the Greek camp was at Besik Bay, and the plain of Troy lay between Besik Bay and Hisarlik. This plain was compared with our theoretical map by trying to find the 12 important features listed in Chapter 4. These were:

1. The bay and beach
2. The rising in the plain
3. The watersmeet
4. The Simois
5. Kallikolone
6. The Wall of Herakles
7. The distance between the camp and Troy
8. The ford
9. The Tomb of Ilus
10. The bend in the river
11. The tomb of Old Aesyetes
12. The Tomb of Myrine

If Hisarlik was Troy, all of these should be found as, and where, described in the Iliad.

The verdict

The landscape between Besik Bay and Hisarlik offers a very poor match when compared with the Trojan landscape. The river layout is all wrong. The Scamander is not found near both the Greek camp and Troy. There is no Simois in the plain, and no 'watersmeet'. There is an unconvincing 'throsmos', but no good candidates for prominent features such as Kallikolone, the Wall of Herakles, the Tomb of Ilus, or the tombs of Old Aesyetes and Myrine in the plain before Troy. Much of what is described in the Iliad had therefore to be put down to poetic imaginings. The view from there of Samothrace, and the proximity of Imbros and Tenedos, have blinded all to the possibility that a much better matching alternative site could be found. This explains why no serious attempt appears to have been made, until now, to find Troy elsewhere.

Chapter 6

Here I explored the possibility that Troy could be somewhere else. The geographical signposts pointing towards Troy are listed as follows:

1. Troy was visible to Poseidon from the top of Mt Fengari on Samothrace
2. Troy was not far from Tenedos and Imbros
3. Troy was visible to Zeus from Gargarus, the highest peak of Mt. Ida
4. The harbour of Troy was beside the Hellespont
5. The location of the allies of Troy
6. Troy's location in relation to the places raided by Achilles
7. Troy lay between Lesbos and Phrygia
8. The location of Troy from the journey there by Iphidamas from Thrace

Conclusions

These eight geographical clues in the Iliad are not all pointing in the same direction. The first two point to Troy at Hisarlik. Points 3 and 4 could apply to Troy at either Hisarlik or in Mysia, and points 5-8 suggest Troy was in Mysia. Overall, this evidence is therefore inconsistent. This inconstistency could suggest that some of these signposts are later interpolations.

The Mysian War legend

This geographical evidence receives some support from literary sources. That the Achaeans fought at Teuthrania is supported by the Mysian War legend. Two senior scholars, Carpenter and Beekes, conclude that the Mysian War and Trojan War stories were originally the same story, which became attached to two different places. The earliest story was of the Achaeans fighting at Teuthrania in Mysia, and in the later story this war was moved to Ilion at Hisarlik. However, both scholars assume the later story was the Homeric version. On the other hand, I will be presenting evidence to show that it is the earlier, not the later, story that is Homeric

Chapter 7

Someone wishing to 'move' Iliadic Troy from Mysia to Hisarlik would have to insert a few really prominent clues into the Iliad which made Troy at Hisarlik seem irrefutable. Looking for these clues we look first at the Samothrace connection, found at the start of Book 13. A study of these lines does indeed lead to the conclusion that the name 'Samothrace' may well have been a later addition. I conclude that the original poet had probably intended 'Samos', not 'Samothrace', as the seat of Poseidon. Once the drama of Zeus's turn on Gargarus is understood, it becomes clear that Poseidon, Troy and the Greek camp must all have been behind Zeus's back when he looked at the northern tribes. If accepted, this argument removes the main pillar of support for Troy at Hisarlik. The mentions of Tenedos and Imbros near Troy would therefore also have been interpolations, probably by the same hand.

Chapter 8

If we assume that the poet intended Poseidon to start his journey to the Greek camp from Samos instead of Samothrace, his journey there, via an Aiga or Aigai on the Kara Dag peninsular, may now be better understood.

Part 2. Finding the Trojan plain in Mysia

Chapter 9

Here our reconstructed map is compared with a map of the Bakir Çayi valley. At once a near perfect match is apparent. The Skamander and Simois correspond well with the Bakir Çayi and the Sariasmak. The Bay of Elaia, the ancient port of the Attalid kings, offers a good site for the Greek camp.

Chapters 10 - 13

A visit to the lower Bakir Çayi valley reveals all the 12 features of the Trojan landscape as listed in Chapter 5. These are all found generally as and where described in the Iliad. In addition, no other features were found in this landscape which would have affected the action of the war, but which the poet failed to mention. Kalarga Hill, with its distinctive brow, is a good candidate for Kallikolone. The Simois may once have run along its side facing the battlefield. Impressively, a wall-shaped hill in the foothills on the other side of the plain is found in exactly the right place opposite Kallikolone. This is identified as the Wall of Herakles. The poet of the Iliad apparently knew this valley very well.

Chapter 14

In this chapter I look beyond the Trojan plain. A possible site for the burial place of Achilles on White Island, as described by Apollodorus, is found on Mardalich Adasi, near Candarli. Some fragments of the poems of Sappho, showing Lesbos used as a way station for the Achaean's return journey, may also offer some support for Troy in Mysia.

Chapter 15

A study of the work of Strabo and Walter Leaf yields further evidence in support of Troy in Mysia. Some differences between Homer, Strabo, and Leaf, which are irreconcilable with Troy at Hisarlik, are happily resolved with Troy at Bergama. These include:

a) finding the Larisa of Hippothous,
b) finding the home of Chryseis near Thebe,

c) showing that when the Kilikes fled their home town, Killa near Thebe, to escape from the marauding Achilles, those who settled near Hamaxitos did not settle some 80km nearer Achilles at the Greek Camp, and

d) explaining why, in the middle and upper valleys of the Skamander, the bank of the Mendere nearest Hisarlik was ruled from Dardania, and the furthest (southern) bank was ruled from Troy at Bergama.

Chapter 16

Here some archaeological evidence is presented to confirm that Mysia was occupied in the Late Bronze Age. The legends of the destruction of Teuthrania by the Achaeans, the Mycenaean material in the necropolis at Pitane, and the Mycenaean sword found near Pergamon all may lend some support to the theory that the Trojan War was fought in the lower Bakir Çayi valley.

The evidence of Hittite geography supports the identity of Hittite Wilusa with the Greek Ilios. It also supports the conclusion that, if Troy was not at Hisarlik, then the most probable place for it was in the Bakir Çayi valley.

Summary of Conclusions

1. Homeric Troy cannot be found at Hisarlik. This site has no natural acropolis. It is much too small to be the Troy of the Iliad. Between Besik Bay and Hisarlik, many important features of the landscape of the Trojan Plain are missing.

2. A study of all the geographical clues in the Iliad shows that these give conflicting information. While some point to Troy at Hisarlik, others point to Troy being to the east of Lesbos in ancient Mysia. This is where, according to the Mysian war legend, the Achaeans fought by mistake at Teuthrania, thinking they were at Troy.

3. A study of the beginning of the Iliad Book 13 leads us to conclude that the mention of Samothrace, the main anchor for Troy at Hisarlik, was a later addition. Mentions of Tenedos and Imbros as being near Troy would therefore also be later additions.

4. The evidence suggests that the poet originally intended that Poseidon watched the battle at the ships from Samos, not Samothrace.

5. A near perfect match with the Trojan landscape is found in the lower Bakir Çayi valley. This leads us to conclude that the Homeric Trojan War took place in Mysia, between the Bay of Elaia and the acropolis of Pergamon.

6. Some of the problems raised by Strabo and Leaf concerning Troy-related legends and tribal movements in the Troad are resolved with the Trojan plain in Mysia.

7. A possible alternative island site here for the burial place of Achilles can now be proposed.

8. Archaeological evidence supports the view that Mysia was occupied in the Bronze Age.

In short, all the evidence so far presented appears collectively to show, beyond reasonable doubt, that the Homeric plain of Troy lay in Mysia.

Possible explanations

Finding the plain of Troy of the Iliad in Mysia may be explained in different ways:

a) The poet of the earliest embryo Iliad did not know the whereabouts of Troy of the Trojan War legends, or even if the war really was an historical event. He knew of many different legends about this war, and set his poem about the wrath of Achilles in a landscape in Mysia with which he was familiar.

b) Troy really was at Hisarlik, and the earlier Mysian War was a real event which became the subject of oral poetry. The landscape of the Achaean's battlefield of the Mysian war was later somehow transferred to Hisarlik during the long process of oral transmission of the tale of Troy. This may perhaps have had the effect of making the landscape of the battlefield at Hisarlik more interesting and more memorable to the story-telling bard and his audience.

c) The plain of Troy of the Iliad really was in Mysia. The legendary war the Achaeans fought in Mysia was therefore in reality the Trojan War. Some additions and deletions were later made in the embryo Iliad in order to place both Troy and the Trojan landscape within sight of Samothrace at Hisarlik. This could only have been done by someone who had both a good reason for wanting Troy at Ilion (Hisarlik), and some measure of control over the text of the Iliad.

In my view, the first two possibilities are less likely than the last. If I am right, then both Troy and the magnificent acropolis of Ilios should also lie in this plain. In Volume 2 we will identify Ilios as Pergamon. This acropolis still bears the name of the precinct of Apollo on its highest terrace, called Pergamos in the Iliad. What remains of Troy would therefore lie buried beneath the northern suburbs of Bergama. Perhaps the existence there of one of the most ancient geothermal springs in Western Anatolia, the Asklepion, will help us find nearby what is still left of the walls of Troy.

Addressing the Jury

Ladies and gentlemen of the jury, we have now come to the end of our first enquiry concerning the truth about the Trojan War and the integrity of the poet of the Iliad. Here we have sought, principally by an examination of the evidence of the Iliad, to establish the whereabouts of the plain of Troy. There will be two further enquiries. The second will seek to establish the location of Troy and Ilios from descriptions in the Iliad. It should be a simple task to find Ilios and Troy in relation to the plain of Troy, since by definition they lie at the head of this plain. The third enquiry will be to determine a plausible explanation as to how antiquity came to accept that Troy was once on the site of Classical Ilion at Hisarlik. Armed with this explanation, it should then be possible to understand why this deception has remained undetected for some 2500 years.

The matter before you is one of grave import. The location of the Iliadic Trojan plain, once established, will set the agenda for the remaining two enquiries. The consequences of your decision here will have implications far beyond this room. At stake is nothing less than a change in our understanding of the literary heritage of western civilisation. Out of the mists of antiquity comes the shadowy figure of a poetic genius, known to intelligent antiquity as Homer, credited as being the original poet of much of the Iliad and the Odyssey. And out of the mass of evidence presented to this enquiry may eventually come the dawn of a new understanding and appreciation of this man and his genius.

Since the time of Herodotus the world has been led to believe that Troy was at Ilion, on the site today we call Hisarlik. The main participants in the discovery of Hisarlik as the site of Troy were guided to this spot by a few key signposts in the Iliad. The four most influential of these were a) that Troy stood beside the Hellespont, assumed to mean the Straits, b) it was visible from a mountain top on Samothrace, and it was near c) Imbros and d) Tenedos. It is the integrity of this information that has been challenged during this enquiry.

Most of the detailed information about the Trojan War comes from the Iliad and Odyssey, and these are our primary sources of evidence. The arguments as presented rest mainly upon the evidence of geography and topography. An appreciation of this evidence does not demand a detailed knowledge of ancient Greek history and mythology, the Greek language or archaeology. The landscape of the Trojan plain has not been bulldozed away. We can be confident that it remains largely as it was some 3,000 years ago. The principal questions for you to decide are these: is this landscape, as described in the Iliad, real or imaginary, and if real, is it best seen at Hisarlik or at Pergamon?

You may now retire to consider your verdict.

LITERARY SOURCES RELATING TO THE TROJAN WAR

Introduction. The Epic Cycle. The Trojan Cycle. Other early historians. Strabo.
Apollodorus and the places captured by Achilles. Quintus Smyrnaeus and the Mysian War.
Virgil's The Aeneid. Conclusions

Introduction

As we saw in Chapter 2, much more information about the wider events relating to the war is contained in a series of minor epic poems, collectively referred to as the Epic Cycle. This is a series of compositions by different and later authors, telling of myths and legends covering the whole Heroic period. Incorporated within the Epic Cycle is a series of works known as the Trojan Cycle, which included the Iliad and Odyssey. A few abbreviated accounts of these generally lesser works are all that survive. They may or may not agree in points of detail with each other. They are also assumed to contain many inaccuracies and embellishments. This is perhaps because some of the content may have been based on stories handed down by word of mouth over several centuries. Also, some of the content may have been invented long after the earliest stories were composed.

Information about the Epic and Trojan Cycles of poems is taken from a volume by Evelyn White [1]. This includes a collection of the works of Hesiod and Homer-related writings, republished together in 2002 in the Loeb Classical Library series.

The Epic Cycle

This series of stories, by poets of the Ionic School, covers the period from the origins of the Trojan War to the death of Odysseus. This marks the end of the Heroic Age. The various works included are briefly outlined, with comments quoted largely from Evelyn White's Introduction. After Homer, the quality of the epic style of poetry generally declined. Later poets were dominated by the Homeric tradition. They tried to copy his style and treatment, but they naturally chose to treat legends that preceded or followed the action of Iliad and Odyssey. This led to a body of poetry covering the whole of the Trojan War story. Eventually there existed an epic history of the world from its beginning to the death of Odysseus. Of these sometimes major works, only scant fragments have survived, in the form of abridgements of the synopsis of each poem in the Trojan cycle by Proclus, i.e. Eutychius Procles of Sicca.

Fragments of The Epic Cycle have been collated into the following:

The War of the Titans – concerning the union of heaven and earth, their offspring, the Cyclopes and 100 handed giants. Ascribed by some to Arctinus of Miletus.

Theban Cycle – three poems; the stories of Oedipus, the Thebai, and Epigoni.

The Epigoni – ascribed to Antimachus of Teos, telling of the sack of Thebes.

The Trojan Cycle – eight epic poems, including the Iliad and Odyssey. This comprises The Kypria, The Iliad, The Aethiopis, The Little Iliad, The Sack of Ilium, The Returns, The Odyssey and The Telegony. The other six, apart from the Iliad and Odyssey, are believed to be later than Homer, and their general structure is considered purely imitative.

The Trojan Cycle

The content of these six epics, as far as is known, is explained in a little more outline below, as they are more relevant to the Trojan War:

The Kypria, ascribed to Stasinus of Cyprus. This covered events before the

Iliad. It starts with the first causes of the war, the 'apple of discord' and the 'judgement of Paris', and the rape of Helen. It continues with the gathering of the Achaeans at Aulis in Boiotia, to the north of Attica, their first landing in the Kaikos valley by mistake, the capture of Teuthrania, their eviction by Telephos, and return to Aulis. It concludes with the second gathering at Aulis, their eventual landing at Troy, and the story of the war leading up to the quarrel between Agamemnon and Achilles.

'The Aethiopis', a work by Arctinus of Miletus. This included a) the coming of the Amazon Penthesilea to help the Trojans, and her death by Achilles, b) the arrival of the Ethiopian Memnon, also killed by Achilles, c) the death of Achilles after being wounded in the foot by an arrow from the bow of Paris, and d) the dispute between Aias and Odysseus over the arms of Achilles.

The Little Iliad, by Lesches of Pyrrha on Mytilene. This elaborated the story of the Sack of Troy as told by Arctinus. It included a) the arms of Achilles being awarded to Odysseus, b) the madness of Aias, c) the bringing of the wounded Philoctetes from Lemnos and his cure, d) Neoptolemus son of Achilles coming to the war, and his slaying of Eurypylus, son of Telephos, e) the making of the Wooden Horse, f) the spying of Odysseus, g) his theft of the palladium with the help of Diomedes, and h) ending with the Greek fleet sailing away to hide behind Tenedos, and the admission of the Wooden Horse into Troy by the Trojans.

The Sack of Ilium, which gave an account similar to Virgil's version in Aeneid Book 2. It comprised the episodes of the Wooden Horse, of Laocoon, of Sinon, and the return of the Achaeans from Tenedos, the death of Priam, the sacrilege of Aias son of Ileus, the actual sack of Ilios, the division of the spoils and the burning of the city. The Greeks sail away, and Athene plans to destroy them all on the high seas. As an aside, we note that here Evelyn White has taken the view, as apparently did Rieu and others, that the names Ilios and Troy can be interchanged at will. The Greek text of the Odyssey makes it clear that it was Ilios, not Troy, that admitted the Trojan horse. Apollodorus (Epitome 5:16) tells us that this was pulled up beside Priam's palace, known from Homer to have been on the acropolis of Ilios.

The Returns. These four poems rounded off the story of the Trojan War. The Iliad and the Odyssey were connected by a poem in 5 books, ascribed to Aias of Trozen, which begins where the sack of Troy ends. It tells of the dispute between Agamemnon and Menelaus, the departure from Troy of Menelaus, the fortunes of the lesser heroes, the return and tragic death of Agamemnon, murdered by his wife Clytemnestra, and the later vengeance of his son Orestes on his mother and her new husband Aegisthus. The story ends with the return home of Menelaus.

The Telegony, in two books by Pergamon of Cymene (c568 BCE). This answers many of the questions left unanswered by the Odyssey, such as what happened in Ithaca after the slaying of the suitors, and the fate of Odysseus. It tells of the adventures of Odysseus in Thesprotis after killing the suitors, his return to Ithaca, and his death at the hands Telegonus, his son by Circe. The epic ends by disposing of the surviving personages in a double marriage, Telemachus to Circe, and Telegonus to Penelope. [2]

The end of the Cycle marks the end of the Heroic Age.

Other Ancient Historical Sources

Many of the early Greek and Roman historians refer at some point to the Trojan War and the Greek and Trojan participants. Many themes from these poems became the subjects of plays by the great Greek dramatists, although they would probably have been more concerned with dramatic effect than with historical accuracy. All these writers considered the war an historical event. Thucydides, whose family claimed descent from Aias, took both the Heroes and the War as historical. A few of these early historians are referred to in this study. The burden of providing most of the detailed evidence with which to locate Homeric Troy must inevitably fall upon the poet himself.

Strabo
Although a late source, Strabo's Geography, especially his Book 13, is cited frequently as a reference in this book, so need not be discussed further here. Suffice it to say that Strabo regarded Homer as an excellent authority on

geography. Hence, when the Ilians claimed they lived on the site of Troy, Strabo cited evidence to show that Homer's geographical and topographical descriptions did not support this claim.

Strabo (13.1.7) said the lands of the Trojans were divided into nine dynasties, and Achilles, seeing the Trojans safe behind their walls, waged war in these outlying areas. He discusses these areas, naming most of the places named by Apollodorus (see below) along with a few others, but does not mention Colophon. This is the furthest south of those named; some 25 km south of Smyrna and an incredible 400km south of Hisarlik.

Apollodorus, and the places captured by Achilles

Apollodorus of Athens, c180-120BC, was a student of Aristarchus, the famous grammarian and editor of Homer. His 'Library' was dedicated to Attalus II of Pergamon. This could suggest he was less influenced by Athenian propaganda embedded in the Troy-related literature. He may have had access, at Pergamon, to independent sources. The version of his work that survives is thought to have been written by an author of 1st or 2nd century AD. In the Epitome of The Library of Apollodorus [3] we have a summary of the whole story of the Trojan War from the abduction of the twelve-year-old Helen by Theseus to the return of the heroes.

This is a late source, heavily influenced by the Alexandrian editors. Apollodorus also journeyed round the Troad, but his work does not contain much of relevance to us by way of new geographical information. The Troy of Apollodorus was where Novum Ilium stood in his day, and he mentions the tombs of some of the Heroes as being located near Sigeum. By the time he wrote there were many variant versions of the stories in the Epic Cycle, with inconsistencies that strongly suggest the fictitious nature of many of them. To cite just one example, the number of Greeks said to have been squeezed inside the Wooden Horse varied between several authorities from 23 (Tzetzes) to 3,000 (The Little Iliad). Two points from Apollodorus that are particularly relevant to our search are mentioned here.

Apollodorus provides us with a list of places said to have been taken by Achilles after the Greeks had landed and the Trojans had retreated behind their walls. These are given (Epitome, III. 32-34) as Lesbos, Phocaea, Colophon, Smyrna, Clazomenaea, Cyme, Aegialus, Tenos, the so-called Hundred Cities, Adramyttium, Side, Endium, Linaeum, Colone, Hypoplacian Thebes, Lyrnessus, Antandrus, 'and many other cities'. They left Philoctetes on Lemnos, so we must assume it was already a Greek not an Asian colony. In addition, the Iliad (11.625) gives Tenedos, [4] and the Kypria gives Pedasus. This makes a total of 18 named towns sacked by Achilles. This compares with Achilles' statement (Il 9:325-330) that he 'captured twelve towns from the sea, besides eleven that I took by land in the deep soiled realm of Troy', a total of twenty-three places.

We assume that Achilles captured these places (including Colophon if this is not named in error, or if it referred to a second Colophon now lost) during the early years of the war. If Troy was near the centre of its territory, and if the places he took lay roughly equally on either side of it, then Troy would have to be placed some 150-200km further south. If Troy was at Hisarlik, we may also ask why Abydos, Sestos and Perkote were not also taken by Achilles.

Quintus Smyrnaeus and the Mysian War

Quintus lived at Smyrna probably around 400AD, but apart from this very little is known about him. He wrote a poem in the style of Homer, covering the events of the Trojan War after the death of Hector at the close of the Iliad. Writing at such a late date and in such an imitative style, we may expect his work simply to mimic the stories of the Cyclic poets, and accordingly be of little interest to us. However, it has some interest in that it may reflect the changing Homeric tradition in his day.

The introduction to his work, translated by A.S. Way in the 1970 Loeb Edition [5], provides some useful background information. Quintus was clearly familiar with many natural features of the western part of Asia Minor. However, from his poem it is quickly apparent that his Troy was at Novum Ilium. This is confirmed by such references as the high mound of Aias, Rhoteium's headland [6], and the return trip with Neoptolemus with the landmarks approaching Troy described, [7]: 'they sighted Ida, Chrysa next, and Smintheus' fane, then

Sigean strand, and then the tomb of Aeacus' son…They passed Calydnae's isles, left Tenedos behind, and now was seen the fane of Eleus, where stands Protesilaus' tomb…'. He is also, if the translation is to be trusted, happy to include such possible anachronisms as [8] combatants 'slashing with swords', and [9] Tydeides saying to those who agreed they should give up and go home, that he would smite their heads off with 'sharp blue steel'. Swords strong and long enough for slashing rather than stabbing, and 'blue steel', are thought to have been unknown until well after the time of Homer. Although Tenedos is mentioned in the Odyssey as a passing port of call, it is only the Little Iliad and Quintus who tell us about leaving the Wooden Horse on the beach and sailing away to hide the fleet behind this island.

His references to the Mysian misadventure and the wide plain of the Kaikos are singular. The Kypria tells us that the Achaeans, when they first sailed for Troy with Achilles as a 15yr old admiral on board, landed by mistake at Mysia. They '…reach Teuthrania and sack it, taking it for Troy.' The idea that a confederation of seafaring nations went to Mysia instead of Troy by mistake and sacked the wrong city is so improbable as to be absurd. The most probable reason for the invention of this story, as part of the Troy deception, is argued in Volume 2. Quintus describes Mysia specifically as the wide plain of the river Kaikos. After Teuthrania was sacked, their king, Telephos, '…comes out to the rescue and kills Thersander, son of Polyneices, and is himself wounded by Achilles.' The Achaeans were forced to retreat to their ships and sail home. Telephos was left nursing a wound from the spear of Achilles that refused to heal.

From the Kypria, therefore, we learn that Teuthrania was a kingdom within Mysia. In the Iliad's list of Trojan allies, Chromius and Ennomus, sons of Arsinous, were sent to Troy from Mysia according to Apollodorus (Epitome, III. 34.), which agrees with Homer. So why were the Teuthranians not mentioned among the Trojan allies? Were all mentions of Teuthrania erased from the Iliad and Odyssey by the later Athenian editors, to help retain the illusion of Troy far away at Hisarlik?

After the death of Hector, one of the would-be saviours of Troy to arrive there was Eurypylus from Mysia, [10] son of Telephos and grandson of Herakles. 'A great host followed him, in battle skilled, all that by long Caicus' outflow dwelt.' But the poet of the Iliad apparently knew nothing of the Teuthranians as a separate dynasty. The mention in the Odyssey of Eurypylus, son of Telephos, is in the speech that eulogises Neoptolemus and names Memnon (Od. 9:520ff), so perhaps it was a later interpolation, invented to complement and extend Homer's original work.

To conclude, scholars think that Quintus may have had access to some previously unknown source material. Although of some historical interest, Quintus offers us no useful additional geographical information about Troy.

Virgil's The Aeneid

Virgil (70-19BC) wrote the Aeneid as a successful panegyric to the great Roman Emperor Augustus, the name that the Emperor Octavian chose for himself as from 27BC. Virgil worked on it for the last 10 years of his life, but it still lacked the finishing touches when he died in 19BC. His dying instructions were for it to be destroyed. The reason for this instruction was not made clear, and remains a matter for speculation. Fortunately Augustus did not allow this to happen.

The Aeneid tells the story of how Aeneas, son of Anchises, leader of the Dardanians and now king of the Trojans after the murder of Priam and his family, escaped from Troy. First over land, and then by ship, he had many triumphs over adversity before he and his surviving crew members arrived on the west coast of Italy. There they founded a new Troy, and his descendants later built Rome. This was the beginning of the Latin state.

The poet's indirect themes, however, were the glories of Rome, and of the house of Julian. This included the family and descendants of the great Julius Caesar, to which Augustus belonged. The poem contains many allusions to the history of Rome, and it predicts the future rivalry between Carthage and Rome, and Rome's eventual triumph. It is apparent that Virgil's aim is to confirm and embellish the popular tradition of the Trojan origin of the Roman state, and the descent of the house of Julian from Venus, or Aphrodite as she was known to the Greeks, and the Dardanians. Contrary to earlier traditions, Virgil would have us believe that Dardanus, the founder of Troy, went there from Italy. Since Julius Caesar took great pride in his Trojan ancestry, he endowed the site of Novum Ilium with considerable privileges. Virgil could, therefore, hardly do other than base his geography of the legendary Troy upon that of Ilium.

This becomes immediately apparent from his description of the sack of Troy. In the Aeneid Book 2, Aeneas, having travelled as far as Carthage, recounted the fall of Troy to Queen Dido. Despite some fabulous heroics, Aeneas was unable to prevent the city going up in flames. He finally escaped carrying his father on his back, his son in one hand and the temple treasures in the other. As the city burnt, he told Dido that he could see the flames from the burning houses reflected in the waters of the strait of Sigeion. As Virgil must have known, this would only have been possible if his Troy was on the coast, which was not the case for Novum Ilium in his day. Was he perhaps believing Hestaiai's claim that 'the plain now to be seen in front of the present Ilium is a later deposit of the rivers'? Or was he using his own poetic licence, and imagining a fictitious Troy by the sea, having never visited Novum Ilium? While we cannot answer these questions, we can be certain that Virgil's Ilium was not Homer's Ilium, from which the Achaean ships could not be seen. The Aeneid, therefore, will not provide us with any useful geographical evidence concerning Homeric Troy.

Conclusions

This brief overview of literary sources concerning the Trojan War confirms that the Iliad itself must remain our primary source of on-site geographical and topographical information concerning the Trojan plain. The Odyssey may endorse some of this information. However, where it contradicts the Iliad, information from the Iliad will take precedence. Of the later sources, only those which include information derived from sources dating to before mid 6C may contain useful additional geographical evidence concerning the real location of Troy.

THE STORY OF THE ILIAD, WITH LANDSCAPE DETAILS EMPHASISED

Introduction

This much abbreviated version of the Iliad is for those wishing to become more familiar with the story. It is based upon the translation by Rieu [1] in his deservedly popular Penguin Classics Edition. However, in the interests of accuracy, some quotations from the Iliad are taken from the more literal translation by Murray given in the Loeb Edition [2]. I hope that, even from this very shortened version, the reader will gain some appreciation of the nature and spirit of Homer's writing. In it I have included all the most important geographical references and mentions of features in the Trojan landscape, so you can see how these references are woven into the fabric of the story. These are quoted in bold type, and are collected together in Chapter 3 so as to give a good picture of the Trojan plain. This will help us when we are looking for the real site of Homeric Troy.

The Iliad has a sub-title, 'The Wrath of Achilles'. This anger and its terrible consequences, at first introverted, but later unleashed upon the Trojans, forms a thread which runs right through the Iliad. This thread is the reason why some scholars believe the Iliad to have been created by Homer as one very long epic poem. But others, including Walter Leaf, disagree.

THE STORY OF THE ILIAD

Book 1. Agamemnon insults Achilles.

When the story of the Iliad begins, the Greeks are encamped near their ships on the edge of the Trojan plain, and the war had been going on for over nine years. The Greek forces had all arrived at the coast of Asia by ship, and these were now drawn up on the beach, out of the water. **Over a thousand ships stood in long lines, three ships deep, on a wide sandy beach between two headlands, near the mouth of the river Scamander.** The city of Troy with its high citadel was defended by King Priam and his many allies, who had come mainly from neighbouring countries.

Fighting, it seems, had been intermittent. The Trojans spent most of their time safely behind the strong walls of their city. During such times, Achilles, their greatest warrior, had managed to capture many Trojan cities during campaigns by land and by ship. As was customary, he and his troops took much rich booty from the fallen cities, including many Trojan women. He and his army had recently returned from such a trip, during which he had captured a place called Chryse. A woman taken from there, Chryseis, was awarded by lot to Agamemnon as his share of the booty. Achilles kept for himself another woman named Briseis.

Now it so happened that the father of Chryseis was a local priest of Apollo. Much distressed, he came to the Greek camp with handsome gifts as a ransom payment, and asked for the return of his daughter. When Agamemnon refused, the priest went home and prayed to Apollo for help. Apollo was deeply offended by Agamemnon's behaviour, so he sent a plague among the Achaeans.

With his men starting to die around him, Agamemnon sought an explanation from Chalcas, the seer who had accompanied the Greek expedition. Chalcas told him that the deaths were the punishment of Apollo for the mistreatment of his priest. To prevent further losses among his men, Agamemnon was forced to give her up, which he did with bad grace. She was returned to Chryse by Odysseus in a fast ship, along with suitable offerings to propitiate the angry god. Now, left with no prize, Agamemnon decided to confiscate Briseis, the woman chosen by Achilles. This made Achilles so angry that he vowed that he would not fight for the Achaeans until Briseis was returned to him. He returned to his tent, and there he wept and prayed for vengeance to his divine mother Thetis. In his anger he asked her to try to persuade the gods to help the Trojans fling the Achaeans back to their ships, pen them in against the sea and slaughter them. Thus they would be taught to appreciate their greatest fighter, and Agamemnon would realize what a fool he had been to insult the noblest of them all. Thetis answered his prayer. She waited until she found Zeus alone, then appealed to him to do as she asked, and he reluctantly agreed.

Book 2. The Greek and Trojan armies.
To achieve what he had promised, Zeus first sent a false dream to Agamemnon, persuading him that now was a good time to assemble all his forces and fight the Trojans. Zeus had once solemnly told Agamemnon that he should never sail home until he had brought the towers of Ilium tumbling down, so Agamemnon followed the advice of the dream. First, to test the will of his men to fight he suggested they give up and go home. When the men, who had become disheartened over the last nine years, rushed towards the ships, it was the bright eyed Athene who swooped down beside Odysseus and told him to use his wits to persuade the men to stay. When order was restored and the men had returned to the meeting place, Odysseus addressed the men and called on them to stand their ground, and fight until Priam's spacious town was captured. With the help of a speech by aged Nestor, king of Pylos, they won over the support of the men, and after a sacrifice to Zeus, King Agamemnon had his troops assemble for inspection. Homer writes (Il. 2. 464ff) 'So their many tribes poured out of the ships and huts into **the plain of Scamander…and they stood in the flowery meadow…**, countless, as are the leaves and flowers of their season.'

There then follows a long list of all the Greek forces, known to scholars as the 'Catalogue of Ships'. This Homer introduces with the words 'Now I will tell the leaders of the ships, and all the ships.' He starts with the Boeotians, who came in fifty ships, 'with a hundred and twenty young Boeotians in each.' Next he gives the men from Aspledon and Minyaean Orchomenos, with thirty hollow ships. The list continues with the men from Phocis with forty black ships, and cites many more places before ending with the Magnetes who lived by Mount Pelion.

While the great Achaean army started rolling across the plain towards the walls of Troy, the goddess Iris was sent to Priam's doors to warn the Trojans and their allies to gather together and go out and do battle. She spoke to Priam disguised as his son Polites who, we are told, **'sat as a lookout for the**

Trojans, trusting to his fleetness of foot, on the topmost part of the grave mound of aged Aesyetes, watching for the time when the Achaeans should start out from their ships.' Hector, Priam's son and their greatest warrior, recognised the voice as that of the goddess, and the men rushed to arms. We are then told of another geographic feature. **'There is in front of the city a steep mound far out in the plain, with a clear space round it on all sides; this men call Batieia, but the immortals call it the tomb of dancing Myrine'**. It was here that the Trojans and their allies now formed up in battle order.

Homer then lists the forces on the Trojan side. He starts with the Trojans, led by the great Hector, leading the best and largest force, and the keenest spearmen of them all. Then came **the Dardanians, a colony led by Aeneas, from 'among the spurs of Ida.'** After the Dardanians, the rest of the Trojan allies are listed, ending with the Mysians, Phrygians, the Carians who possessed Miletus, and the Lycians 'from distant Lycia and the swirling streams of Xanthus.' The Trojan army hailed from many parts and were without a common language.

Both lists contain names of places that cannot be identified today, but also many places that are well known. From these, it is reasonably clear that Homer has listed the Trojan allies from the mainland of Western Asia generally from north to south. He starts with the Dardanians, coming from the region around Gargarus, the highest mountain in the hills of Ida to the north of Lesbos. The list ends with forces from Lycia in the SW corner of Anatolia.

Book 3. Menelaus fights Paris.

When all the Trojans were drawn up in battle order, they advanced towards the Achaeans, making as much noise as possible. The Achaeans, on the other hand, marched in silence, filled with resolve. Just as they were about to clash, Paris stepped out from the Trojan ranks and pledged single combat against any Argive they cared to choose. This challenge was met by the mighty Menelaus, who longed for revenge against the man who had stolen his beautiful wife. When he saw his opponent, Paris's heart failed him and he fled. His brother Hector sought him out and persuaded him to honour his pledge, so Paris returned to the battlefield. Priam and his friend Antenor were brought to the field in a chariot to witness the outcome. The pair drew lots to decide who should be the first to cast his spear, this falling to Paris. Then the fight commenced. Menelaus parried the spear with his shield, and then cast his own spear. This pierced the shield of Paris, who twisted and so avoided death. Menelaus then struck Paris a mighty blow with his silver-studded bronze sword on the helmet, but the sword shattered into several pieces. Menelaus rushed forward, seized the dazed Paris by the thick crest of horse hair on his helmet, and was about to drag him off and claim victory, when Aphrodite enveloped Paris, her favourite, in a mist and transported him from the field to the safety of his own bedroom.

When it became clear to Menelaus that Paris had fled the battlefield, Agamemnon announced that the victor was Menelaus, and demanded that the Trojans give up Helen.

Book 4. Pandarus breaks the truce.

With Menelaus the victor, Zeus had now to decide whether or not to allow Helen to be handed over, and allow the Trojans and Achaeans to part on friendly terms. Such a resolution pleased neither Athene nor Hera, and it was Athene who flashed down into the midst of the armies. There she found a fine Trojan archer called Pandarus, and talked him into shooting Menelaus with an arrow. When the arrow was about to find its target, she directed it so that it caused only a shallow wound. However, this outrage caused an immediate end to the truce. While Menelaus was being attended to, the Trojan battle line advanced to attack. Agamemnon then showed his mettle, and went round all his troops with words of encouragement to inspire them. In the ensuing battle, Ares, the god of war, spurred on the Trojans, and Athene helped the Achaeans. After a while the Trojans started to fall back, which did not please **Apollo, who was watching from Pergamus**. He started calling out encouragement to the Trojans, reminding them that Achilles was not fighting, but lay sulking back at the ships. It was a day when many a Trojan prince and many an Achaean noble fell, lying stretched out side by side.

Book 5. The heroic deeds of Diomedes.

As the battle continued, Athene called on Ares to join her in leaving the field, and letting Zeus decide who should win. The Danaans then started to push back the Trojans, each captain killing his man. Athene remained ready as usual to answer the prayers of the Achaeans, and to help them if needed. Diomedes, the Argive son of Tydeus, was causing much havoc among the Trojans. In desperation Aeneas sought out their best archer Pandarus, and asked him to shoot Diomedes. Pandarus replied that he had already shot him in the shoulder, and it must be some god who was making him so indomitable. Diomedes would have killed Aeneas as well, after wounding him with a great rock, but Aphrodite came to his aid. However, Diomedes even managed to wound Aphrodite, and it needed the help of Apollo to save both Aphrodite and Aeneas from the spear of the powerful Achaean. Aphrodite fled back to Olympus on a chariot provided by Ares, while **Apollo removed Aeneas from the field to the holy citadel of Pergamus, where his temple stood**.

Then Ares went among the Trojans to give them new heart, and the Trojans began to stand and hold their ground. They were soon reinforced by the return of Aeneas, who had been healed by Apollo. Champions on both sides fought and fell. Then, faced by Ares and Hector, the Achaeans fell back steadily. Ares was slaughtering so many Argives that Hera and Athene agreed to join the battle. First they obtained Zeus's agreement to them driving Ares from the battlefield. Then they went to Troy from Olympus in their gold and silver chariot. Soon they **'came to the land of Troy and the two flowing rivers, where the Simois and Scamander join their streams, there the goddess, white armed Hera, stayed her horses, and loosed them from the chariot**...' From there the two goddesses set out on foot to help the Argives, and encouraged them to redouble their efforts. Hera, in the likeness of a warrior, reminded them that when Achilles was in the field, the Trojans dared not even show themselves in front of the Dardanian Gates, '...but **now far from the city they are fighting at the hollow ships.'** Athene found Diomedes, told him not to fear even Ares with her at his side, and together they drove a chariot towards Ares. Ares hurled his spear at Diomedes, but Athene pushed it upwards so that it missed its target. Athene then guided the spear of Diomedes into the belly of Ares, and saw the wounded god whirl up towards heaven in a hazy cloud. Having achieved the task they set themselves, Hera and Athene also left the battlefield and returned to Mount Olympus and the palace of Zeus.

Book 6. Hector and Andromache.

Left to themselves, free of interference from the gods, the Trojans and Achaeans carried on the grim struggle. **The battle swayed to and fro across the plain, 'midway between Simois and the streams of Xanthus.'** The Achaeans then started to gain the upper hand. Menelaus captured a Trojan named Adrestus alive, who begged to buy his freedom with a large ransom. But Agamemnon appeared as Menelaus was hesitating, and told him that not one of the Trojans should be left alive, down to the babies in their mother's womb. '…let all perish together from Ilios, unmourned and unseen.' As an aside here, we note that Agamemnon's words show that genocide was his intention. We should remember this when later we follow Aeneas, a survivor from Troy, who escaped and eventually became regarded as one of the founders of Rome and the Roman Empire.

Then, when the Trojans had been pushed back towards Ilium, they were rallied again by Hector into making a stand before they reached the gates. The older women were told to collect at the temple of Athene on the Acropolis, place a precious robe on the knees of the seated goddess, and beg her 'to keep the savage spearman, Diomedes, clear of holy Ilium.' The Trojans rallied to such an extent that they started to push back the Achaeans, who thought some god must have come down from the starry sky to help them.

Meanwhile Hector made his way **through the Scaean Gate to Priam's palace, a magnificent house with a marble colonnaded front, behind which were 50 apartments, one for each of his sons, and 12 apartments for his daughters.** There he told his mother Hecabe also to take a precious robe and join the other women in prayer at Athene's temple in the acropolis. This she did, taking with her a robe embroidered by women from Sidon in Phoenicia. Hector then went to Paris's bedroom, and told him to go down and help on the battlefield. He then went to find his wife Andromache. When he heard that she had climbed the 'great tower of Ilium', **he retraced his steps down the well-built streets, crossing the great city till he reached the Scaean Gate**, where Andromache came running up to meet him carrying their baby son. She begged him not to return to the battle. Instead she told him to **'Rally the Trojans by the fig tree there, where the wall is easiest to scale and the town most open to attack.'** Three times the Atreidae had tried to break in there. Hector held his wife and son briefly, then sent her back to her house while he made his way with Paris back to the field of battle.

Book 7. Aias fights Hector.

Each soon killed an opponent. When Athene saw the Argives again being slaughtered, **she flew down from Olympus** to sacred Ilium. **Apollo saw her from Pergamus** and started out to intercept her. He, being desirous of a Trojan victory, persuaded her to agree to arrange a truce, and for the battle to be decided by single combat between Hector and one of the Achaeans. This was duly arranged, and the lot fell to mighty Aias to fight Hector. When Hector saw his great size, dressed in full armour and carrying his huge tower shield, even Hector's heart gave a flutter. They fought long and hard, until Aias wounded Hector, whereupon Apollo stepped in to give Hector new strength. At last the heralds raised their staves between the combatants and called for the fight to end. Aias and Hector exchanged gifts of honour, and a truce was declared so that both sides could collect and bury their dead.

The Trojan elders later gathered at the doors of Priam's palace. One of them proposed they now return Helen along with her property, since no good would come by continuing the fight. Paris opposed this suggestion, but offered instead to give the Achaeans all the goods he had brought back with him from Argos, and to add something of his own. Priam agreed that Paris's offer be conveyed to the Achaeans, and that the truce should hold until their dead were buried. The Achaeans refused the offer, but agreed to the truce. This allowed the Achaeans to burn their dead brethren with full honours on the customary funeral pyre, then using carts drawn by oxen and mules **they raised a single barrow over them, using such material as the plain provides. Using this mound for a base, they then built high walls to protect the ships and themselves, with strong gates let into them, leaving carriage-ways for the chariots. Then outside the walls they dug a deep parallel trench, with a line of stakes along it as an obstruction to chariots and infantry,** should the Trojans press them hard against their ships.

The Imperial Earthshaker Poseidon was peeved that the Achaeans had built their wall without offering the proper sacrifices to the gods. He complained to Zeus that people would talk about this wall long after they had forgotten the wall of Troy that he and Apollo had built for Laomedon. Zeus reassured him that his misgivings over 'this contraption' were absurd. Poseidon was perfectly capable, once the Achaeans had sailed for home, of sending a flood or an earthquake to break down the wall and obliterate these defences. That night the Achaeans feasted. They drank wine that had just come in by ship from Lemnos, a gift from a son of Jason, the great captain of the Argonauts. In the city the Trojans and their allies also feasted, but Zeus, 'brewing evil in his heart for them, kept thundering ominously.'

Note - Homer's reference here is to Jason, the famous captain of the Argonauts who, accompanied by Herakles (also known to the Romans as Hercules), sought to find and bring back the Golden Fleece. Was the story of Jason and the Argonauts purely a made-up and fantastic legend? Or did the legend reflect a real historical venture to Colchis on the SE shore of the Black Sea? Homer clearly gave the story some historical credibility, and places the war barely two generations after Jason's famous expedition.

Book 8. The Greeks withdraw to their ships.

Zeus then called a meeting, and told the other gods of his decision to bring the matter to a speedy close. He said that if he found any god taking an independent course and going to help the Trojans or Danaans, he would throw them out of heaven altogether. He then went off to the top of Mount Gararus, a peak of Ida, from where he looked out over the Trojan city and the ships of the Achaeans.

The next day, as the converging forces met once more, he held a symbolic balance of fate in his hands, and the scales came down on the side of the Achaeans, spelling a day of doom for them. He sent a flash of lightening down among the Achaean troops, and terror coloured the cheeks of every man. Although Nestor and Diomedes in their chariot made a brave sortie against the Trojans which nearly won the day, Zeus stopped them by hurling a thunderbolt in front of the horses of their chariot, and the smell of burning sulphur filling the air. Realising that Zeus was against them, they turned their chariot around and joined the rest of their comrades in a steady retreat towards their ships.

Spurred on by Zeus, the Trojans gradually pushed the Greeks back across their defensive ditch, and onto the shore among their own ships.

Hera and Athene were distressed at the sight of so many Danaans being slaughtered, so agreed to go to their aid together in a flaming chariot. But Zeus saw their intentions, and sent Iris as a messenger with an instruction to tell them to stop, which they had no choice but to obey. Zeus left his vantage spot at Mount Gargarus and returned to Olympus to speak with them. He told them that more Achaeans would die the following day, and they would have no rest until Achilles came out from his ship to fight for them. This was decreed by heaven, and neither Hera nor Athene could do anything about it. And as night fell, Hector withdrew his troops, telling them that only the failing light had prevented them from destroying all the Achaeans and their ships. So the Trojans collected food by chariot from the town, and **camped across the corridors of battle, between the ships and the streams of Xanthus**. All night long a thousand fires flickered expectantly at what the morning would bring.

Note. The lines 8.517-524 suggest that the Trojans had not camped away from the city before. Having hemmed the Greeks in by their ships, the Trojans could not afford to return to Troy for the night, so they camped on the ground they had just taken.

Book 9. Agamemnon's peace embassy to Achilles.

While the Trojans kept watch, the Achaeans were close to despair. Agamemnon proposed they leave that night. With half the army lost, Troy with its broad streets would never fall to them now. But Diomedes would have none of it. 'Go if you wish,' he told the king, 'but the rest of us will stay until Troy is sacked.' After they had eaten, they held a conference, at which Agamemnon admitted that he now bitterly regretted his treatment of Achilles. He promised to return Briseis along with seven other women all suitably skilled, if Achilles would forgive him and join them in battle. It was agreed this offer would be carried to Achilles by Aias and Odysseus.

Accompanied by Phoenix, Achilles' old charioteer, the three made their way to the end of the line of ships, where they found Achilles and his close friend

Patroclus sitting together. Achilles welcomed them warmly, and cooked them a meal. After drinking to the health of Achilles, Odysseus relayed the message from Agamemnon in a fine speech. Achilles responded with one equally as fine, and his message was simple. Neither Agamemnon nor the rest of the Danaans would ever win him over, since it appeared to him that nothing he had ever done for his countrymen had been properly appreciated. He loved Briseis with all his heart, but she had been snatched away from him by an ungrateful king. That king should not try his tricks on him again, for he would not succeed. Achilles intended to sail back to his home in Phthia the very next day.

Another long speech, this time from Phoenix, failed to persuade Achilles to conquer his pride. Although he thawed somewhat, he said he had no use for the good opinion of the Achaeans. He was content instead with the approbation of Zeus. He invited Phoenix to stay with him until morning, when they would decide whether to stay or go. Aias then told Odysseus they should go and report back to the king. He admonished Achilles for holding a grudge for so long, and for his inhumanity in not giving a thought for the affection of his colleagues who had made him the idol of their camp. Their wish was nothing more than to remain his dearest friends. Achilles admitted there was much in what Aias had said, but was of the opinion that Hector would be brought up short of his own hut and his black ship. While Achilles, Patroclus and Phoenix settled down for the night in Achilles' hut, Odysseus and Aias reported the blunt response from Achilles back to Agamemnon. They told the king that Achilles believed that they would never achieve their goal 'in the steep streets of Ilium', for Zeus was protecting that city. So they took the advice from Diomedes, and went to bed, intending at the first light of dawn to deploy their forces as best they could to protect the ships.

Book 10. A successful spying mission.
But Agamemnon could not sleep for worry. He woke his old friend Nestor and together they decided to send spies into the Trojan camp to learn their plans and troop dispositions. Diomedes and Odysseus were chosen for the task, and Nestor went to awaken Diomedes. Nestor reminded him of how close the Trojans were. **'Do you not realize that the Trojans on the rising ground of the plain are camped hard by the ships, and but scant space**

still holds them off?' After making a tour of their outposts to check all their sentries were awake, they held a brief meeting to plan their reconnaissance. Then Odysseus and Diomedes went off into the night. They were unaware that Hector had held a similar meeting, and sent a spy, Dolon, to visit the Achaean camp. However, they saw Dolon before he saw them, and managed to capture him. From Dolon, who answered all their questions truthfully, they learnt where to find the Trojan allies sleeping in their separate camps. He told them that **five groups of allies, including the 'noble Pelasgi', were lying towards the sea, and another four, including the Mysians and Phrygians, were situated towards 'Thymbre'.** He also told them that **Hector '... was holding council by the tomb of godlike Ilus, away from all the turmoil...'** After rewarding Dolon with a quick death, they raided the camp of the Thracians, killing thirteen and riding back to the ships on a pair of very fine thoroughbred white horses. They were greeted by Nestor, and Odysseus told him all that had taken place. He added that **the horses they brought back were 'newly come from Thrace'.**

Note that, despite the Greeks being camped in large numbers before Troy, reinforcements such as these Thracian horses were readily able to reach Troy by another route. This must have been via an overland route through the hills of Ida.

Book 11. Achilles becomes concerned.

When dawn came, Agamemnon summoned his forces to prepare for battle, and the men put on their armour, gathered up their weapons, and took up their positions. On their side, '**the Trojans facing them on the rising ground of the plain were arrayed about great Hector...**' Then the two sides clashed, and throughout the morning the fighting continued with the Achaeans gradually getting the better of their opponents. Then, around mid-day, the Danaans decisively gained the upper hand, and the Trojan ranks were finally broken. They were soon in rout before Agamemnon and the Argives. As Zeus drew Hector away from the din of battle, so Agamemnon and his army chased the fleeing Trojans, who sought safety behind their walls. '**And past the tomb of ancient Ilus, son of Dardanus, over the middle of the plain, past the wild fig tree they sped, straining towards the city**...But when they came to the Scaean Gates and the oak tree, there the two armies halted and awaited one another, but some were still being driven in rout over the middle of the plain like cattle…'

At this point Zeus came down, and **'sat on the peaks of many fountained Ida; and in his hands he held the thunder bolt.'** From there he sent Iris to Hector with a message telling him to give ground as long as Agamemnon was in full war-cry. But as soon as the king was hit by a spear or arrow and retired from the field, Zeus would give Hector the strength to drive the Achaeans right back to their ships by the time the sun set. And so it came to pass. The last Trojan killed by Agamemnon was **Iphidamas, who had recently come from Thrace with twelve beaked ships, which he had left at Perkote and come by foot to Troy.** Then, as Zeus had promised, Agamemnon was caught unawares by a spear which passed through his forearm. He was then driven back to the ships to have his wound tended. This was the signal for the Trojans to redouble their efforts. Irreparable disaster now threatened the Achaeans.

Realising that Zeus had turned against them, they retreated, and quickly fell back towards the ships. They lost another captain when **Diomedes was hit in the foot by an arrow shot by Paris, who was supporting himself against a pillar on the mound of Ilus.** Then, after helping to rescue Diomedes, Odysseus was wounded in the thigh, and had to be rescued from death by Menelaus and Aias. So, with more of their captains wounded, the Achaeans continued to retreat. Then Aias, on his side of the battlefield, halted the Trojans with a brave counterattack before they could reach the ships. Hector meanwhile knew nothing of this, '…since he was **fighting on the far left of the battle by the banks of the river Scamander…'** where the slaughter was heaviest.

As the Achaeans fell back towards their camp, Achilles had been watching the rout from the stern of his ship. He saw Nestor helping a wounded man, and sent his friend Patroclus to find out who this was. Patroclus then had to listen to the wrath of Nestor over Achilles' refusal to fight. Why did Achilles show no concern or pity for his fallen countrymen? Nestor reminded Patroclus that he and Achilles had come to Troy together. Achilles' father Peleus had instructed that Patroclus, as the older man, should give Achilles sound advice, set him an example, and 'take the lead, which he will follow to his own advantage.' Patroclus, much moved by Nestor's speech, started out to return to Achilles, but was soon diverted to help treat the wounds of one of his comrades.

Book 12. Hector storms the Achaean camp wall.

Meanwhile the Argives and Trojans fought on. The wall that was built without the goodwill of the gods groaned under the weight of missiles hurled against it, and Hector continued to encourage the Trojans to cross the Argive trench. Then to save risking their chariots across the trench, they dismounted, left the horses behind with their squires, formed themselves into five companies, and charged the trench on foot. There were places where the Achaeans had left a causeway between the trenches for the safe passage of their own troops, and these were protected by gates. These were stoutly defended for a time, but the Trojans, keeping the upper hand, attacked other gates also. Hector and Polydamus were about to cross the trench when an eagle, bitten by a snake he was carrying in his talons, dropped it among the Trojans. This was taken as a bad omen, and Polydamus advised Hector not to advance and fight for the ships that day. Hector, however, put his faith in Zeus, and gave the order to advance. A gust of wind blew dust in the face of the Achaeans, and the Trojans made a determined effort to breach the wall. After further mighty struggles, a Trojan ally from Lycia named Sarpendon, beloved son of Zeus, made the first breach in the wall, big enough for a company to pass through. Then despite desperate defending by the Achaeans, the Trojans began to swarm over the wall, while others poured in through the gate itself. 'The Danaans were driven in rout among the hollow ships, and an unceasing din arose.'

Book 13. The battle at the ships.

Having forbidden the other gods of Olympus to interfere in the fighting, Zeus **'turned away his gleaming eyes, and looked afar at the land of the Thracian horsemen, and of the Mysians who fight in close combat, and of the lordly Hippemolgi who drink the milk of mares... To Troy he no longer turned his gleaming eyes at all...'** for he did not expect any of the gods to go against his command to keep away. But Poseidon was watching from afar. He had risen from the sea and **'sat marvelling at the war and the battle, high on the topmost peak of wooded Samothrace, for** from there all Ida was plain to see, and plain to see were the city of Priam and the ships of the Achaeans.' He pitied the Achaeans and was enraged with Zeus. As soon as he saw that Zeus was no longer watching, he decided to intervene on their behalf. He strode down the mountainside, **'and the high mountains and the woodland trembled beneath the immortal feet of Poseidon as he went.' With his fourth stride he reached his palace at Aegae, where he harnessed his chariot and drove majestically across the waves towards the battle. He left his horses in a large cavern mid-way between Tenedos and Imbros, then made his way to the Achaeans' camp.**

As the Trojans were massing behind Hector, Poseidon in the form of an Achaean captain began to revitalise the Greeks. Thus inspired, the Achaeans rallied enough to halt the Trojan charge. The fighting became general by the stern of the ships, with many casualties on both sides, as first one side then the other pushed forward then fell back. Then on the left side of the ships the Argives began to get the upper hand. But on another front, Hector still tried to press forward, opposed by picked men from Athens. Then Polydamus suggested the Trojans withdraw for a meeting to agree tactics; whether to carry on the attack or to withdraw and regroup and make plans for the morrow. He was worried in case Achilles should be persuaded to come out and fight. But Hector wanted a quick victory. Time and again the Trojans attacked and probed at many places, but the Achaean defences stood firm against them.

Book 14. The deception of Zeus.
When the Achaean wall fell, Nestor was with the wounded royal lords Agamemnon, Odysseus and Diomedes. **The beach, 'wide as it was, had proved unable to hold all the ships, and the Achaeans, cramped for room, had drawn them up in tiers, covering the whole seaboard of the long bay from headland to headland.'** Agamemnon, fearing that Zeus had turned against them and they would all perish, suggested dragging the line of ships closest to the sea into the water, and anchoring them out to sea. The others could then be launched during the night, and they could make safe their escape. Odysseus talked him out of issuing an order to this effect, and instead they went round giving encouragement to the troops.

Hera had seen Poseidon scurrying among the Achaeans, and Zeus sitting on the topmost peak of Ida. She conceived a ruse to bemuse the wits of the king of the gods, so that he would not notice Poseidon helping the Achaeans. She succeeded in causing him to fall into a deep and gentle sleep after lying with her, thereby distracting his attention away from the battlefield. While he was asleep Poseidon was encouraged to help the Achaeans more vigorously. Aias succeeded in injuring Hector with a huge rock, so he was withdrawn stunned from the field of battle. **Hector was carried off to 'the ford of eddying Xanthus, the noble River whose father is immortal Zeus'**, where he was laid on the ground and revived with splashes of cold water. Spurred on by this success, and inspired by Poseidon, the Argives gradually regrouped, their newfound strength taking its toll on the flesh of many a Trojan fighter. Once again the battle had swung in their favour.

Book 15. The Achaeans at their ships.

When Zeus awoke and surveyed the battlefield, he saw the Trojans fleeing back across the palisade and trench towards their chariots, suffering heavy losses. There also was Hector lying on the ground, and Poseidon was helping the Achaeans as they chased after the Trojans. Zeus turned to blame his queen Hera, but she denied that the awakening of Poseidon was her doing. Quickly he sent a message to Poseidon to instruct him to leave the field and go home, and sent Apollo to give new strength to Hector. Then Zeus told Hera how the battle would go. He intended that the Achaeans should fall back among the ships of Achilles, who would then send his friend Patroclus into the fight. It would be only after the death of his dear friend Patroclus that Achilles would be roused sufficiently to fight again for his countrymen, and eventually he would kill Hector. This was all in accordance with a promise he had earlier given Achilles, and a nod of his head had made the promise solemn and binding.

With the other gods banned from interfering, Apollo soon set about his task of bringing panic to the ranks of Achaeans. He revitalised Hector to such effect that the astonished Achaeans recognised at once the hand of Zeus behind this recovery. Dismayed, they again started to fall back towards their ships. Despite staunch resistance, the Trojan advance proved unstoppable, and the Achaeans were pushed back across the trench and palisade in disorder, and took refuge behind their wall. But Apollo with ease 'kicked down the banks of the deep trench and piled them in the middle to make a wide causeway', and with equal ease knocked down the Achaean wall.

Patroclus, who was tending the wounded when he heard of the pending danger, went to join Achilles beside his ship. Then the Trojans, despite yet more heroic defensive fighting, now stormed the ships. At last Hector managed to reach the stern of one of them, and called upon the Trojans to bring fire to set it alight. Only the mighty Aias still stood firm before them.

Book 16. Patroclus fights and dies.

When he reached his master, Patroclus appealed to Achilles at least to allow him to take the field with Achilles' forces, known also as the Myrmidons. Achilles was now roused, and ready to put his grudge behind him. He agreed Patroclus should lead the Myrmidons, and gave him his armour.

At that point, Hector managed to break the spear of Aias, who then had to retire out of range. The Trojans then started to throw blazing brands at the ships, one of which caught fire and started to burn. Achilles saw the flames, recognised their significance, and hastened Patroclus to finish preparing for battle. Then Achilles went round the huts and got all his men under arms. He told Patroclus to push the Trojans back from the ships, and then return. With these instructions, the Myrmidons went into battle. Achilles prayed to Zeus for success on the field and for the safe return of Patroclus, but Zeus, who heard this prayer, answered only half of it, but not the rest.

The sight of Patroclus wearing Achilles' armour, accompanied by the Myrmidons, caused the Trojans' hearts to sink. They thought that, at last, Achilles had settled his feud with Agamemnon and had come out to fight. They thought about retreat, and their lines began to waver. Under the fresh assault from Patroclus and his men, and with the Achaeans revitalised by their support, the Trojans began to withdraw from the ships. Patroclus then killed the mighty Sarpendon, and soon the withdrawal became a rout. Then Patroclus got carried away with his successes, and forgot his orders from Achilles to return to the ship. This was his undoing. He felled many more Trojans, and chased them back as far as Troy. There he and his followers tried to take 'high-

gated Troy'. **'Thrice did Patroclus set foot on a corner (literally 'elbow')
of the high wall, and thrice did Apollo fling him back...'** When he tried
a fourth time, Apollo warned him that neither he nor Achilles would sack Troy,
and Patroclus stepped back in fear. Soon afterwards he was struck violently in
the back by the strong hand of Apollo. He fell, dazed, his spear broken, and his
helmet lost. As he stood up, he was wounded by a spear in his back. He tried to
escape into the throng, but was finally killed by a thrust from the bronze spear
of Hector. The fine armour of Achilles was stripped from his body and sent
back to Troy. Meanwhile the immortal horses that drew Achilles' chariot, a gift
from the gods to his father Peleus, stood motionless and wept at the loss of
their charioteer Patroclus.

Book 17. The battle over the body of Patroclus.
The Trojans wanted to defile the body of Patroclus and feed it to the dogs of
Troy, while the Achaeans were determined to recover his body for a proper
burial. So a fight ensued over the body, which became the centre of the
battle between both sides. The grim struggle raged all day long, and
Menelaus and the gigantic Aias, aided by Athene, were mainly responsible
for saving his body. Achilles had as yet no idea that his great friend had been
killed, for **the fighting was a long way from the ships, under the walls
of Troy**. But with Apollo supporting Hector and the Trojans, it was the
Achaeans, carrying the body of Patroclus, who were slowly but surely driven
back to their ships.

Book 18. New armour for Achilles.
When Achilles was told that Patroclus had been killed, a great sadness and
despair descended upon him. And he raged, for he knew he must now go out
and kill Hector, to avenge the death of his friend. But he had no armour, for
this he had given to Patroclus, and even now it was being carried triumphantly
back to Troy. But, in his hour of need, his immortal mother Thetis came to
him and promised him a new suit of armour, made by the lame god Hephaestus
himself. She would return with it at dawn the next morning.

Achilles feared that by then the battle might be lost. So, protected by Athene,
he went beyond the wall and showed himself to the Trojans, causing much
consternation in their hearts. Hector ignored advice to retire to Troy, and

ordered the men to set up camp and prepare their supper. All night long the Achaeans mourned loudly the death of Patroclus, and Achilles swore he would not hold his funeral until he had killed Hector. He knew that his own early death had been ordained by the gods, but now he wanted to avenge the death of Patroclus, and to ensure he was given a proper burial.

The wonderful description of how Hephaestus made the armour for Achilles is not relevant to the aims of this book, but it is hoped that the reader will enjoy this when reading a full version. It also offers a valuable insight into the state of metalworking technology as it was known in Trojan times according to Homer.

Book 19. The end of the feud.
The next morning Thetis returned as promised with the new armour for Achilles, and stayed to treat the body of Patroclus with ambrosia and red nectar to keep it from decomposing until the time came for his funeral. Then Achilles went among the troops, and sat down with them in front of Agamemnon. Then he spoke saying that as far as he was concerned, his feud with Agamemnon was at an end. All he wanted now was to fight the Trojans and kill Hector. Agamemnon, in his reply, first said he was not to blame for his unfair treatment of Achilles, for it was the gods who had blinded him of his wits and judgement. He was now willing to make amends, and to return to Achilles his woman Briseis, as well as many added gifts as atonement for his suffering.

With the feud ended, it was agreed that the men should wait until they had eaten before they resumed battle. But Achilles was too full of anger and remorse to eat anything. Agamemnon arranged for the gifts to be taken to Achilles' hut while the meal was taken, and when the men were ready, they lined up in battle formation. While the men ate, Achilles continued to mourn the loss of his best friend. When the meal was over, the men prepared for war, and Achilles donned his new armour. And just before he went out to fight, Athene 'shed into his breast nectar and sweet ambrosia so that hunger may not come upon him.'

Book 20. The gods join in the war.
While the Achaeans lined up for battle by the ships, the Trojans took up their positions 'on the rising ground of the plain.' Zeus, concerned at

what might happen next, called the gods to a meeting. Left to themselves, the Trojans would quickly flee back to seek safety in their city, and Achilles might then start storming the walls, thus cheating his destiny. To avoid this, he told the gods they were free to go down to the battlefield, and help whichever side they most favoured.

When the armies clashed, it was indeed a clash of the gods. While Athene led support for the Achaeans, Ares, the god of war, encouraged the Trojans, **urging them on, 'at one moment from the heights of the citadel, and at the next from the banks of the Simois, as he ran along the slopes of Kallikolone'.** Then Poseidon caused an earthquake, and the gods came and arrayed themselves against each other, according to the sides they had chosen. Poseidon spoke to Hera, and called the gods aiding the Achaeans to now withdraw from the field, but to rejoin the battle if Apollo and Ares started interfering with the fighting. **'...let us then go apart from the track to some look-out spot and sit there, and war will be the concern of men.'** He led the way **'to the heaped up wall of godlike Herakles, the high wall that the Trojans and Pallas Athene had built for him so that he might flee there and escape from the monster of the deep when it drove him from the seashore to the plain.'** Their divine opponents also **'sat opposite on the brows of Kallicolone'**, both sides pausing to reflect on the scene before them.

On the field, Aeneas and Achilles came face to face. Before they fought each recounted their heritage. Aeneas gave his lineage from Dardanus, founder of Dardania **'at a time before the sacred city of Ilium had been built to shelter people on the plain.'** But destiny had ordained that Aeneas would survive to save the House of Dardanus, much beloved by Zeus, from extinction. He would become king of Troy, to be followed by his children's children in the time to come. It was Poseidon who saved Aeneas from the spear of Achilles by whisking him off to the edge of the battlefield. Later that day Apollo also intervened to save the life of Hector from the deathly hand of Achilles, while the Trojan's troops continued their retreat across the plain.

Book 21. Achilles fights Scamander.
When they reached the ford of the Scamander, Achilles cut the Trojan

force into two groups, 'one he drove to the plain toward the city...but half were forced into the deep-flowing river with its silver eddies.' Here, trapped in the river and cowering under its overhanging banks, many were killed by the untiring spear of Achilles.

Note – Rieu, in the Penguin Classics edition, making best sense of the text, says that half were chased into 'a bend in the river where Xanthus of the silver pools ran deep.' This would explain why, instead of just crossing the river, many got trapped in it.

Then the river god Xanthus appealed to Apollo for help in stopping the slaughter, and together they brought down a flash flood, hurling rushing waters around Achilles. **The floods caused a full grown elm tree to fall into the river, bridging it from side to side**. Achilles managed to climb out of the river channel, but the river roared after him over the land. He was rescued by the gods. Hephaestus set fire to the plain and the trees by the river, while **Hera summoned a SW wind from the sea to spread the fire over the plain.** Thus Xanthus was consumed by fire, and his waters dried up. Then the gods started fighting again. Ares was flattened by a boundary stone hurled by Athene, and was led away by Aphrodite. Poseidon challenged Apollo's misplaced loyalty by reminding him of how they laboured together at the command of Zeus to build the walls of Ilium, and how king Laomedon refused them their promised payment. He and Apollo agreed to call off the gods and leave the fighting to the mortals, and they retired to Olympus. Achilles then resumed his killing of the Trojans as they fled back towards their city. Priam, high on the walls of Ilium, watched in horror and called out for the gates to be thrown open to allow his forces to reach safety within the walls. And Apollo again played his part for the Trojans. While they were crowding back through the gates into the city, he appeared in front of Achilles disguised as Agenor to distract him, causing Achilles to chase after him in vain across the wheat fields, heading him off towards Scamander of the deep pools.

Book 22. The death of Hector.
When most of the Trojans were safe behind the walls, Apollo revealed himself to Achilles, who was furious to think of all the Trojans he might have killed before they reached Ilium. He started running towards the city, and King Priam

saw him coming across the fields. But the fates had left Hector outside the walls, where he had decided to make a stand against Achilles. A heart-rending appeal from his father failed to shake Hector's resolve, and Hecuba, his mother, fared no better. But when Hector saw Achilles approaching god-like in his bronze armour, his heart failed him and he ran. With Achilles in pursuit Hector fled under the walls of Troy, while the gods watched in silence. Then Zeus, having a soft spot for Hector and remembering the many sacrifices Hector had made in his honour, asked the other gods if he should now save him from death at the hands of Achilles. But Athene reminded him that Hector's doom had already been settled. There could be no reprieve. And so, aided by Apollo for the last time, Hector kept ahead of Achilles while fleeing round the city walls. Passing the lookout and the windswept fig tree and **'ever away from under the wall along the wagon track, and came to the two fair flowing fountains, where well up the two springs that feed eddying Scamander.' One flows with warm water, the other cold, even in the heat of summer. 'And there near the springs are the broad washing troughs, fair and wrought of stone, where the wives and fair daughters of the Trojans were used to wash bright clothes in time of peace...'** Three times they circled the walls, and more than once **Hector made a dash for the Dardanian Gates** hoping to be saved by the archers from above. But each time Achilles headed him off. Then, when they reached the springs for the fourth time, Zeus held out his golden scales. The beam came down on Hector's side, and his fate was sealed. He turned and stood his ground, but the fight was short. When Hector's body tumbled into the dust, the whole town gave a cry of grief.

Book 23. The funeral and the funeral games.

While Troy wept, Achilles dragged Hector's much wounded body back to their camp by the ships. The Achaeans feasted, but Achilles vowed not even to cleanse himself of the gore of battle until the body of Patroclus was burned and his ashes buried under a mound. The ghost of Patroclus visited Achilles while he was asleep, reminded him that he too was destined to die under the walls of Troy, and asked that, when that happened, their bones should be buried together.

The next day wood was fetched from the slopes of Ida and a huge funeral pyre was built. On it were cast other offerings, including horses, dogs and, as

Achilles had promised to Patroclus, the corpses of twelve noble sons of Troy. The fire was then lit and, fanned by the immortal winds, it burned through the night. In the morning the flames died down, and the bones of Patroclus were recovered for later burial with Achilles. Then a round barrow of modest size was built over the pyre in honour of the dead hero. Afterwards, as was the custom, games were held in his honour, including chariot racing and contests of skill and strength.

Note - The description of the games, a summary of which is not attempted here, is one of the finest pieces of writing in the whole epic. The important point for us to note is that **near the Greek camp there was enough space to hold such games, and for a chariot race course, perhaps about 4-5km long. It took place on open ground, starting near the ships and heading inland, turning round a marker post – a tall tree stump - then heading back towards the sea.**

Book 24. Priam meets Achilles, and Hector's burial.
In the days that followed, Achilles continued to grieve. Every day he dragged the body of Hector three times round the barrow of Patroclus. But on the morning of the twelfth day, Apollo appealed to Zeus for this dishonour to cease. Zeus acknowledged that Hector was a favourite of the gods in Ilium, and that when offerings were made, his own altar never went without its share. So he agreed that Priam should go to Achilles and, in return for a ransom, bring back Hector's body. **He sent for Thetis, and brought her to him from her deep cavern between Samos and Imbros.** She did as he asked, and went to her son Achilles to tell him he must accept a ransom for the return of Hector's body. Then Iris was sent to Priam in Ilium to tell him he could recover his son's body by going to Achilles and offering him a large ransom. Priam agreed to do this, after offering a prayer to Zeus for a sympathetic reception from Achilles. Zeus sent out an eagle, as a sign of reassurance to Priam, who then started to arrange the visit.

This was duly arranged. Later that day, Priam in his chariot with horses yoked behind, and the herald Idaeus driving the treasure laden mule cart, headed out for the Achaean camp. **When it grew dark they reached the great barrow of Ilus and stopped so the mules and horses could drink from the river.**

There they were met by Hermes, the Ambassador of the gods, who guided Priam and his driver unseen through the gates of the Achaean camp, and to the hut of Achilles. As Hermes vanished into the night, Priam entered unobserved, went up to Achilles, grasped his knees and prayed for the return of his son. Achilles thought with great sadness of his own father, and took pity on the old man before him. He bade Priam and his driver to sit and eat, and stay overnight with him before going home. He had his men unload the gifts Priam had brought. Then they cleansed and wrapped up the body of Hector, still protected from decay by the gods, and placed it in the mule cart. After dinner, Achilles asked Priam how long he proposed to devote to Hector's funeral. Hector asked for nine days' mourning, then they would bury him on the tenth and hold a feast, then build him a mound on the eleventh. So Achilles agreed to refrain from fighting for twelve days while the funeral rites were being observed. Not long after Priam had gone to sleep, Hermes, worried about how Priam would get back without being discovered by Agamemnon and the other captains, came and woke him up. So they set out at once for Troy, stopping at the ford of eddying Xanthus, where Hermes took his leave, then continuing towards the town.

Priam's daughter Cassandra was the first to see them coming in the early morning light, from her vantage point at the top of Pergamus. Soon she had roused the whole town, who flooded out onto the plain to welcome home their beloved king. The family brought Hector to the palace, laid him on a bed, and brought in the musicians to play dirges to accompany the weeping and wailing women. His wife Andromache held his head in her arms, and mourned both him and their newly born son, who she feared would be murdered when Troy fell to the Achaeans. Even Helen was distraught with grief, saying that, during the nineteen years she had been among them, of all her Trojan brothers she loved Hector most for his kindness and gentleness. And then Priam told his people what he had agreed with Achilles, and sent them out to fetch wood for the funeral pyre. And on the tenth day, the body of Hector was placed on top of the pyre, and the flames consumed him. The next morning the fire was quenched with wine, his white bones recovered, and these were buried in a golden urn. **This they 'laid in a hollow grave, and covered it over with great close-set stones. Then quickly they heaped the mound…',** keeping a close watch against attack. And when this was done they went back into Troy, and enjoyed a splendid banquet in the palace of king Priam, in honour of Hector, tamer of horses.

Concluding Comments.

The Iliad ends abruptly at this point. Yet most readers today may feel, with some justification, that this is not the ending they had been led to expect. Having read so often of the impending death of Achilles and the fall of Troy, they may feel disappointed that the epic does not conclude with these events. I think we should assume that Homer's audience already knew about these from other stories. Perhaps these were so well known that they had become old hat even in their day. It was the new story composed by Homer that they had come to hear. The ending we are given is what we would expect if it related to a much shorter epic about the 'wrath of Achilles'.

As already mentioned, the Odyssey describes Achilles' death and the fall of Troy in some detail, but here our concern is with the Iliad and the Trojan landscape. Readers will by now, it is hoped, have some idea of the flavour of one of the world's greatest literary masterpieces. They will also have some appreciation of the nature and layout of the Trojan plain, with its two rivers. They will remember some of the features of the local topography, such as Kallikolone, the Tomb of Ilus and the rising in the plain before the ships that Homer has introduced into the story. This evidence can be collated to present a full picture of the Trojan landscape as described by Homer. This picture can then be compared with the landscapes at Hisarlik and Bergama, to see which offers the best fit.

Notes

Prologue

1. Here is not the place to dwell on the troubled past relations between Greece and Turkey, which are briefly documented in the better guidebooks. However, it does explain why, with the repatriation of the Greeks following the 1923 Treaty of Lausanne, the old Greek names have been replaced with Turkish ones.
2. Radt, W. (1999)

Chapter 1

1. Teuthrania and the Mysian war story are found in the Cypria, one of the Epic Cycle of poems relating to the Trojan War. Quintus of Smyrna (Loeb Edn. 1970) tells us in more detail about the battle beside the Kaikos. Teuthrania was known in historical times, and Pausanias (1.4.5.) said it was the earlier name for Pergamon, although modern scholars do not agree with him.
2. The minor Troy-related epic poems are listed and briefly discussed in Chapter 2.
3. The Catalogue of Ships in Book 2 of the Iliad lists the places which sent forces to Troy, the number of ships sent, and the names of the captains of the troops. It is from this list that we can estimate that over a thousand ships sailed to Troy to recover Helen.
4. Wood, M. (1985) p.19.
5. The name Mendere appears to be ancient. 'Dere' is an ancient name meaning 'river', still in use in Asia today. But how this river was named may never be known. It seems unlikely that this name was imposed by Athens in mid 6C, as being plausibly similar to Skamander, although a motive for so doing will become obvious in Volume 2.
6. Allen, S.H. (1999) p.77-79. This wonderfully researched book is full of fascinating details about the early days of the discovery of Troy at Hisarlik in general, and of the life of Frank Calvert in particular.
7. Allen, S.H. (1999) p.101.

8. Blegen, C.W. (1963) p.111ff

9. ibid. p.165.

10. ibid. p.157.

11. Page, D.L. (1959) p.96. There are a number of different 'traditional' dates for the Trojan War. All of these, according to Page, 'are mere speculative guesses, based at best on shifty and quarrelsome genealogical traditions, especially the Lacedaemonian (i.e. Spartan) king-lists. No Greek in historical times ever possessed reliable evidence from which a scientific approximation to the date of the Trojan War might have been calculated. There is no point in trying to harmonise such guesses with the results of archaeological research: ...the date given by Eratosthenes is nothing but a guess proceeding from flimsy premises which could not possibly have led to a scientific calculation.'

12. Korfmann, M (1986)

13. Journal of Hellenic Studies, Vol. 3 1882. p.69ff. Mahaffy's paper was entitled 'The Site and Antiquity of Hellenic Ilion'. The paper in response by Jebb was in two parts: 1. The Ruins at Hisarlik, and 2. Their Relation to the Iliad. While revisiting this debate we should remember that in 1882 there was little evidence from archaeology, and none from Linear B texts, the earliest Greek writing, or from Hittite texts, to support today's view that the Iliad contained much historical fact. Many therefore still regarded Homer's work as pure fiction, and the events and peoples of the Trojan War as mythological. Furthermore, the date of the war was then not linked through Mycenaean pottery to Egyptian dates. The concept of a Dark Age of Greece was not yet a cloud on the horizon of the ancient historians.

14. Croesus was the last king of Lydia before it fell to the Persian king Cyrus the Great in 546. Mahaffy said there were other indications which point to the Aeolic occupation of the site being earlier, perhaps c700, but did not say what these were. He may have been thinking of the story of the Locrian Maidens, discussed in Volume 2, which according to Polybius implies that the temple to Athena at Ilion may have dated to around 700.

15. Mahaffy, J.P. (1882) p.69-70.

16. Jebb, R.C. (1881) and (1882) p.185ff.

17. King Priam had come to the Greek camp at night to meet Achilles, to plead for the return of the body of Hector, his eldest son. In one of the most moving passages in the whole of the Iliad, Achilles shows deep sympathy for the old king who is about to lose his once great kingdom.

18. One such example is given by J. Latacz (2004) p.273. Latacz claims Lesbos belongs unambiguously to the realm of Priam. He quotes 24.543-6 as proving this, as follows –

'And you old sir, we are told you prospered once; for as much as Lesbos... confines to the north above it, and Phrygia from the north confines, and enormous Hellespont, of these old sir, you were lord once in your wealth and children.'

19. Leaf, W. in Lunn (1925) p.76.

Chapter 2

1. Graves, R. (1955) Section 159h. The reason why Paris was chosen by Zeus to be the judge is explained by Graves. Paris, while a herdsman on Ida, had a prize fighting bull, and 'offered to set a golden crown upon the horns of any bull that could overcome his own.' The god Ares, for a jest, turned himself into a bull and won the prize. Paris without hesitation gave the crown to Ares, and his integrity won him favour with the gods who were watching from Olympus.

2. Watkins, C. (1986) p.51. 'Some general impressions from Homer – linguistic pluralism of men from many lands...Il 2.803-804, 4.437-438 and 4.433-435, show Trojans were not Greek speakers. The epic convention is, of course, that Trojans spoke Greek – Arabs speak Spanish in 'El Cid' and French in the 'Song of Roland'. 'It is probable that the Greek names borne by most Trojans, major and minor, are 'fictions', as are quite consciously the names 'Hektor' and his son 'Astyanax'. Il 6.402-403 'Hektor would call him Skamandrios, but other men Astyanax – for only Hektor guarded Ilios'. Hektor could have had a real Anatolian name that never surfaced...'

3. The Epic Cycle may be read in English in the invaluable Loeb Classical Library series. See Evelyn-White, H.G. (1936) and subsequent reprints.

4. Nagy, G. (1996) p.38. He said that the earliest references to 'Homeros' say he wrote the whole cycle. But by the time of Aristotle the epics of the Cycle are conventionally ascribed to different authors. The Alexandrian scholar Zenodotus accepted that the Odyssey and Iliad were Homeric and the rest were not. Some later scholars have tried to narrow the corpus further by saying that the Iliad and Odyssey had separate authors.

5. March, J. (1998) p.231.

6. Graves, R. (1955) Section 158ff.
7. Graves, R. (1955) Section 158.2.
8. Rieu, E.V. (1950).
9. Murray, A.T. (1924) Edition revised by W. F. Wyatt, 1999.
10. Bowra, C.M. (1972). p.105.
11. Shewring, W.H. (1980)

Chapter 3

1. Taplin, O. (1991)
2. It seems generally believed that the Catalogue of Ships has exaggerated the number of ships sent to Troy. The use of the number 40 by peoples of the East in early times should commonly be taken as meaning 'many', and not be taken literally.
3. A discussion of the question as to whether or not, and when, the Achaeans built a wall to protect their ships is found in Page, D.L. (1959).
4. The 'double fountains' are called 'the source of eddying Scamander' in the World's Classics edition of Homer, the Iliad', Fitzgerald, R. (1984).
5. Leaf, W. (1892) p.360.
6. I met Professor Wolfgang Radt in 2003, at his office in Istanbul, some two years before he retired. He listened to my seemingly outlandish ideas with kindness and courtesy, and provided much helpful information. For those who can read German, his brilliantly detailed and illustrated book 'Pergamon' has proved a veritable mine of invaluable information for this study.

Chapter 4

1. Lorimer, H.L. (1959) p.497-498.

Chapter 5

1. Leaf, W. (1912)
2. Strabo (13.1.36) quotes the authority of Demetrius - 'Demetrius cites also Hestiaia of Alexanderia as a witness, a woman who wrote a work on Homer's Iliad and inquired whether the war took place round the present Ilium and the Trojan plain, which latter the poet places between the city and the sea; for, she

says, the plain now to be seen in front of the present Ilium is a later deposit of the rivers.'

Chapter 6

1. March, J. (1999)
2. Strabo, Book 7 frag. 58. He was writing probably around 10-20AD.
3. Korfmann, M. (1986). This paper gives the initial results of his archaeological findings in Besik Bay. Others, including Dorpfeld, had earlier argued that the traditional site at the river mouth was unsatisfactory, and proposed Besik Bay as a more likely alternative. On p.41 Korfmann wrote: 'Numerous finds had clearly established that this bay had long been part of Troy. This was Troy's harbour. In all logic and probability, this harbour provided the foundations for the rise of the city.'
4. Ibid. On page 11, he quoted Wilhelm Sieglin (1898) re Hellespont.
5. Luce, E.V. (1998) Notes p.237 and note 2.15, quoting Janko (1992) in the Cambridge Commentary on the Iliad, Vol.4 on Il. 15.233-235.
6. Leaf, W. (1892) p.227.
7. Page, D.L. (1959) p.138 for Fig.5.1. The Trojan Allies.
8. Leaf, W. (1923), p.xlii. The eight separate dynasties were, according to Demetrios : i) the Troas under Hector, ii) the Dardanians under Aeneas, iii) the Lykian Troas under Pandaros, iv) the Troas near Abydos under Asios, v) the Troas under the two sons of Merops in Perkote, making five districts under separate dynasties. He adds three dynasties in the southern Troad – vi) the Kilikes of Thebe under Etion, vii) the Kilikes of Lyrnessos under the husband of Briseis, and viii) the Leleges of Pedasos. Thus he gets eight dynasties, and Leaf supports these. Demetrios found the Kilikes and Leleges not from the Catalogue but from the list of places taken by Achilles. He said they must have been part of Priam's Troyland, probably by intermarriage. They are not in the Catalogue, he said, because they were completely destroyed as Homer says. However, Leaf disagreed, claiming they were in the Catalogue, but included under the general name Pelasgians, led by Hippothoos from Larisa on the west coast just north of Lekton Point.
9. Nilsson, M.P. (1933) p.26. Also Beekes, R.S.P. (2003) p.22. He wrote 'Homer does not have the name Lydians, only MeOEiones. One wonders how this is to be explained. Most probably Homer knew the term Lydians, so

he must have consciously ignored it. But why were they not mentioned as allies of Troy, like the Lycians? He also ignored the presence of the Greeks along the coast of Lydia, which may be because Homer knew (or better thought) that there were no Greeks in Asia Minor at the time of the story about Troy, or in general the Greek expeditions against Asia Minor. The general idea is that the Ludoi [Lydians] lived to the south and at a later date became more important.' Here Beekes seems to imply that the Lydians existed in Western Anatolia before the Trojan War. This would make them a LBA civilisation, which seems earlier than implied by the associated legends.

10. Apollodorus, Epitome, III. 32-34.

11. Carpenter, R. (1946) p.54. He wrote that 'From other fragmentary accounts and allusions, ranging from Pindar to Pausanias, Quintus Smyrnaus, and scholia on the Iliad, we can piece together something more of the lost tradition about this wretchedly mistaken expedition against Troy.'

12. Beekes, R.S.P. (2003) p.22. He writes 'On the other hand we have the strange story that the Greeks, going to Troy, made a mistake [sic!] and went to Teuthrania (near Pergamon), in which expedition Achilles and Patroklos had similar roles as in the Iliad. It is improbable that after the Iliad a second story was made which largely imitates it, and was presented as an error! An obvious conclusion is that in the oldest story the Greeks went to Teuthrania, and that this expedition was only later transferred to Ilios, because Ilios was much more considerable, a much greater undertaking, giving much more fame. This agrees with the fact that Achilles took (in the Iliad, I. 328) 23 cities, all in the extreme south of the Troas, which is near Teuthrania; this undertaking seems unconnected with Troy. Achilles probably operated from Lesbos; it is now agreed that this island (in Hittite called 'Lazpas') was the first Greek position in the north.

13. R. Graves, in 43.1, discusses the myths of Macareus / Macar / Makar. The name means 'happy'.

14. Latacz, J. (2004) p273.

Chapter 7

1. These three tribes dwell in the area to the west of the Black Sea. These 'Mysians' are the Mysi (Moesi), the people of Moesia, in N Thrace near the lower Danube. The 'Hippemolgai' (mare-milkers) and the 'Abii' are believed

to be Scythian tribes from broadly the same region of the lower Danube. The former are the predecessors of the Tartars, who may to this day still drink koumiss or fermented mares milk. Collectively they are sometimes referred to by Homeric scholars as 'the northern tribes'.

2.   Carpenter, Rhys. (1946) p.78-79.

3.   Bryant, J. (1797). Note also that Bryant was supported by Hobhouse, later Lord Broughton. He had travelled with Lord Byron to the area, where they both spent a month living at Abydos. Allen, S.H. (1999) gives Broughton (1813), p.684, as following Bryant in placing Troy on the coast opposite Tenedos. Note also that in Hobhouse's plan of the plain of Troy, 'The probable site of Ilium' is shown at Hisarlik, although the promontory bearing these ruins is not named. This may have given Maclaren, C. (1822) the initial idea that Troy should be on this spot.

4.   Leaf, W. (1892) p.227.

5.   Janko, R. (1992) p.42.

6.   Lascelles, J. (2005) p.134-139.

7.   Lorimer, H.L. (1950) p.469.

8.   Evelyn White, H.G. (1914). Hymn to the Delian Apollo p327. These hymns are described as Homeric, but some scholars think they are more probably the work of a later epic school of poets. They retain a strong romantic element, with the influences of Homer and Hesiod well marked in diction and style.

9.   Levi, P. (1971). In 7.4.1, Pausanias tells of an early Achaean legend about Prokles and his son Leogoros. According to Pausanias this Prokles was an Ionian leader, son of Pityreus, an Epidaurian, who was driven out of Argos along with others by the Argives under their leader Deiphon. Prokles was descended from Ion, son of Xouthos, and it was this Ion who had given his name to his people by calling them Ionians. It seems likely that, having been driven out of Argos, Prokles went to western Anatolia, to the coastal region which later became known as Ionia. Whether or not this was so, his son Leogoros became king of Samos. While he was king, the people of Ephesos, led by Androklos, attacked and defeated him, and drove the Samians off the island. Pausanias then writes 'Some of the Samian refugees settled the island off Thrace, called Samothrace, earlier called Dardania, after that settlement; others under Leogoros put a wall round Anaia on the mainland opposite, and ten years later they crossed over to Samos, threw out the Ephesians, and recovered the island' (Pausanias, 7.4.3.). Levi suggests in footnote 24, that a

possible date for the foundation of Samothrace was c690. In footnote 22 he adds that these events may well be historical, rather than legendary.

10. Lascelles, J. (2005) p.136 on the view from Samos.

11. At this point I cannot help speculating a little further as to why Poseidon may have gone to Samos in the first place. Homer may simply have arranged this so that Poseidon could go from there to help the Greeks as soon as Zeus's back was turned. But Samos was home to a very early temple or shrine dedicated to Hera. Pausanias (7.4.4) tells us that some say the sanctuary was founded by the crew of the Argo, who brought the statue from Argos, but the Samians tell a different story. The statue was one of the most ancient, made by Smilis of Aigina, in the age of Daidalos, who was contemporary with King Minos of Crete. Hope-Simpson, R. (2003, p.214) reports that this 'Heraion apparently had fortifications in LH III...', and noted the presence of a LH IIIA chamber tomb at Myloi nearby. Given this archaeological evidence, a Mycenaean presence on Samos appears attested before the time of the Trojan War, which probably dates to LH3B. It seems likely therefore that Homer would have known of its existence. Did Homer intend Poseidon to visit Hera on Samos so that there they could hatch a plot as to how she might distract Zeus's attention, thus enabling Poseidon to help the Achaeans while he was not looking? This is indeed what Hera does later in Book 14, where Zeus succumbs for a while to the feminine charms of his beautiful wife. This story is well known to Homeric scholars as the 'Deceiving of Zeus'. May there once have been some now lost lines by Homer telling us more about this deception? And were these deliberately omitted later because they would have revealed that Poseidon was on Samos, not Samothrace?

12. In Il. 24.78 the underwater cave home of Thetis is placed 'between Samos and Imbros'. She was there with Poseidon and her 'goddesses of the sea', the Nereids, who were daughters of Nereus. Some were named in Il 18.38-51. When they heard a deep cry of mourning from Achilles, they went to the Greek Camp and Thetis spoke words of comfort to him. Was there a home of Poseidon not far from the Greek camp? Here Samos is assumed to mean Samothrace, which was not written in full because it did not fit the meter. But there was a cult centre of the Nereids on Lesbos, within the immortal's earshot of Achilles, and this would fit the proposed new geography much better.

Chapter 8

1. Leaf, W. (1892) p.227/8.
2. Luce, E.V. (1998) p.22 and p.27.
3. Luce, E.V. (1998) p.26. He quotes Huxley's claim that the ancient lexicographer Stephanos of Byzantium located an Aigai on the Thracian Chersonese.
4. In discussing the view from Samothrace, Janko says 'The poet who placed the god there had seen it from the plain of Troy himself; such a detail is hardly traditional.' Noting that the island is called 'Samos of Thrace', he says that this epithet 'proves that Homer knew of the Ionian Samos also.' This agrees with my suggestion that Homer probably knew that the top of the Samian Mount Kerkis was visible on the southern horizon from somewhere near Smyrna, where he is thought to have spent his childhood.
5. Huxley, G.L. (1969) p.5-11. The floruit of both Sappho and Alcaeus was perhaps around 600, and both were doubtless steeped in the legendary history of their island home. On Lesbos, which earlier had suffered dreadfully at the hands of the marauding Achilles, one would expect a local residual memory of the Trojan War to have lasted for many generations. In his paper, Huxley tries to explain, from the meagre sources available, that both Sappho and Alcaeus seemed to be referring to early Lesbian legends, telling of the storms that first befell the returning Achaeans soon after they left Troy. The Lesbian version differs from the story told in the Odyssey, and this was discussed in Chapter 14. My primary purpose here in quoting the two sources, Huxley and Strabo, is to show that there is evidence that an ancient Aiga/Aigai existed near Elaia. But we may pose the question: if the Achaeans returned home via Lesbos, which was the more likely that they came from a) Besik Bay, or b) from Elaia?
6. The pattern 'thrice... and the fourth time' was used elsewhere by Homer. Patroklos tried three times to scale the walls of Troy, before a fourth attempt led to his downfall. And Hector ran three times round the walls of Troy, only to be killed as he started his fourth circuit.
7. Leaf, W. (1892) p.225. One major interruption in the story of the Deceiving of Zeus was a parallel story known as the 'Aristeia (i.e. story) of Idomeneus'. This tells how Idomeneus, King of Crete, achieved glory by fighting and getting the better of two gods who were supporting the Trojans. See the Iliad 13.306-519 for more on this story.

8. Page, D.L. (1965) p.46 n.1.
9. See photographs in Chapter 14.

Chapter 9

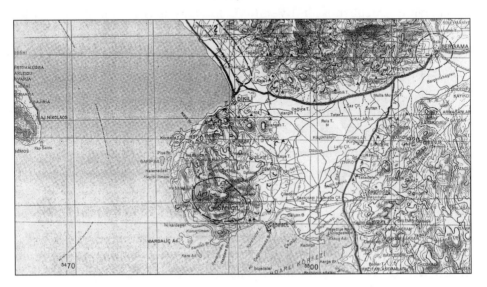

Fig. 9.2. The 1941 Military Map

1. Map reference D30:3(8), Map Room, Bodleian Library, Oxford University. This map of the lower Bakir Çayi valley region is part of a German military map dated 1941, which in turn is based on a Turkish map of 1936, scale 1:200,000. It shows the plain from Bergama to the Eleatic Gulf, now given its Turkish name of Candarli Korfezi. The Kara Dag hills lie to the west of the plain, on which the Germans have indicated a possible artillery emplacement. It is a maze of black lines which make it very difficult to distinguish between minor roads and small streams, so I have not included the whole map in the main text.

2. This river is named Sariasmak Dere on a British Admiralty Chart No. 1665 (1962), information courtesy of John Lascelles.

Chapter 10

1. Bowra, M. (1972) p.92.
2. Bowra. M. (1972) p.37/8. Believing that Hisarlik was Homer's Troy, Bowra explained the apparent confusion over the wall by reference to Homer's way of telling a story. 'Each point,' he said, 'is made emphatically in its own place because it is relevant to the context...there is no real contradiction.' Others may disagree.
3. Bean, G. (1966, p112-114) gives a description and sketch map of ancient Elaia.
4. Hansen, E.V. (1971) p.80. In late 191BC, after forcing the commander of the Seleucid fleet, Polyxenidas, to admit defeat at Ephesus, the fleets of the Rhodians and Eumenes II went home, but 'the Roman fleet stayed over winter at Kane, protected by a line of entrenchments.'
5. Of this claim, Leaf wrote (1923) p.178, 'Now that we know for certain that the 'ancient site' was at Hisarlik, the arguments of Demetrios to the contrary have lost their interest, except in so far as they illustrate the flimsy grounds on which Strabo, blindly following, was able for many centuries to mislead and confuse all enquirers into the history of the Trojan War.' Leaf discussed some alternative suggestions for the site of Thymbra proposed by others, and commented on the etymological similarity of the names 'Thymbra' and the river 'Dombrek', identified near Hisarlik as the Trojan Simois. He mentioned that Calvert had apparently found an inscription recording the treasures of Apollo Thymbraios at his farm. He suggested that the original site of Thymbra probably fell into obscurity and the name was transferred to the stream just north of Hisarlik, where it survived 'in the mutilated Turkish form', i.e. Dombrek. Thymbra, Leaf added, was 'one of the little towns of the Troad which numismatists claim coined c350-300.'
6. Cook, J.M. (1973) p.118-9. During his study of the Troad, Cook could find no evidence there of a town called Thymbra. He wrote that, despite the general belief held by Calvert, Schliemann, Dorpfeld, Leaf and numismatists, a Thymbra in the plain of Troy, whose sanctuary to Apollo was associated in legend with Achilles, cannot be supported. He also found no pre-Classical remains at what he believed to have been the site of the Village of the Ilians. His survey work also led him to believe the conventional placement of Sigeion, Achilleum and the tomb of Achilles were wrong. These, he thought, should be moved further

south, nearer to Besik Bay. This is evidence of yet more uncertainty concerning the so-called tombs of Homer's heroes at Hisarlik.

7. As an alternative scenario, it is possible to imagine the Trojans camped along the 'throsmos' in a long line. Those 'towards the sea' would then be those nearest the river mouth, and those 'towards Thymbra' would be those nearest the foothills. In this case, Thymbra could have been the name of a small settlement to the north of, or even on the site of, the later port of Elaea. It is helpful to know that Hansen (1971, p4.) tells us that the earlier name of Elaea was Cidanis. This name is not mentioned in the Iliad we have today, so if it was there originally, it must have been left out or changed as a later alteration.

Chapter 11

1. Luce, J. V. (1998) p.157.
2. Rieu, E.V. (1950) p.380.

Chapter 12

1. Sketch map based on British Admiralty Chart No. 1665 (1962).
2. As translated by Rieu (1950) p.380.

Chapter 13

1. Rieu's Iliad p.60.
2. Hansen, E.V. (1971) p.84. A brief history of Pergamon and the Attalid kings is given in Volume 2.
3. Bean, G.E. (1966) p.94.
4. Hansen, E.V. (1971) p.283.
5. Lascelles, J. (2005) p.41.
6. Hansen, E.V. (1971) p.284.
7. This photograph is shown by Radt, W. (1999), fig 211. p.269.
8. Hansen, E.V. (1971) p.283.
9. Radt, W. (1999) p.269.

10. Radt, W. (1999) p.267ff gives in German a good general discussion of the Bergama tomb mounds and graves.

11. Hansen, E.V. (1971) p.246 makes a few brief comments about this water supply scheme.

12. For more information on these Hellenistic and Roman aqueducts see Jones, C.P. (1991).

13. Hansen, E.V. (1971) p.4 on earlier name of Caicus.

14. Hansen, E.V. (1971) p.4. Note that she quotes E. Thramer, P.W. Kretschmer and E. Schweizer for this paragraph, all late 19th C scholars. More modern scholars may have a different view.

15. Koester, Helmut. (Ed.) (1998). This was a collection of conference papers, and contained a lot of what was, for me at that time, new and very useful information about Pergamon.

16. Cook, J.M. (1973) p.109. For a more general discussion, see Cook, J.M. (1988).

17. Nohlen, Klaus in Koester, Helmut (Ed.) (1998), Chapter 4, p84.

18. Roof vents would also help release pressure and pockets of air trapped during very high flood flows when the culverts ran full. This would have helped reduce damage inside the tunnels by erosion and water hammer. Clever chaps, these Romans.

19. Hertel, D. Personal communication.13th December 2008.

Chapter 14

1. Apollodorus, Epitome, v.5-6. Translated by J.G.Fraser, Loeb Edition (first published 1919), 2002 edition. The different Achilles' funeral stories are discussed in note 1 on page 216. According to Tzetzes and Dictys Cretensis the golden urn containing his ashes was buried at the headland of Sigeion, which shows that, by their time, the Troy deception was already accepted. Fraser concludes that, 'As the mortal remains of Achilles were buried in the Troad, and only his immortal spirit was said to dwell in the White Island, the statement of Apollodorus that the Greeks interred him in the White Island must be erroneous, whether the error is due to Apollodorus himself, or, as is more probable, either to his abbreviator or to a copyist. Perhaps in the original form of his work Apollodorus followed Arctinus in describing how Thetis snatched the body of Achilles from the pyre and transported it to the White Island.'

2. Page, D.L. (1965) p.280 tells us that Achilles' burial place was apparently also claimed by the Scythians. He discusses a small fragment of a poem attributed to Alcaeus, in which Achilles is called the Lord of Scythia. This apparently shows that Alcaeus is acquainted with 'that eccentric legend in which Achilles was transported at death to White Island near the mouths of the Danube, where he lived in a sort of Elysium, with Medea, or alternatively Helen, for his consort. His cult spread far and wide in those remote and barbarous territories. Ruler of Pontos was his later title, and lord of Scythia means roughly the same. But nothing more survives…' As Page's comment suggests, the mythmakers have been busy. There may doubtless be other competing, and equally speculative, locations for the tomb of this great warrior.

3. Leaf. W. (1923) p.335.
4. Leaf, W. (1923) p.336.
5. Leaf, W. (1923) p.xxiv, and p.333ff.
6. Page, D.L. (1965) p.58, discussing Sappho, Fragment 17.
7. Ibid. Alcaeus Frag. G I, p.162.

Chapter 15

1. Leaf, W. (1923).
2. ibid p. xxiii.
3. ibid p.xv.
4. ibid p.xx.
5. Cook, J.M. (1988).
6. What better way is there to explain the loss of a beloved son than to tell posterity that he was chosen for immortality by Zeus, to serve him as a cup bearer at Olympus? In the legend of the rape of Ganymede, Zeus, in return for taking his son, gave King Tros a pair of immortal horses. Yet in another version, concerning Eurypylus coming to Troy and being killed by Neoptolemus, Zeus gave Tros a golden vine. This apparent mistake led to speculation that this line was a later interpolation. Perhaps this legend was brought to a site near Ilion by Pisistratus. Yet another legend, which told that Ganymede died in Mysia after being captured by Tantalus, King of Phrygia, seems more credible. This story may possibly be linked with one that tells us that Ilus, the next king of Troy and a brother of Ganymede, attacked Pelops, son of Tantalus, causing him to flee from Sipylus to southern Greece. This

was later named the Peloponnese, meaning Pelop's 'nesos' or 'island'. Ilus could have launched such an attack on Sipylus, in the Hermus valley next door, much more easily from Bergama than if Troy was at distant Ilion.

7.   There is a local legend that Skepsis was established as a city after the fall of Troy by Scamandrios, son of Hector, and Askanios, son of Aeneas. This contradicts the one told by Virgil, that Askanios went to Italy and became one of the founders of Rome.

8.   Leaf, W. (1923) p.177.

9.   Jebb, R.C. (1882).

10. Leaf (1923) p.59ff. Discussing Strabo 13.1.7, he said that the Telephos Myth is wholly post-Homeric except for one Greek word in one place. This was not in the Tale of Troy, 'but in that curious by-way, the Nekyia (i.e. Book 10) of the Odyssey, which contains much mythical matter from an unknown source. There is nothing in the passage to connect Eurypylus either with the Mysians or Teuthrania; no town is named, the people are called Keteioi, and an enigmatic expression [concerning them] has no explanation in ancient mythology. Thus the later mythologists had a free hand...' He explained that they rejected Demetrios' idea that Neoptolemus attacked Eurypylus' town, and assumed Eurypylus came as an ally to Troy, where he was killed by Neoptolemus, as Memnon and the Amazon Queen Penthesileia had been killed by Achilles. From the collected evidence about Telephos, I think it becomes more likely that he was a real historical leader of the Keteians/Keteioi from the valley of the Keteios. Perhaps he was known to Homer, but was later expunged from the Iliad. In short, some stories about Telephos were later inventions, but it remains possible that a person of that name around that time may have been historical.

11. Leaf (1923) p.343. One such 'silly fable' was by Aristarchos, who claimed 'Keteians' was not a proper name but an adjective meaning 'monstrous'. He went on to say that 'the name continues to attract speculators. Prime Minister Gladstone was perhaps the first to suggest that they were the Hittites, known from the Egyptian monuments as the Kheta, who certainly at one time penetrated to these regions. This view was also held, but later abandoned, by the German Egyptologist E. Meyer. They have also been identified with the Qedi, a people living in East Kilikia and named among the followers of the Hittite king Chattusil [Hattusilis] in his war against Ramesses II.' Leaf's erudite discussion of Strabo on the Keteians gives a flavour, to the general

reader, of the diversity of opinion and confusion that can arise over the name of one tribe, mentioned once only by Homer.

12. Hansen, E.V. (1971) p.4 on the earlier name of the Caicus (Kaikos).

13. Bowra (1972) p. 165. 'Homer told of a heroic age, which he regarded as much superior than his own. Not being a historian, he does not place in it any datable past, and though we can find a historical foundation for it, Homer's picture is compounded of so many different elements that it corresponds to nothing real.' Troy at Bergama deserves a different verdict.

Chapter 16

1. Lloyd, S. (1989) p.34.

2. Wood, M. (1985) p.138.

3. Hawkins, D. (2002).

4. Lloyd, S. (1989) p.77.

5. Spencer, N. (1995). The main message from this paper is that the Bronze Age and early Iron Age cultural influences of settlements on Lesbos seem, from the archaeological evidence, to be Anatolian rather than Greek. This is what we would expect from the Iliad, the Trojan War legends, and the Hittite texts, which suggests that it was once part of the Hittite empire. There are also some place names, including 'Pyrrhus', another name for Achilles, which may reflect the island's Homeric heritage.

6. Hansen, E.V. (1971) p.6 and p.21. On p.6 she cites three references: a) Preller, L. Griechische Mythologie, II, 3,2 (Berlin, 1923), 1139. b) E. Meyer, Geschichte des Altertums III (2nd edn Stuttgart and Berlin, (1937) 392-396. and c) K. Bittel, IF. XVII in Kleinasien und Byanz (Berlin, 1950), 25-27.

7. Bean, G.E. (1966) p.112-117.

8. Bittel, K. 'Zur ältesten Besiedlungsgeschichte der unteren Kaikos-Ebene', in Kleinasien und Byzanz (Berlin: Walter de Gruyter & Co., 1950), p.10-29. I am indebted to Eric van Dongen for providing a translation of part of this paper.

9. Spencer, N. Personal communication, June 2011. Nigel kindly informed me that another example of the 'horned' type of Mycenaean sword (one of which was reported by Bittel as possibly coming from the region of Pergamum) had been found by Winifred Lamb in her 1930s excavations at Thermi on the east coast of Lesbos (Lamb, 1936, pl. XXV, 32.63).

Appendix 1

1. Evelyn-White, H.G. (1914). 'Hesiod, Homeric Hymns, Epic Cycle, Homerica.' This includes a collection of the works of Hesiod and Homer-related writings, republished together in 2002 in the Loeb Classical Library series.
2. Ibid. p.xxxiii.
3. Apollodorus, Loeb edition (1921).
4. We will include Tenedos here although, in my view, mentions of Tenedos may well have been interpolated into the Iliad later by the Athenians as part of the Troy deception. Did Apollodorus share our suspicions?
5. Quintus Smyrnaeus (1970).
6. Ibid. p.253.
7. Ibid. p.327.
8. Ibid. p.281.
9. Ibid. p.259.
10. Ibid. p.265.

Appendix 2

1. Rieu, E.V. (1950).
2. Murray, A.T. (1999).

GLOSSARY
(all dates BC unless otherwise stated)

Achaeans. Also Argives, and Danaans. These are the three different names used by Homer to refer collectively to the Greek forces deployed at Troy. Achaea and Argos, the homes of the Achaeans and Argives, are two city states in the Peloponnese. Danaos was a legendary king of Argos, so the term 'Danaans' may be applied generally to Argives and to descendents of the clan of Danaos.

Achilles. Son of Peleus, Achilles was the greatest of the Greek warriors. His quarrel with Agamemnon and its eventual resolution provides the main theme for 'The Iliad', which has the sub-title 'The wrath of Achilles'.

Aeneas. Son of Anchises, and third cousin of Hector and Paris. According to the Roman author Virgil he survived the war, migrated to Italy via Carthage (where he met the Phoenician Queen Dido) and became a founder figure for Rome. By this imaginative story, Rome acquired a Homeric heritage.

Agamemnon. Son of Atreus, was king of Mycenae in Lakonia in southern Greece, and brother of Menelaus. Agamemnon was the leader of a confederation of Greek states that sailed with a large fleet of warships across to Troy to recover Helen.

Agora. The market square or civic centre of a city state.

Aias or Ajax. Son of Telamon and King of Salamis. One of the strongest and tallest of the Achaean heroes. Another Ajax, 'the lesser', came from Locris.

Akkadian. The main Semitic language of Ancient Mesopotamia. Replaced by Aramaic c6-500.

Alexander, son of Priam. See under Paris.

Anatolia. The ancient region of north-west Asia roughly the area of modern Turkey.

Archaic Greece. The early historical Greek period, starting from the first Olympics (conventional date c776 to the start of the Classical age, c500.

Archilochus. An Archaic or Classical Greek poet and mercenary, c680-645, perhaps the earliest known lyric poet.

Archon. Magistrate in Athens. The chief Archon gave his name to the year.

Arctinus of Miletus. A very early legendary Greek epic poet, said to have been a pupil of Homer. He is credited as the author of the epics 'The Aethiopis' and 'The Sack of Troy', both part of the Trojan War epic cycle.

Ares. Son of Zeus and Hera, and divine supporter of the Trojans.

Argives. See Achaeans.

Atreus. Father of Agamemnon and Menelaus, hence both are sometimes called Atreides.

Autochthonous. Native or aboriginal.

Bronze Age. The era before the Iron Age, when some tools and weapons of war were made of bronze. Bronze was usually an alloy of copper and tin, but early some early bronze was made from an alloy of bronze and arsenic. The Bronze Age in the Near East is generally said to have started c3,300 and ended c1200, but these dates are not universally applicable.

Central Greece. This includes the regions of Attica, whose capital is Athens, and Phokis, home of the famous oracle at Delphi. Other states include Boiotia, Locris, Doris and the Island of Euboia.

Ceramic period. A period in which a certain type or style of pottery was in use, used to date the strata in which it is found.

Classical Greece. Usually refers to the period from 500 to 300, generally accepted as the high point of early Greek culture.

Colchis. An ancient country at the south eastern end of the Black Sea, in the present Georgia and Abkhazia.

Cuneiform. An ancient script developed in Mesopotamia, using nail-shaped reed ends pressed into soft clay to form wedge-shaped depressions. It dates from as early as the 4th millennium BC.

Danaans. See Achaeans.

Dark Ages of Greece. The name given to the period between the fall of the Mycenaean palaces in 12C to the beginning of the Archaic period in 8C.

Diodorus Siculus. Greek historian from Sicily c80 – 20.

Diomedes. Son of Tydeus, an Argive, and one of the strongest warriors.

Dorians. A Greek tribe from north-western Greece, thought by many to have occupied most of southern Greece in 12C.

Dorpfeld, Wilhelm. German architect and archaeologist who helped Schliemann at Hisarlik, and led excavations there for two seasons in 1893-4. He established the vital connection between the site and Mycenae when he identified Mycenaean pottery in Troy settlement layers 6 and 7. He later spent a few seasons excavating at Pergamon.

Ephor. A Spartan magistrate. Five were elected annually.

Epic Cycle. Name given to a group of epic poems developing a central theme.

Epigoni. 'after-born'. The sons of the 'Seven against Thebes', the heroes who had tried but failed to capture Thebes. The Epigoni succeeded where their fathers had failed, perhaps a generation before the Trojan War.

Eratosthenes. Greek scholar and librarian of the great library at Alexandria in Egypt, c275-195. He was the first Greek to calculate the circumference of the earth, and the tilt of its axis.

Ethiopia. Name given by the Greeks to two places inhabited by black peoples. The best known is the region to the south of Egypt, and the other was ancient Elam.

Etruscan. A people in ancient central Italy. Generally believed by Greek and Romans writers to have come from Lydia in northwest Anatolia.

Eupatridai. Ancient Greek nobles or aristocrats.

Hatti. Ancient name for the home land of the Hittites in central Anatolia and later in N Syria.

Hector. Son of Priam, and the greatest of the Trojan warriors. His fight with Achilles, in which he is killed, provides the climax of the Trojan War as described in 'The Iliad'.

Helen. Wife of Menelaus, whose abduction to Troy by Paris was the cause of the Trojan War.

Helladic. A name for a ceramic period on mainland Greece. Normally divided into Early, Middle, and Late Helladic which roughly equates to the three similar Minoan periods. Based on the Old, Middle and New Kingdoms of ancient Egypt.

Hellenic. Greek or Greek-speaking.

Hellenistic. Name given to the mixture of Hellenic and Eastern culture of Western Anatolia and Eastern Mediterranean regions of the era from the conquests of Alexander to the time of Roman rule.

Hellespont. Name applied to the Straits of the Dardanelles since the time of Herodotus c450. But, as argued in this book, in Homer's day it probably applied to the whole of the Northern Aegean.

Helot. A Spartan serf

Herakles. (Heracles, Roman Hercules) son of Zeus by mortal Alkmene, daughter of Electryon, King of Mycenae.

Herodotus. Author of 'The Histories', the earliest existing history of the Greek-speaking world and their neighbours. c485-425.

Hesiod. Greek poet from Boeotia, thought roughly contemporary with Homer, c7th C. Some would place him earlier. Author of 'Theogony', a poem about the birth and ancestry of the Greek gods.

Hittite. An empire in central Anatolia, conventionally dated from c1700 to c1200BC. Its language was mostly written in cuneiform, but a hieroglyphic version has now been recognised.

Homer. Legendary epic poet, most commonly placed in the late 8th or early 7th century. Known in antiquity as the composer of the Iliad and Odyssey.

Hoplite. A heavily armed infantryman, usually carrying a round shield on the arm fitted with two holding straps.

Idomeneus. King of Crete, son of Deucalion, and grandson of the legendary king Minos. One of the great heroes of the Trojan War who returned safely to Crete.

Indo-European. Name given to a large group of languages, including nearly all of those spoken in Europe, northern India and Iran. It is a subset of the Indo-Hittite languages, which also include those spoken across much of Anatolia.

Ilios. The holy acropolis of Troy. Widely accepted as being the same place as Wilusa, named in the Hittite texts.

Ionians. Central Greek tribe who survived the Dorian invasion, and some of whom settled on the western coast of Anatolia.

Iron Age. A term used for the period following the Bronze Age, when most tools and weapons were made of iron. This term is usually used for the few centuries between the Bronze Age and the Archaic or Geometric periods.

Kecrops/Cecrops. Legendary king and founder of Athens.

Lakedaimonian. A Spartan.

Late Helladic or Mycenaean. Ceramic period in mainland Greece, c1600-1000.

Late Minoan. Ceramic period in Crete, dating roughly from c1650 to 1450, when Crete became dominated by Mycenaean Greeks.

Linear B. A form of the earliest Greek writing, mostly found on burnt clay tablets. The script is formed as a series of signs representing either a) syllables, usually of a pattern representing a consonant + a vowel, rather than single letters, or b) determinatives or pictograms, which are intended as pictures to illustrate the meaning of the word. The earliest examples of its use are said to date from 17th C. Thought to have developed from the earlier, less common, and less well understood Linear A.

Lydia. Region in NW Anatolia. In 6C its last king was Croesus, who ruled from Sardis. In earlier times it may have extended considerably further north, and been the homeland of the Etruscans before they migrated to central Italy.

Menelaus. Brother of Agamemnon and king of Sparta, a Lakonian city some 100km south of Mycenae. Married to Helen, later known as Helen of Troy.

Mesopotamia. Region between the two rivers Euphrates and Tigris, roughly corresponding to modern Iraq.

Minoan. Modern name derived from King Minos, for the early people of Crete.

Minos. Famous king of Crete, who kept the dreaded minotaur, half bull and half man, in the Labyrinth at his palace until it was killed by Theseus.

Mycenae. Ancient city near Argos in the northeastern Peloponnese, famous as the home of King Agamemnon who led the Achaeans at Troy.

Mycenaean. Name given to the Mid-Late Bronze Age Greek culture as revealed by the finds in the city of Mycenae, including the rich Shaft Grave burials found there by Schliemann.

Northern Greece. These include Thessaly (home of Achilles), Macedonia (home of Alexander the Great), and Thrace. Ancient Thrace bordered on the western side of the Straits opposite 'Troy', but is now occupied largely by Turkey and Bulgaria in the north.

Odysseus. Son of Laertes and king of Ithaca. He is the hero of 'The Odyssey', Homer's epic about the ten-year-long journey home from the war of this clever and resourceful hero.

Paris. Son of king Priam. Also called Alexander by Homer. He abducted Helen while on a trading mission to Sparta, after staying as a guest in her home for a few days with king Menelaus.

Pausanias. Greek writer from 2C AD, author of an extensive and detailed Guide to Greece, which contains a wealth of information about early Greek history, myths, and legends.

Pelasgians. The legendary earliest inhabitants of Greece.

Peloponnese. The southern part of Greece, which is almost an island. It is connected to the mainland by a narrow neck of land known as the Isthmus of Corinth. Achaia and Argos (or the Argolis) lie along the northern boundary of the Peloponnese. The other states are Elis, Messenia and Lakonia, with Arcadia occupying much of the mountainous central area.

Phrygia. Region in northern and western Anatolia. A powerful state from c800 to when it was conquered by the Cimmerians in c680-670.

Polemarch. War leader, one of the archons in Athens.

Polis. A city state.

Priam. King of the Trojans. He had 'fifty' sons, including Hector and Paris.

Prytaneion. Town hall.

Pythia. The priestess at Delphi.

Schliemann, Heinrich. A wealthy German businessman credited with discovering Troy at Hisarlik in 1873. He completed 12 seasons of excavation at Hisarlik between 1870-1889. He also discovered the Shaft Grave royal burials at Mycenae in the Peloponnese in 1876, where he believed he had found the gold death mask of Agamemnon.

Seleucid. Name of the dynasty of kings established in Syria and Mesopotamia after the death of Alexander the Great, by Seleukos, one of his generals. It lasted from 322 to 64.

Sidon. A Phoenician coastal city in the Eastern Mediterranean, north of Tyre, now in present day Lebanon. In Homer's time it was the leading Phoenician city, and 'Sidonian' was another name for 'Phoenician'.

Stele. Upright stone slab bearing inscriptions and/or sculptured designs.

Strabo. A Greek geographer, c60BC to 20AD. His surviving works provide the most comprehensive geographical coverage of the Greek-speaking world and her neighbours.

Synoecism. The union of several towns to form a single state.

Thucydides. c460-400. Greek historian of the Peloponnesian Wars.

Troad. Name meaning 'Troy lands', generally referring to the western peninsular of northern Anatolia.

Troy. City in north-western Anatolia conquered by the Achaeans at the end of the Trojan War, as described by Homer. Accepted by some as the 'Taruisa' of the Hittite texts, where it is associated with, or adjacent to, Wilusa. Schliemann claimed to have found the site of Troy at a hill locally known as 'Hisarlik', a few kilometres south of modern Canakkale. The site was known as Ilion to the Classical Greeks and became important as Novum Ilium under the Romans.

Tyrant. A ruler with no hereditary right to rule.

Ugarit. An important city state and naval trading centre north of Lebanon, where a major archive of ancient texts of baked clay tablets was found in the last century. Flourished in the late 2M.

Ugaritic. The Semitic language spoken at Ugarit, and written in an alphabetic form of cuneiform.

BIBLIOGRAPHY

Allen, S.H. (1999) *Finding the Walls of Troy.* University of California.

Apollodorus, *The Library*, Volume II, Loeb Classical Edition, Vol. 122. 1921.

Bean, G. E. (1968) *Aegean Turkey: An Archaeological Guide.* Ernest Benn, London,

Beekes, R.S.P. *The Origin of the Etruscans.* Koninklijke Nederlandse Akademie van Wetenschappen, 2003. Paper. ISBN: 90-6984-369-2.

Blegen et al. (1959) in *Troy Vol. 4* (Princeton 1959, p.250).

Blegen, C. W. (1963) *Troy and the Trojans.* Thames and Hudson, 1963, and edition by Barnes and Noble, 1995.

Bowra, C. M. (1972) *Homer.* Duckworth, 1972.

Bittel, K. '*Zur ältesten Besiedlungsgeschichte der unteren Kaikos-Ebene*'. In Kleinasien und Byzanz: (Berlin: Walter de Gruyter & Co., 1950), p.10-29.

Broughton, Lord (John C, Hobhouse 1813). *A Journey through Albania and Other Provinces of Turkey in Europe and Asia to Constantinople during the Years 1809 and 1810.* 2 Vols. London.

Bruckner, A. (1912) Archaeologi Ainziger.

Bryant, J. (1797) *Dissertation Concerning the War of Troy.*

Carpenter, R. (1946) *Folk tale, fiction, saga in Homeric epics. UCLA, 1946.*

Cook, J.M. (1973) *The Troad, An Archaeological and Topographical Study.* Clarendon Press, Oxford, 1973.

Cook, J.M. (1988) *Cities in and around the Troad.* BSA83.

Easton, D. F. et al. (2002) *Troy in Recent Perspective.* Anatolian Studies 52, pp75-109.

Evelyn-White, H.G. (2002) *The Homeric Hymns, Hesiod, Epic Cycle, Homerica.* Loeb Classical Library Edition, Vol 57, 1914, revised in 1932 and reprinted in 2002.

Fitzgerald, R. (1984) *Homer The Iliad.* Translated by Robert Fitzgerald for The World Classics Edition.

Graves, R. (1955) *The Greek Myths.* (Two volumes). Penguin Books.

Grote, G. (1846 and 1869) *A History of Greece.* Vol 1.

Hansen, E.V. (1971) *The Attalids of Pergamon.* Cornell University Press.

Hawkins, J.D. (2002) In Easton et al, *Troy in Recent Perspective*. Anatolian Studies, p75-109.

Herodotus *The Histories*, translated by Aubrey de Selincourt, Penguin Classics, 1954.

Homer The Odyssey, translated by Shewring, Walter. The World Classics.

Hope-Simpson, R. *The Dodecanese and the Ahhiyawa Question* ARSA 98. 2003 p.214.

Huxley, G.L. (1969) *Aigai in Alkaios*, Greek, Roman, and Byzantine Studies. Vol.10.

Janko, R. (1992) *The Iliad : A Commentary*. Vol. IV Books 13-16. General Editor G.S.Kirk. Cambridge University Press.

Jebb, R.C. (1881) *Homeric and Hellenic Ilium*. Journal of Hellenic Studies, Vol.2.

Jebb, R.C. (1882) *i.The ruins at Hisarlik; ii. Their relation to the Iliad.*' Journal of Hellenic Studies, Vol. 3 p.185ff.

Jones, C.P. (1991) *Aelius Aristides on the Water in Pergamon*. Arch Anzeiger

Koester, Helmut (Ed.) (1997) *Pergamon, Citadel of the Gods*. Archaeological Record, Literary Description, and Religious Development. Harvard Theological Studies. Trinity Press International, Harrisburg, Pennsylvania. 1997.

Korfmann, M. (1986) *Troy, Topography and Navigation*. In Mellink, Machteld J. (ed.) *Troy and the Trojan War*. Bryn Mawr, Pa.

Lascelles, John (2002) *Troy – The World Deceived*. Draft unpublished manuscript.

Lascelles, John (2005) *Troy – The World Deceived: Homer's Guide to Pergamum*. Published by, and obtainable from, Trafford Publishing. www.Trafford.com/05-0729.

Latacz, J. (2004) *Troy and Homer*. OUP. First published in German in 2001.

Leaf, W. (1892) *Companion to the Iliad*. Macmillan, London.

Leaf, W. (1912) *A Study in Homeric Geography*. Macmillan, London.

Leaf, W. (1923) *Strabo on the Troad*. Cambridge U.P.

Lloyd, Seton (1989) *Ancient Turkey, A Traveller's History of Anatolia*. Guild Publishing, London.

Lorimer, H.L. (1950) *Homer and the Monuments*. Macmillan.

Luce, J.V. (1998) *Celebrating Homer's Landscapes*, Yale University.

Lunn, Sir Henry (1925) *Aegean Civilisations*. Ernest Benn, London.

Maclaren, C. (1822) *A Dissertation on the Topography of Troy*.'

Mahaffy, J.P. (1882) Journal of Hellenic Studies 3 p.70.

March, J. (1999) *Dictionary of Classical Mythology*. Cassell.

Murray, A.T. (1999) *Homer Iliad*. Loeb Classical Library Edition, 1924. Edition revised by W. F. Wyatt.

Nagy, G. (1996) *Homeric Questions*. University of Texas Press, Austin.

Nilsson, M.P. (1933) *Homer and Mycenae*. Methuen, London.

Page, D.L. (1959) *The Historical Sack of Troy*. Antiquity Vol. XXXIII.

Page, D .L. (1965) *Sappho and Alcaeus*. 1955, 1965 edition Oxford Clarendon Press

Pausanias, *Guide to Greece*. Translated by P Levi, Penguin Classics, 1971.

Quintus Smyrnaeus, *Ta Meta Ton Homeron*. trans by Arthur S Way, Loeb Classical Library, Heinmann, London, 1970.

Radt, W. (1999) *Pergamon*. DuMont Buchverlag, Cologne, 1988 and 1999.

Rieu, E.V. (1950) *Homer The Iliad*. Penguin Classics.

Shewring, W.H. (1980) *The Odyssey*. The World's Classics edition, with an introduction by G.S. Kirk.

Spencer, N. (1995) *Early Lesbos between East and West*, Journal of British School of Athens, p.269-29.

Taplin, O. (1991) in Boardman, J. et al. *The Oxford History of the Classical World*. p.51ff.

Watkins, C. (1986) 'The Language of the Trojans' in Mellink, M.J. ed., *Troy and the Trojan War*. p.45-62.

Wood, M. (1985) *In Search of the Trojan War*. Guild Publishing, London.

INDEX